# ORGANIZATIONS IN SOCIETY

**Edward Gross**
University of Washington

**Amitai Etzioni**
George Washington University

Prentice-Hall, Inc., Englewood Cliffs, New Jersey 07632

**Library of Congress Cataloging in Publication Data**

Gross, Edward.
  Organizations in society.

  Based on: Modern organizations / Amitai Etzioni.
  Bibliography: p.
  Includes index.
  1. Organization.  2. Management.  I. Etzioni,
Amitai.    II. Title.
HM131.G71765    1985      302.3′5     84-22354
ISBN 0-13-641853-8

The Joseph Berliner quotation which appears on pp. 14–15 is reprinted with the permission of Administrative Science Quarterly.

The Gary Marx quotation which appears on p. 37 comes from Emilio Viano (ed.), *Criminal Justice Research* (Lexington, MA.: Lexington Books, 1975), and it is reprinted with the permission of Gary T. Marx.

The Edward Glaser quotation which appears on page 56 is used by permission of the publisher. Copyright © 1971 by The Psychological Corporation. All Rights Reserved.

Table 4.1, which appears on page 57, is reprinted from John F. Witte, *Democracy, Authority and Alienation in Work: Workers' Participation in an American Corporation*, Table 16, p. 80. © 1980 by the University of Chicago. All Rights Reserved. Reprinted by permission of the University of Chicago Press.

The Ralph Turner quotation which appears on p. 58 is reprinted by permission of the author and the American Sociological Association.

Figures 6-1 (page 94) and 6-2 (p. 95) are reprinted by permission from Joan Woodward, *Industrial Organization: Theory and Practice* (New York: Oxford University Press, 1965).

The Barbara Garson quotation which appears on p. 100 is excerpted from *All The Livelong Day*. Copyright © 1972, 1973, 1974, 1975 by Barbara Garson. Reprinted by permission of Doubleday and Company, Inc.

Cover design: Ben Santora
Manufacturing buyer: Barbara Kittle

Printed in the United States of America

10  9  8  7  6  5  4  3  2  1

ISBN 0-13-641853-8   01

Prentice-Hall International, Inc., *London*
Prentice-Hall of Australia Pty. Limited, *Sydney*
Editora Prentice-Hall do Brasil, Ltda., *Rio de Janeiro*
Prentice-Hall Canada Inc., *Toronto*
Prentice-Hall Hispanoamericana, S.A., *Mexico*
Prentice-Hall of India Private Limited, *New Delhi*
Prentice-Hall of Japan, Inc., *Tokyo*
Prentice-Hall of Southeast Asia Pte. Ltd., *Singapore*
Whitehall Books Limited, *Wellington, New Zealand*

# CONTENTS

# PREFACE

This book started out as a plan to update a book by one of the authors, Etzioni's *Modern Organizations,* published in 1964. Many new works, both quantitative and case studies, had enriched our knowledge since that date. However, there had been other changes too which made it clear that more than an updating would be required to suit the book to the needs of contemporary students.

The 1964 book had served as a brief but concentrated introduction, and remained relevant for the original ideas and point of view it contained, especially the "compliance" perspective, which dealt with relationships between forms of power and commitment or alienation in organizations. Further, research since 1964 has tended to offer continued support for the perspective. But other approaches, offering different models, had become increasingly important. *Modern Organizations* traced, historically, a path from classical organizational theory and scientific management, through human relations theory, on to the work of Max Weber and later structuralists. We re-tell that story in this book, though in more concentrated form. In the meantime, classical theory, particularly that involving rational models, has become highly sophisticated. Human relations theory, in turn, has led to a variety of fascinating interactionist models, and structuralist approaches demonstrated growing explanatory power, as well as methodological rigor.

In sum, the field of organization study has not only become richer in research studies, but has also become more complex, and more exciting, in stimulating empirical approaches. Using *Modern Organizations* as a base, Gross made use of his own ideas as well as suggestions from Etzioni to do the writing and research for this version. The result is a new introduction to the area of organizational research and ideas.

**Edward Gross/Amitai Etzioni**
*May 1984*

# CHAPTER ONE
# RATIONALITY
# AND HAPPINESS
## *The Organizational Dilemma*

Our society is an organizational society (Presthus, 1978). We are born in organizations, educated by organizations, and most of us spend much of our lives working for organizations. We spend a good deal of our leisure time paying, playing, and praying in organizations. Most of us will die in an organization, and when the time comes for burial, the largest organization of all—the state—must grant official permission.

In contrast to earlier societies, modern society has placed a high moral value on rationality, effectiveness, and efficiency. Modern civilization depends largely on organizations as the most rational and efficient form of social grouping known. By coordinating a large number of human actions, the organization creates a powerful social tool. It combines its personnel with its resources, weaving together leaders, experts, workers, machines, and raw materials. At the same time, it continually evaluates its performance and tries to adjust itself accordingly in order to achieve its goals. As we shall see, all these characteristics allow organizations to serve the various needs of society and its citizens more efficiently than smaller and more natural human groupings such as families, friendship groups, and communities.

Organizations are not a modern invention. The Pharaohs used them to build the pyramids. The emperors of China used them a thousand years ago to construct great irrigation systems. And the first Popes created a universal church to serve a world religion. Modern society, however, has more organizations, and they fulfill a greater variety of societal and personal needs, involve a greater proportion of citizens, and affect a larger segment of their lives. In fact, modern society has so many organizations that a whole set of second-order organizations is needed to organize and supervise them. In the United States, such regulatory commissions as the Securities and Exchange Commission and the National Labor Relations Board are examples.

Finally, the modern organization is generally more efficient than the ancient or medieval species. Changes in the nature of society have made the social environment more congenial to organizations, and the art of planning, coordinating, and controlling has become more disciplined with the development of the study of administration.

The fact that the social environment has become more congenial to organizations has changed the very face of that environment. For not only do individuals find themselves immersed in organizations, but organizations themselves must act in a world thick with *other* organizations. They are now actors in their own right—what Coleman (1982) calls "corporate actors." They can take actions on their behalf, utilize (and plunder) resources, own property, and even commit crimes. That way of putting it may sound strange, but the courts have no difficulty in charging firms or even government bureaus with crimes such as air pollution, price-fixing, responsibility for mine accidents, and corruption. They are then punished by fines, injunctions, and occasionally even by being put out of operation (Ermann and Lundman, 1978; Clinard and Yeager, 1980).

These developments mean that there are two kinds of actors on the world scene today—living persons (like you and me) and corporate actors—which leads to some new kinds of relationships, as shown in Figure 1-1. Coleman (1974) sums up the relationships among these persons and actors in an elegant statement: "[E]ach type of person seems to give preferential treatment to its own kind" (p. 89). That is, living persons prefer to deal with other living persons (people prefer to deal with other people, face to face), and corporate persons prefer to deal with other corporate persons. For example, people may willingly help a neighbor clean up an eyesore near their property, but they may be much slower to respond to a city appeal to conserve water or electricity. A local Better Business Bureau may be quite reluctant to give out damaging information about one of its member firms to a caller, even while it (quietly) chastises that firm or otherwise sanctions it. Similarly, one study (Smigel, 1956) reported that while people generally disapproved of stealing, when asked what their order of preference would be if they had to steal, they replied they would be most unwilling to steal from small business, less unwilling to steal from government, and least unwilling to steal from big business. This means that though organizations, especially large ones, are ever more prominent in our everyday lives, we feel distant from them, even to the point of being willing to relax our customary moral standards in dealing with them.

| | | FROM LIVING PERSONS | FROM CORPORATE ACTORS |
|---|---|---|---|
| TO | LIVING PERSONS | *1* E.g., persons exchange courtesies on an elevator. E.g., lovers kiss. | *2* E.g., the Internal Revenue Service sends you a demand for more taxes. E.g., you are required to register for the draft. |
| TO | CORPORATE ACTORS | *4* E.g., a client presents herself to a social-work agency. E.g., a student seeks to register for a course. | *3* E.g., oligopolies. E.g., a government department investigates suspected improprieties in a factory. |

**FIGURE 1–1 Relationships between living persons and corporate actors.** A living person may approach a corporate actor, as in Cell 4, or the reverse, as in Cell 2. The persons or actors in Cells 1 and 3 seem to prefer to deal with others in the same cell. Problems arise in Cells 2 and 4, particularly since one party is usually much weaker than the other. The scheme is modeled on one in Coleman, 1974, p. 88. The particular examples inserted are by the authors.

## COSTS OF ORGANIZATION: CAN THEY BE AVOIDED?

The increase in the scope and rationality of organizations has not come without social and human costs. Many people who work for organizations are deeply frustrated and alienated from their work. The organization, instead of being society's obedient servant, sometimes becomes its master. Modern society, far from being a *gemeinschaft* town meeting, often seems closer to a battleground where organizational giants clash. But it is widely agreed that the undesirable side effects do not outweigh the considerable benefits of organizations. Although a few people advocate returning to a more traditional society in which human groupings are small, intimate, and inefficient, most critics of modern organizations seek to reduce the frustrating and distorting side effects of these huge social instruments while maintaining, even enhancing, their efficacy.

At this point we must confront a major misunderstanding. *Not* all that enhances rationality reduces happiness, and *not* all that increases happiness reduces efficiency. Human resources are among the major means used by the organization to achieve its goals. Generally, the less the organization alienates its personnel, the more efficient it is. Satisfied workers usually work harder and better than frustrated ones. Within limits, happiness heightens efficiency in organizations; and conversely, without efficient organizations, much of our happiness is unthinkable. Without well-run organizations our standard of living, our level of culture, and our democratic life could not be maintained. Thus, to a degree, *organizational rationality and human happiness go hand in hand.* But a point is reached in every organization where happiness and efficiency cease to support each other. Not all work can be well paid or gratifying, and not all regulations and orders can be made acceptable. Here we face a true dilemma.

Consider some of the major criticisms that have been made of organizations and the attempts to answer them.

**WHAT THE CRITICS SAY**

1. Organizations force workers to do simplified, meaningless tasks, so robbing them of initiative, creativity, and independence. Look at the assembly line.

**WHAT THE DEFENDERS SAY**

We can enrich jobs by deliberately building in autonomy and discretion. In Sweden, the assembly line has been modified to do just this. In any case, very few people actually work on assembly lines anymore. We are becoming a service society.

2. Organizations do not serve society or consumers well. Automobiles are unsafe, factories pollute the air, and the sheer size of organizations makes them dangerous. The multinationals dominate life in company towns and even overthrow governments.

We can control pollution, and make better products with quality-control circles and other advances pioneered by Japan and other countries. Large size produces economies of scale. Besides, only very large organizations can afford to do research on new products.

3. Organizations don't even work well. Cars break down before you get them home from the showroom, prisons don't rehabilitate, and schools turn out illiterates. We need alternative institutions.

You go too far. Cars give trouble because you want so much from them—trouble-free driving at high speeds with minimal maintenance. If we produced a serviceable car with minimum features, you wouldn't buy it. Prisons could rehabilitate if you would pay the price for vocational counseling and training. The schools do a great job—name another country in which over a third of all high-school students go on to higher education.

4. Organizations are out of control. An arrogant power elite of interlocking directors controls them, and an army of ever-increasing bureaucrats administers them. The client or citizen is powerless against organizations.

The evidence for any monolithic power elite is exaggerated or so biased as to be invalid. Client and citizen power, they are increasing. Look at the detail on contents now provided on labels at the supermarket. Look at the growth of consumer action groups.

As we shall see, this is not a debate that can be settled by an impartial set of judges. The problem of modern organizations is how to construct human groupings that are as rational as possible, and at the same time produce a minimum of undesirable side effects and a maximum of satisfaction. Both sides, then, have something to claim for their arguments, and both are partly wrong. We find a record of progress and setbacks in the search for the best combination of the values that the parties to the dispute hold dear.

As we make our way through the mine field between these combatants, we must stay close to reliable research. For example, a careful study by Kohn (1971) reported that the more bureaucratized the organization, the more the people working in it value self-direction:

> They [the workers] are more open-minded, have more personally responsible standards of morality, and are more receptive to change than are men who work in nonbureaucratic settings. (p. 465)

A more educated work force partly explains this finding, which is so contrary to the critics' claims about conformity. But a more significant part of the explanation is to be found in the nature of employment in a large organization—greater job protections, higher income, and more complex and challenging work.

On the other hand, the critics' contention that the proportion of administrators is increasing *is* valid, but only under certain conditions: when the organization is increasing in complexity,[1] as, for example, when a clothing manufacturer that has been producing for a mass market decides to shift to designer-quality clothes for high-fashion boutiques, or when a university introduces new programs in minority or area studies. Such genuine changes in structure and complexity require new professions, specialists, and administrators to organize and monitor them. While careful examination of the research will hardly settle the argument, it will give us a more realistic appreciation of both sides and help make the search for solutions more rewarding.

## ORGANIZATIONS DEFINED

Organizations are social units (or human groupings) deliberately constructed and reconstructed to seek specific goals. Corporations, armies, schools, hospitals, churches, and prisons are included in the definition; tribes, classes, ethnic groups, friendship groups, and families are excluded.[2] Organizations are characterized by: (1) divisions of labor, power, and communication responsibilities that are not random or traditionally patterned, but deliberately planned to enhance the realization of specific goals; (2) the presence of one or more power centers to control the concerted efforts of the organization and direct them toward its goals, as well as to review continuously the organization's performance and repattern its structure, where necessary, to increase its efficiency; (3) substitution of personnel, i.e., the removal of unsatisfactory persons and the assignment of others to their tasks, as well as the recombination of personnel through transfer and promotion.

Other social units are marked by some degree of conscious planning (e.g., the family budget), by the existence of power centers (e.g., tribal chiefs), and by replaceable membership (e.g., through divorce), but to a much lesser extent than the social units we are calling *organizations*. Hence organizations are much more in control of their nature and destiny than any other social grouping.

There are many synonyms for the term *organization*. One, *bureaucracy*, has two disadvantages. First, it often carries a negative connotation for the layperson (cf. Albrow, 1970); and second, it implies for those familiar with Weber's work (which we will discuss later) that the unit is organized according to the principles he specified. But many organizations, including many modern ones, are not bureaucratic in this technical sense. Hospitals and universities, for instance, do not have one center of decision making, whereas bureaucracies, by definition, do. Another term, *formal organization*, refers to only one set of characteristics of organizations (cf. Hall, 1982, pp. 30–31). We discuss this aspect later; here it suffices to say that this term does not refer to an organization as an entity, but only to a part of it. *Institution* is sometimes used to refer to certain types of organizations, either quite respectable ones, as in "GM is an institution," or quite unrespectable ones, as in "He is in an institution." Sometimes *institution* refers to a very different phenomenon—namely, a normative principle that culturally defines behavior, such as marriage or property. Because of these two conflicting usages, this term has probably caused more confusion than *formal organization* and *bureaucracy* together. All three might well be avoided in favor of the simple term *organization*.

Since many social groupings have some degree of patterning and some control structure—e.g., in contrast to a mob—*social organization* has been used to characterize these phenomena. But in recent years *social structure* has been increasingly employed to describe these characteristics of social units. Thus we can safely reserve the term *organizations* to refer to planned units that are deliberately structured for the purpose of attaining specific goals, and do without the term *social organizations* altogether.

## NOTES

1. Cf. Blau, 1970; Blau and Schoenherr 1971; Blau, 1977. These findings are based mainly on cross-sectional studies (comparing more complex with less complex organizations at

the same point in time). A critique of such studies that presents genuine longitudinal data is offered by Meyer, 1972.

2. Whether goals should be part of a definition of organizations is the subject of considerable controversy. Yuchtman and Seashore (1967) prefer to evaluate organizations in terms of their ability to exploit their environments in "the acquisition of scarce and valued resources." But the word *valued* suggests that the resources must be valued *for* some end or goal. Similarly, Georgiou (1973) proposes thinking of organizations as units that "exchange activities for incentives." But the activities have to be specified and the incentives focused on some objectives. Neither of these alternatives escapes concern with some degree of goal emphasis or performance. Scott (1981) offers three different definitions, each designed to fit a different "perspective": high goal specificity and formalization (rational systems perspective), survival as the main end (natural systems perspective), and shifting goals attained by negotiation (open systems perspective). None of these alternatives escapes a concern with goals. How important goals are and how they change is an empirical matter, as we shall see.

# CHAPTER TWO
# ORGANIZATIONAL GOALS
*Masters or Servants?*

The goals of organizations serve many functions. They provide orientation by depicting a future state of affairs that the organization as a whole might attain. Thus they set down guidelines for organizational activity. Goals also constitute a source of legitimacy that justifies the activities of an organization, and indeed, its very existence. Moreover, goals serve as standards by which members of an organization and outsiders can assess the success of the organization—i.e., its effectiveness and efficiency. Goals serve in a similar manner as measuring rods for the student of organizations who tries to determine how well the organization is doing.

Since they serve so many functions, goals can tell many stories, though they do not reveal all that goes on inside the organization. For example, Kamens (1977), in discussing educational organizations, contends that schools must legitimate their claims to certain goals by dramatizing them in a myth (something believed to be true whether or not it is). Thus, a school claiming to be producing elites may foster the belief that it flunks out a large number of students in the first year to correct "mistakes" in admission. Meyer and Rowan (1977) go even further in asserting that the formal structure of the organization itself may serve a *symbolic function,* assuring clients or relevant constituencies that organization goals are being aggressively pursued. For example, a modern large organization must provide up-to-date medical facilities for its workers or risk being seen not simply as negligent (by insurers or courts), but as unprogressive, and therefore not the place for bright, creative executives to seek rewarding careers. Since economics is now regarded as a science (with Nobel Prizes being routinely given to economists), no modern prime minister can make any serious proposal for the welfare of his country without first consulting leading economists. Similarly, for organizations of all kinds, Mêyer and Rowan (1977) assert:

> Though no one may read, understand, or believe them, econometric analyses help legitimate the organization's plans in the eyes of investors, customers (as with Defense Department contractors), and internal participants. Such analyses can also provide rational accountings after failures occur: managers whose plans have failed can demonstrate to investors, stockholders, and superiors that procedures were prudent and that decisions were made by rational means. (p. 350)

We need not be altogether cynical about such claims, for organizations *do* pay some attention to econometric analyses. All that is being asserted here is that they are careful to make sure the attention is visible to all concerned persons.

However symbolic may be the uses of goals, it remains true that the very *raison d'être* of organizations is the service of such goals. But once formed, organizations acquire their own needs[1] or imperatives, and these sometimes become the masters of the organization. This happens, for example, when a fund-raising organization spends nearly as much money on staff, buildings, and publicity as on the charity for which funds are purportedly being raised. In such instances, organizations reduce the service to their initial goals in order to satisfy their acquired needs. Sometimes organizations go so far as to abandon their initial goals and pursue new ones more suited to their needs. This is what we mean when we say that the organizational goal becomes the servant of its master.

In this chapter, we consider the following questions: What are organizational goals? Under what conditions can they be met? When do organizational needs become masters, subverting the initial goals? How are organizational effectiveness and efficiency defined, and what organizational problem does their very measurement raise? The chapter closes with a discussion of the danger of using goals as the prime tool for studying and evaluating an organization, and suggests an alternative.

## THE NATURE OF ORGANIZATIONAL GOALS

An organizational goal is a desired state of affairs that the organization attempts to realize. The organization may or may not be able to bring about this desired image of the future. But if the goal is reached, it ceases to be a guiding image for the organization and is assimilated to the organization or its environment. For example, an early goal of the women's movement in the United States was the achievement of the franchise for women. Once the 19th Amendment to the Constitution was ratified, the vote for women ceased to be a goal and the movement moved on to other goals or objectives. A goal, then, is a state that we seek, not one we have. Such future states of affairs, though images, have a very real sociological force that affects contemporary actions and reactions.

But whose image of the future does the organization pursue? That of top executives? The board of directors or trustees? The majority of the members? Actually none of these. The organizational goal is that future state of affairs that the organization as a collectivity is trying to bring about. It is in part affected by the aims of the top executives, those of the board of directors, and those of the rank and file. Sometimes it is determined through peaceful consultation, at other times it is the outcome of a power play among the various organizational divisions, plants, cabals, ranks, and "personalities."

How, then, does one determine what the goal of an organization is? In part, the participants may act as informants. We may interview executives and employees of various departments to establish what they see as the organization's goals. In interviewing them, however, we must carefully distinguish their personal goals from the goals of the collectivity. An executive's goal might be to gain a larger stock option; that of the finance department to balance the budget; the employees', to obtain a raise. Still, all might view the organizational goal as making a profit. Profit making might be selected because they believe that is the way for them to fulfill their personal or departmental goals, or because they believe in principle that every private enterprise should make a profit. In either case, their goals should not be confused with the organizational ones. The participants should be specifically asked what they see as the organization's goals, as distinct from their own or from those they think the organization ought[2] to pursue. We may also get relevant information by studying minutes of board meetings and by examining other documents of the organization. In addition, we can analyze the division of labor of the organization, its flow of work, and its allocation of resources, as reflected in its budget.

Especially revealing are those situations in which the distribution of manpower and material resources clearly suggests a direction of effort different from that expressed by the informants. For instance, if the administrator of a mental hospital informs us that his hospital is in the business of curing people, and we find that there are but 4 doctors (only one of whom has had psychiatric training) serving 5,000 patients, that the hospital aides have no more training or interest in therapy than prison guards, that 90 percent of the patients—many of them suffering from senile disorders generally considered incurable—have spent 10 years or more in the hospital, then we might infer that the hospital's real goal is to keep the level of public disturbance down or to care for the aged.

A useful way of conceptualizing the disjunction between verbalized statements and organization activities is offered by Perrow (1961), who distinguishes "official" from "operative" goals.[3] Official goals are general statements of purpose or of contributions to society, such as "improving the health of the community," "making a profit," or "providing in-depth appreciation of the intellectual achievements of Western civilization." Such broad statements do not provide much guidance for those who actually are to perform those activities. Statements of "operative goals" are much more specific, spelling out whether "health" is to be improved by research or treatment (and if so, with how much money and with what kinds of employees and patients); how much profit is expected; what kinds of products for what kinds of markets will be produced; whether the "intellectual achievements" shall be restricted to philosophical and ethical concepts, or whether logic, mathematics, and computer science are also to be taught.

At the same time, we must be careful not to discount "official goals" as irrelevant. They are *purposely* vague and general since their intent is not to provide detailed instructions to employees, but rather to offer a rationale for the organization's existence to the wider public or interested constituency. Administrators of state prisons or mental hospitals will get little response from a legislative committee if they testify that their job is to keep dangerous people off the streets (unless there has recently been a prison escape, for example). They will speak, instead, of the importance of rehabilitation and of their long-range hope that persons now incarcerated will someday be able to return to society as retrained useful citizens and taxpayers.

## HOW GOALS ARE SET

Virtually all organizations have a formal, explicitly recognized, sometimes legally specified organ for setting initial goals and for their amendment. In some organizations, goals are set formally by a vote of the stockholders; in others, by a vote of the membership (e.g., some labor unions); in still others, by a small number of trustees; and in a few, by an individual who owns and runs the organization.

In practice, goals are often set in a complicated power play involving various individuals and groups within and outside the organization, and by reference to values that govern behavior in general as well as the specific behavior of the relevant individuals and groups in a particular society.

Many factors enter into the struggle to determine an organization's goal or goals. Sometimes dominant personalities may, through charismatic qualities or the simple fact of ownership, impose their own goals on the organization. This factor was especially important historically, when firms were small, and is a feature in small businesses and family-owned enterprises even now.

More commonly, goal determination is the outcome of a power struggle among factions or departments. In a study of plastics firms facing competitive environments, Lawrence and Lorsch (1967) report that the sales, production, and research departments had highly different orientations. Sales was particularly concerned with consumer problems and price, production with costs and efficiency, and research with long-range innovations and changes. Production was the most highly formalized department, research much less so. Such differences in orientation brought the three departments into conflict as each sought to influence the firm's goals. For example, production preferred products allowing for long runs, with few scientific innovations and few design changes, while sales wanted products adapted to particular customer needs or to fast changes in market preferences or style. Yet the researchers report that the most successful firms were not those that tried to reduce these differences in orientation, but rather those that preserved them, while also developing strategies for resolving resulting conflicts.[4]

Ladd and Lipset (1975), analyzing the results of a national survey of institutions of higher education, report strong differences among the various academic disciplines in political behavior, liberal-conservative attitudes, and degree of support for student participation in university policy. Such variation comes to be reflected in committee participation and attempts to influence governance. The result is that the traditional goals of "teaching, research, and community service" turn out to reflect the balance of forces on a campus. Interestingly, the researchers find that, contrary to traditional thinking going back at least to Marx and Engels, it is the *most* satisfied among the faculty who are the most liberal and critical in their political orientation.

In addition to personalities and factions, an important role is played by environmental forces. Most organizations are less autonomous than they seem. Consider a prison that will have to drastically reduce its security precautions if it carries out its plan to allow inmates to work in the fields—a measure deemed helpful in the shift from the goal of custody (keep them in) to that of rehabilitation (change them while they are in). The surrounding community will often object strongly to such a relaxation of security measures, especially after an escape, and will exert considerable political pressure to prevent a change of the prison's goals from custodial to rehabilitative. If necessary, the community will work to remove the warden and other prison staff. Other environmental forces—such as antitrust laws, the Department of Health, and labor unions—also set limits, not only on the means an organization may use, but on the goals it may pursue as well.

When the environment consists of other organizations, as tends to be increasingly the case, an organization may find its goals defined in spite of itself. Maniha and Perrow (1965) describe a "reluctant organization," a small-town Youth Commission that was set up (because of the enthusiasm of a city councilman) with the vague mandate of "promoting the best interests of children and youth in the city." The commission soon found itself assisting the Juvenile Division of the Police Department by backing an ordinance to control youth disturbances, cosponsoring a seminar advocated by the United Fund, and then seeking state support for protective services for youth. No one on the commission really wanted to become active in these matters, but the commission was turned to by local citizens as the "logical" agency.

The picture of goal determination that emerges from such research is that goals are the outcome of a dynamic, ever-changing set of alliances as groups seek to pursue their own interests, even using the organization as a weapon (Selznick, 1952) if the opportunity arises. Cyert and March (1963) have called this viewpoint that of seeing goals as the result of efforts by "dominant coalitions."[5]

One must search for the key power holders (or power-holding factions or departments), a search that has given rise to a new set of studies on the loci of organizational power. For example, Hickson, Hinings, Lee, Schneck, and Pennings (1971) have tested the hypothesis that the most powerful subunits or departments are likely to be those offering the least "substitutability" and those managing uncertainty most successfully. The focus on uncertainty has been a continuing concern of researchers ever since Crozier (1964) isolated its importance in his classic study of a French tobacco monopoly. The work in that organization is highly mechanized and bureaucratized, except for machine breakdown, which cannot be easily predicted or planned for. Therefore, says Crozier, the mechanics take on strategic power by virtue of their special expertise.[6]

This approach has given rise to what Zald (1970) calls a "political economy" view of organizations, and even to a resurgence of Marxist approaches (Benson, 1977; Heydebrand, 1977). But we need not go so far as to create new theories or resurrect old ones to account for goal determination. The role of conflict is clearly articulated in the Structuralist position, which we discuss in Chapter 5.

Conflict goes on continually, but at the same time, persons and groups bargain for some say in determining organizational goals, though often such bargaining is implicit or "silent" (Fagerhaugh & Strauss, 1977). The net result is that what happen to be the goals of an organization at a particular time may be seen as the features of a bargain struck among negotiators, or as the terms of a truce among combatants. The goals are always temporary, likely to be modified whenever the power balance shifts, either inside the organization or in the environment.[7]

## MEASURING SUCCESSFUL PERFORMANCE

Because organizations are set up to achieve goals and so satisfy needs, they are under continuous pressure to demonstrate that they are doing their jobs well. A host of monitors keeps close watch—accountants, legal staffs, computer systems analysts, and legislative committees, not to speak of ordinary consumers, who pass final judgment when they try out the product or utilize the service. Satisfying all of these groups is far from easy.

If there is consensus on a major goal, and if it is achievable once and for all, there may be little problem. For example, in a military battle, one army may force the other to capitulate, leading to a clear victory. But even in this instance, military and political analysts will examine the casualty figures and other damage and ask whether the victory was not bought at too heavy a price. Still, there was a clear outcome, however it is evaluated. If, on the other hand, the organizational goal is a continuous one, measurement is much more difficult. If the purpose of the corporation is to make a profit, and it makes a 3 percent profit one year, 4 percent the next year, and no profit the third year, how successful is that corporation? Here one must specify a standard, such as "profit compared to that of similar corporations in the same period." Finally, when we come to organizations whose output is not material (e.g., churches), statements about success are extremely difficult to validate. Since keeping costs down is often used as a way of comparing otherwise noncomparable organizations (for example, a state legislature may compare "costs per patient day" in a mental hospital with "costs per student credit hour" in a university, then rate one organization as "better" if it has reduced costs by a larger percentage than the other), administrators may be tempted to adopt severe cost-cutting practices that threaten the integrity of the organization itself.[8]

Many organizations under pressure to be rational are eager to measure their efficiency. Curiously, the very effort to establish how they are doing—and to find ways of improving if they are not doing as well as they ought to—often has quite undesired effects on organizational goals. For one thing, frequent measuring can distort an organization's efforts because, as a rule, some aspects of its output are more measurable than others. Therefore, frequent measuring tends to encourage overproduction of highly measurable items and neglect of less measurable ones. For example, when a factory puts great pressure on its production people to increase their efficiency, they might well produce more items, but of a lower quality. If quality control is then tightened, the production people might neglect the maintenance of their equipment to put more effort into satisfying the increased pressure to maintain quality.

These problems are particularly severe in socialist countries where a master plan forces targets and quotas on all major organizations. In summing up the achievements of Soviet industry before World War II, the premier complained of a practice called "storming" in the following words:

> The Kolomensk Machinery Works in Moscow County worked this way in 1940: in the first ten days of every month it produced 5 to 7 per cent of its output, in the second ten days, 10 to 15 per cent, and in the third ten days, 75 to 80 percent.
> The Karl Marx–Leningrad Plant, in December 1940, produced 2 per cent

of its monthly output in the first ten days, 8 per cent in the second ten days, and 90 per cent in the third ten days.

In the Moscow Pump and Compressor Plant, in December 1940, 3.4 per cent of the month's output was produced in the first ten days, 27.5 per cent in the second ten days, and 69.1 per cent in the third ten days.

We must put an end to this lack of planning, to this uneven rate of production, to this storming in the work of enterprises. (Berliner, 1956, pp. 87–88)

Alas, 14 years later, another Soviet premier quoted almost identical statistics for other organizations, lamenting the lack of progress in solving the problem. The culprit is the monthly target itself. As it approaches, work is intensified, workers are pressured, and machinery is run without needed maintenance checks in order to meet the quota. Then at the end of the month, everyone relaxes (having earned a break), people take time off, machines are removed from production for servicing, and thus production drops, before the workers realize they had better get moving again.

The possible anomalies introduced by overattention to measuring are especially serious when it is impossible or impractical to quantify the more central, substantive output of an organization, and when at the same time some exterior aspects of the product, which are superficially related to its substance, are readily measurable. High schools that measure the quality of their curricula by the number of students who pass Regents examinations (stressing here one component of effectiveness) find that some teachers neglect the character development of their students to drill them for the tests. If a pastor is frequently surveyed by his superiors on how much money he has raised for a new cathedral or how many children attend Sunday school in his parish, he soon becomes more occupied with fund-raising and class size than with the spiritual guidance of his parishioners.

A study of a hospital (Perrow, 1961) points up the difficulty its officials faced in providing measures of such general goals as "promoting the health of the community through care of patients, teaching and research of high quality." At first, the administrators considered publicizing the names of its contractors and research grantors, but these agencies and organizations were reluctant to allow the hospital to use their names to back up validating claims. The administrators then tried discreet promotion about their specialized equipment, the amount of free care the hospital gave to patients, and the reputation of hospital personnel. These measures had limited effectiveness, so the hospital had to resort to "extrinsic referents": comforts available to physicians who use the hospital; "hotel" aspects, such as wine with meals and a beauty salon for maternity patients; extended visiting hours and circulating coffee carts for visitors; elaborate devices to suppress noise; and meticulous housekeeping. The relationship of these amenities to patient care, teaching, and research is far from clear. In fact, they might even interfere with these goals, quite apart from the extra cost involved.

There is no complete solution to the problem of measuring success. Organizations do best to recognize that many measures are far from accurate, and that attributing too much importance to some indicators of organizational success and not enough to others may lead to considerable undermining and distortion of organizational goals. Using measures of several aspects of the product (e.g., quantity and quality, as well as maintenance control) and stressing those features that come closest to the organizational goal reduces the problem of measuring organizational success, although it does not succeed in eliminating it.

The distortion of goals that arises from overmeasurement of some aspects of the organization's output to the detriment of others is one of a larger category of distortions that arise in the relations of organizations to their goals. In the following sections we are concerned with several other varieties of the distortion phenomenon. Distortions due to overmeasurement are comparatively mild, since the main goals of the organization remain intact, though certain aspects of those goals become overemphasized at the expense of other, sometimes more important ones. Goal displacement is much more detrimental.

## DISPLACEMENT OF GOALS

Goal displacement[9] refers to the situation that arises when an organization substitutes for its legitimate or recognized goal some other goal for which it was not created, for which resources were not allocated to it, and which it is not known to serve.

The mildest and most common form of displacement is the process whereby an organization reverses the priority between its goals and means in a way that makes the means a goal and the goal a means. The most common means so displaced is the organization itself. Organizations are instruments; they are created to serve one or more specific goals. But in the process of forming them, of granting them resources, and of recruiting personnel, interest groups are formed that are frequently concerned more with preserving and building up the organization itself than in helping it to serve its initial purpose. These interest groups use the organizational goals as a means to recruit funds, to obtain tax exemptions or status in the community—in short, as means to their own goals.

Although he did not use the term *goal displacement,* the German sociologist Robert Michels (1962, first published in 1911) is credited with the first extensive description and analysis of this phenomenon. Michels studied the Socialist parties and labor unions in Europe before World War I. He pointed out that they were formed to forward the Socialist revolution and to establish a democratic regime in authoritarian countries, such as Bismarck's Germany. The parties and unions demanded leadership; the leaders soon developed vested interests in maintaining their organizational positions, since without them they would have been forced to return to manual labor, and this would have meant a life of low prestige and wages, with none of the psychological gratifications of leadership. Michels showed that the leaders were, for these reasons, careful to establish themselves firmly in office. By controlling the means of communication within the organization and by either absorbing or "purging" young, ambitious leaders, the established leaders strove to secure their positions. In this process, which Michels referred to as the "Iron Law of Oligarchy" (*iron* because presumably without exception, and *oligarchy* because of the imposition of rule by a few), the organization's democratic goals were subverted. Furthermore, the leaders were less and less induced to take risks in their revolutionary activities for fear of angering the government and thereby endangering the organization's existence. The party or union abandoned its militant activities in favor of developing a smoothly working organizational machine. More and more frequently, revolutionary action was delayed to allow for "further preparations," which amounted to a large buildup of the organization, its assets, and the positions of its leaders. Thus, Michels suggested, organizations with revolutionary goals became quite conservative in their conduct.

Since Michels' statement of the Iron Law of Oligarchy, this organizational tendency has been repeatedly documented. In many countries and in a variety of organizational types—even those in which the leadership is elected and can be changed by the membership—oligarchies prevail.[10]

It is important to note that there are two kinds of settings in which we might hope to establish democratic participation: (1) within organizations, and (2) in the larger society outside of organizations. Michels was clearly describing the first, and he seemed to think that it was somehow necessary for the second. But actually, an organization that is internally undemocratic might still serve the goal of forwarding the establishment of a democratic regime in the society in which it operates (Lipset, Trow, & Coleman, 1956, pp. 411–412). It is even possible that an oligarchy, by preventing wasted efforts on internal strife, might direct the organizational membership more effectively in attaining democratic goals. Still, whatever its implications for democracy in the larger society, Michels' study did show how Socialist organizations acted to persistently delay the Socialist goal of revolution and how that goal was eventually sacrificed in favor of preserving the organization.

Since Michels' work, goal displacement has been noted in a large variety of organizations. Clark (1948) revealed it in his study of the Salvation Army in Canada. He showed that as the organization grew larger and became more successful at obtaining members and funds, the leadership began to devote more and more attention and resources to maintaining the organization. It even gave up evangelical work in those parts of Canada where there was insufficient local financial support to maintain a chapter, presumably because such a chapter might become a drain on the organization's national resources.

Merton (1957, pp. 197 ff) discusses another major source of the same displacement tendency that Michels stressed. Here, goal displacement does not occur at the top of the organization but in its very body, and it occurs not in voluntary associations but in public and private bureaucracies. Merton suggested that bureaucracy has certain effects on its members' personalities, that it encourages the tendency to adhere rigidly to rules and regulations for their own sake, even when the organization formally or informally encourages flexibility in the application of the rules. For example, welfare workers may fear the risks of making a decision on their own; they may play it safe by observing the organization's rules and policies minutely, with the result that more important treatment considerations are underplayed. Thus, a social worker, in violation of his own judgment of what would be most beneficial for his clients, may recommend that a mentally disturbed child remain with her family because the agency has a policy of not breaking up family units, even though the child's presence at home may disrupt the adjustment of the other children in the family. Instead of making procedures "means" to the organization's goal, this social worker is making them "ends" in themselves. The policy is the prevailing criterion for his decision, and he bends the clients' needs to fit the policy. Adherence to the organization's policy has become the organizational goal of the bureaucrat.

In a study of a federal agency, Blau (1963) discovered that under certain conditions such bureaucratic ritualism may be minimized. He found, for example, that interest in innovation increases as persons feel more secure, especially when that security is based on competence. He studied the attitudes of a group of officials toward frequent changes in regulations, and related those attitudes to competence. Most of the objections came from the *less* competent officials, even though the more competent officials might have been expected to object because change meant learning new procedures after they had already mastered the existing ones. But their competence had increased their security, and their resulting self-confidence created an interest in improvements and change.[11]

Still, the pressure toward goal displacement is ever present and must be watched for by those interested in democratic participation in their organization. The tendency is well known to any mother or father who has participated in a PTA or other parent group. A small number of parents runs things, despite their unwillingness to do so and their continued pleading with other parents to *please* volunteer to serve on the annual bazaar committee or to *please* run for office. Even the most ideological and dedicated organizations face this problem. We need not rely on such historical examples as the Socialist parties and unions studied by Michels some 70 years ago. Newman (1980) studied 12 California urban collectives, including health food stores, leather shops, child-care centers, rape prevention clinics, and other countercultural groups. These collectives were determined to avoid hierarchy, paperwork, and anything smacking of bureaucracy. At first, they were run by volunteers who held full-time jobs outside and put in extra hours at the collective. Decisions were made on the spot, and no records were kept. But then the members decided the collective could function better if they got grant money, which would allow people to give up their outside jobs and devote full time to the collective. Alas, that was a fatal decision. For they now found themselves accountable to the fund source. To demonstrate competence and responsibility to outside auditors, they had to keep careful records, and most important, since the grant money was not enough to put *all* volunteers on the payroll, a wedge was driven between the paid and unpaid staff (who still had outside jobs). Soon the familiar Michelsian processes began to creep in. The paid full-time people came to know more about what needed to be done and grew impatient with the volunteers, who often spoke from ignorance. Before long, a hierarchy grew up, with the competent, experienced persons running the organization. Although the myth of "democratic participation" and communalism continued to be spoken of, it became increasingly difficult for members of the organization to believe in it.

## GOAL SUCCESSION, MULTIPLICATION, AND EXPANSION

Similar to goal displacement in its sociological and psychological sources, but quite different from the standpoint of meeting goals, is the tendency of organizations to find new goals when the old ones have been realized or cannot be attained. A case in point is Sills' (1957) study of the Foundation for Infantile Paralysis, which is popularly known for its annual March of Dimes campaign. The major goal of the foundation was to recruit public support for the medical research needed to fight polio and to provide assistance for its victims. As Sills reports, the foundation was not diverted from its goal. On the contrary, in an effort that lasted two decades, it supported much of the medical research that culminated in the famous Salk polio vaccine, which led to the almost complete elimination of polio. The foundation was then, so to speak, "unemployed." Here was a vast network of volunteers who experienced a variety of social and normative gratifications by working for the foundation, and a national leadership and staff—all coordinated in an efficient and obviously effective organizational machine. But the machine was without a purpose. The foundation might simply have been disbanded, but instead it found a new goal—combating arthritis and birth defects. Sills' study illustrates both the deep vested interest that arises in maintaining the organization once it has been firmly established, and the service the goal performs for the organization (rather than the reverse). Without a goal, the foundation had no meaning for its members and no legitimacy in the community. It had to find a new goal or cease to exist.

Such clear-cut cases of goal succession are rare, both because most organizations do not reach their goals in the definitive way the Foundation for Infantile Paralysis did, and because many of those that do achieve their goals are dissolved, as, for example, most anti-Nazi underground organizations were after the collapse of the Third Reich.

A more common form of goal succession occurs when the service of the old goal is highly unsuccessful, forcing the organization to find a new goal to serve if it is to survive. It is even more common for an organization in such a situation to set additional goals or to expand the scope of the old ones. In doing this, the organization acts to increase the dedication of its existing members and to encourage the recruitment of new ones. Thus undergraduate colleges in the United States over the last hundred years took on the goal of graduate training, a goal quite different from their original aim of producing gentlemen "who could read and write and stay out of jail." Many religious organizations added social and community service goals, which have, in some instances, superseded the older spiritual goals: Prayers are cut short to leave more time for square dances. The Red Cross, originally formed to "hold itself in readiness in the event of war or any calamity great enough to be considered national, to inaugurate such practical measures in mitigation of the suffering and for the protection and relief of sick and wounded as may be consistent with the object of the Association" (Sills, 1957, p. 262) found itself underemployed after World War I and lost members, contributions, and public esteem. It overcame that crisis by adding a goal—preserving and improving public health. Zald and Denton (1963) track the striking adaptability of the YMCA, which started as an evangelical association for young men; but because of very broadly stated goals and a decentralized decision-making structure, it responded to the wishes of its clientele and gradually became a general leisure-time organization found in 96 percent of cities with populations of over 50,000.

In fact, goal succession is found in every organization that has short-term goals. A business must state a profit goal for a particular period. Once that is achieved, it must go on to state a new one for a new period. A theatrical repertory group puts on a play, and if it is successful, money is generated to underwrite the production of another play. The armed forces face such a succession problem after a war, when they must develop alternative goals, such as "remaining ready if called upon." This goal is by no means easy to pursue, since it is difficult to maintain the morale of service men and women when they are only going through practice maneuvers or when they see themselves as merely "weekend warriors."[12]

Thus the organization's self-interest may lead not only to displacement of primary goals by other, secondary goals or by means, but also to active pursuit of new goals once the old ones are realized or to the acquisition of additional goals. Additional goals are often justified initially as enhancing the service of the old goals, but frequently they become full-fledged equals if not "masters."

## MULTIPURPOSE ORGANIZATIONS

Many organizations simultaneously and legitimately serve two or more goals. Sometimes this is a sequential development. For example, separate organizations may merge. When one firm buys out another, it may simply add the other's goals to its own. Similarly, government bureaus may be formed by combining previously separate departments, or a new community college may be created by the addition of college preparatory functions to vocational and service programs. In industry, new goals may be added through vertical integration, as when an automobile company buys up a steel production firm (to assure supplies), coal mines (to smelt the iron ore for the steel), and railroads (to transport the automobiles). Chain department stores may buy up manufacturers to assure themselves of supplies or for other reasons. Churches may take on new functions, such as assisting in finding jobs for their unemployed members, or may even move into political activism.

There are also many organizations that were originally formed to serve more than one goal at a time. In the field of scholarship, there are more organizations that combine teaching with research (most universities) than are primarily devoted to teaching (most colleges) or are solely devoted to research (e.g., the Rand Corporation, the Stanford Research Institute). While some hospitals are almost exclusively places where ill people are treated, many also serve as training grounds for the medical profession, and quite a few are also research centers. Most contemporary religious organizations combine social with spiritual goals.

To the extent that such things can be measured, it appears that many multipurpose organizations tend to serve each of their goals separately and all of them together more effectively and efficiently than single-purpose organizations of the same category. For instance, many if not most high-quality hospitals serve three purposes—therapy, research, and teaching—while those that only cure (most community hospitals) generally offer lower-quality medical care (cf. Gross, 1971). Many business conglomerates have been formed from companies whose products have no necessary relationship to one another because the managers believed that the conglomerate, by combining more profitable operations with less profitable ones, would yield administrative advantages, cost savings, or reduced taxes. The net result may be greater profitability for the conglomerate as a whole.

Most of the important scientific discoveries of the past decade and most of the outstanding work in the social sciences have come from the faculties of universities where teaching and research are combined, not from the full-time personnel of research organizations. (Whether teaching is more effective in university colleges where research is emphasized or in colleges that devote themselves primarily to teaching is an open question. In part, the answer depends on the criteria of evaluation used, on whether or not one chooses to include character development in addition to the acquisition of knowledge and skills.) Finally, religious organizations serving middle-class areas in the contemporary United States could hardly fulfill their spiritual purposes without adding some social goals, because it is the social goals that attract many participants, at least initially, to dual-purpose churches. It seems that the community that stays together also prays together.

In part, the relationship between an organization's effectiveness and multipurpose goals seems spurious—the result of extrinsic factors. For instance, multipurpose organizations are more often found in the larger urban centers, and single-purpose ones in smaller communities. Most major American universities and medical centers, for instance, are in, or close to, major cities. Since most professionals, when given a choice, prefer to live in urban centers, multipurpose organizations tend to have a larger pool of qualified professionals from which to recruit than single-purpose organizations. But the relationship between effectiveness and multipurposeness seems to hold even if such extrinsic factors are kept constant—for instance, when we compare single- and multipurpose organizations in the same city, say a college or research organization with a multipurpose university in a major American city.

There are several internal reasons why multipurpose organizations tend to be more effective than single-purpose ones. First of all, serving one goal often improves—within limits—the service rendered to another goal. For example, many researchers are stimulated by teaching intelligent, probing students. Researchers, in turn, bring new ideas to their teaching, as well as a first-hand knowledge of the research experience for which they are training their students. Second, as a rule, multipurpose organizations have greater recruitment appeal than single-purpose ones, partly because high quality is often associated with multiservices. It is difficult to think of many monopurpose organizations that have more prestige than their multipurpose counterparts. Third, while some individuals prefer to deal exclusively in one service, many find combining two services more attractive because it allows them to gratify a wider variety of their personality needs. It also leaves more room for life-cycle adjustment, e.g., stress on research in younger years and teaching in later ones, or the opposite.

There are, however, limits to the organization's ability to serve multipurpose goals. Loss of effectiveness seems to occur when all organizations of a specific category are made multipurpose. In fields such as teaching or medicine, which have a cluster of associated activities, a large proportion of professionals prefer to participate in a combination of these activities. Some, however, perform markedly better in one area than another and would rather devote their full attention to that area. For this reason, effectiveness seems to be maximized when there are both single- and multipurpose organizations in the profession, to allow both types of personalities to find the employment most suited to their capacities and psychological needs.

Within multipurpose organizations, certain types of conflict are unavoidable. The various goals often make incompatible demands on the organization. There may be conflicts over the amount of means, time, and energy to be allocated to each goal. For instance, the treatment goal of a hospital may be best served by a policy of open admissions whereby anyone in need of hospitalization is accepted, while the research goal is best served by a policy of selective admissions that provides sufficient numbers of people with the specific types of illness that match the staff's current research interests. The establishment of a set of priorities that clearly defines the relative importance of the various goals reduces the disruptive consequences of such conflicts, though it does not eliminate the problem.

Furthermore, serving a plurality of goals may create strains for personnel. For example, research demands specialization and allows the scholar to devote considerable time to investigating a particular, often seemingly minute, problem. Teaching, on the other hand, demands breadth of knowledge.

There is also the danger that one goal may so subordinate the other, sometimes more primary, one to the point that the latter is no longer served effectively. A church may initiate social activities to attract members to religious services, for instance, but if the social activities consume the greater proportion of the church's resources or become the major focus of the participants' commitments, then they undermine the achievement of the religious goal. Similarly, the research and consulting activities of a cosmopolitan university faculty may lead to the neglect of teaching. In short, multipurpose organizations may develop major strains deriving from the very characteristics that make them, all things considered, more effective than single-purpose ones. Weick (1976) has suggested a way out of some of these conflicts: "loose coupling" among departments or other units in organizations. His point is that tightly knit organizations may create unnecessary coordination costs. If greater autonomy is allowed, units may respond more readily to environmental changes or special needs of members without disturbing the whole organization. Troublesome departments whose goals conflict may be sealed off until the problems are overcome. Although such devices are only applicable in some kinds of organizations, they do offer an alternative.

## EFFECTIVENESS—GOAL AND SYSTEM MODELS

Since organizations are established to accomplish certain ends or satisfy certain societal needs, we should be able to assess their effectiveness by asking how well they are performing. Since we have focused so heavily on goals, the question could be framed: How close did the organization come to achieving its goals?[13] Actually, it turns out that the measurement of effectiveness is a highly complex problem that has so far resisted any simple solution, and, indeed, has created a new research area known as *evaluation research* or simply *effectiveness study*.[14]

Quite apart from any measurement problems,[15] there are some theoretical problems that are much more serious. There are two basic approaches to effectiveness. One may be called the goal model, and the other the systems model.

The *goal model* seems the simpler of the two. Those who use this model ask the simple question: How close did you come to achieving your goals? This model is exemplified in cost-benefit analysis, as when a government evaluation agency compares the relative effectiveness of different programs set up to provide job skills to increase the employability of out-of-school youths. The approach received much publicity from its use in the U.S. Department of Defense in the PPBS programs (Planning-Programming-Budgeting Systems). A popular approach in business administration is known as "management by objectives," meaning managers are urged and assisted to specify clearly the objectives of their departments and then assess their achievements at the end of a specified time. Similarly, teachers are required to set goals for a given unit, and conference participants at workshops are required to decide each morning when they assemble what their goals are for the day. A recent example has been competence testing in schools; students must be able to solve certain standardized problems before they receive a credential.

Although the goal-model approach seems commonsensical, it suffers from some grave defects. To begin with, it assumes that there is agreement on goals or objectives, or that some group of decision makers has the power to unilaterally impose a set of goals on others, who will accept them without resistance. Actually, even in the face of overwhelming power, subordinates can veto imposed goals by dragging their feet or subverting the goals in other ways. So at best such power tactics are likely to be costly, and at worst, counterproductive. Obtaining agreement on goals is even more difficult than simply imposing them, for the simple reason that organizations have multiple goals that, as we noted earlier, will inevitably conflict in all but the simplest entities.[16]

There are further problems with the goal-effectiveness model. It tends, though not invariably, to give organizational studies a tone of social criticism rather than scientific analysis. Since most organizations most of the time do not attain their goals in any final sense, organizational monographs frequently detour into lengthy discussions about this lack of success to the exclusion of more penetrating types of analysis (cf. Etzioni, 1960). Low effectiveness is a general characteristic of organizations. Since goals are ideals that are more attractive than the reality the organization attains, the organization can almost always be reported to be a failure. While this approach is valid, it is only valid from the particular viewpoint chosen by the researcher. The goal model defines success as the complete or at least substantial realization of the organizational goal. Thus the researcher is analogous to an electrical engineer who would rate all light bulbs "ineffective" because they convert only about 20 percent of their electrical energy into light, "wasting" the rest on heat. It is much more meaningful to compare light bulbs to one another rather than to some ideal "superbulb" that would turn all energy into light. In practice, then, it is significant that Brand "A" converts only 15 percent of the energy into light, while Brand "B" converts 25 percent. From the Olympian height of the goal—light without heat—both results are hopelessly inadequate. From the realistic level of comparative analysis, one bulb is 66 percent more effective than the other (and may even be the best light bulb available).

The second basic approach to evaluating organizational success, therefore, does not compare existing organizations to an ideal, but rather assesses their performances relative to one another. Using this approach, we would not simply say that practically all organizations are oligarchic; instead, we would try to determine which ones are more and which are less oligarchic. The comparative analysis of organizations suggests an alternative approach called the *system model*. It constitutes a statement about relationships that must exist for an organization to operate.

A system model assumes that organizations are usually so complex, and the expectations of their various constituencies (workers, clients, suppliers, legislators) so diverse and often at such cross-purposes, that it is better not to pay exclusive attention to how well the organization attains its goals. For no matter what it does, the organization is bound to disappoint some of its constituencies. The system model assumes that there is *one* point on which all constituencies would agree: The organization itself must survive and continue to at least partially satisfy its constituencies.[17]

Those who take this approach (which includes the present authors) follow the lead of one of its earliest proponents, Philip Selznick, who urged researchers to pay attention to whatever was necessary to "the maintenance of the integrity and continuity of the system itself" (Selznick, 1948, p. 29). That is a large order, but it has led to revealing insights about organizational functioning. For example, in the perspective of the goal model, to suggest that an organization can become more effective by assigning fewer means to goal activities is a contradiction. The system model, however, leads one to conclude that just as there may be an underallocation of resources to meet the goals of the organization, so, too, there may be an overallocation. The system model explicitly recognizes that the organization solves certain problems other than those directly involved in the achievement of its goals. Excessive concern with the latter may, in fact, result in insufficient attention to other necessary organizational activities, and to a lack of coordination between the inflated goal activities and the deemphasized nongoal activities. Thus a bank may pay all its attention to making money and completely ignore the morale of its employees. This lack of attention to nongoal activities may result in staff dissatisfaction, which may express itself in poor work by the clerks, which in turn may result in decreased efficiency or even in a wave of embezzlements that ultimately reduces the bank's effectiveness.

Other researchers have suggested more general requirements for organizational survival and growth or health. They ask: Are the resources of the organization fairly distributed among departments, or are some being starved at the expense of others with more aggressive chiefs? Is the organization, while doing well now, using up its resources at too fast a rate?

The most full-blown theoretical application of the system model is in the classic work of Talcott Parsons.[18] Besides satisfying their own internal needs (securing resources, resolving internal conflicts, and socializing, mobilizing, and motivating its members to pursue the organization's goals), Parsons saw organizations as performing essential functions for society. If an organization did not or could not perform those functions, and therefore did not legitimate itself, it risked loss of support and eventual demise, as illustrated by Clark's (1956) study of an adult education organization in California.

Support for the thesis that a system model can be formulated and fruitfully applied is found in a study of organizational effectiveness by Georgopoulos and Tannenbaum (1957), one of the few studies that distinguish explicitly between the goal and system approaches to the evaluation of effectiveness. Instead of focusing on the goals of the delivery service organizations under study, the researchers constructed three indexes, each measuring one basic element of the system. These were: (1) station productivity; (2) intraorganizational strain, as indicated by the incidence of tension and conflict among organizational subgroups; and (3) organizational flexibility, defined as the ability to adjust to external or internal change. The total score of effectiveness thus produced was significantly correlated with the ratings on effectiveness that various experts and "insiders" gave the 32 stations. The stations were compared to one another on these dimensions rather than to an idealized picture of what a delivery station should be.

Highly technical application of the system model has been adopted by operations researchers (who often employ mathematical models of organizational systems), as well as by practitioners of what is known as Organizational Development (OD). That work came out of the T-groups (*T* for training) and sensitivity training movement of the 1950s—developed into team-building approaches by French and Bell (1978)—and studies of what is called the Managerial Grid by Blake and Mouton (1969). These writers have concluded that certain characteristics define an effective or healthy organization. For example: Is communication relatively undistorted? Do conflicts get solved so that no one is a total loser? Are decisions made by those who have the best information to make them? Still others—especially the colleagues and followers of Rensis Likert (Katz and Kahn, 1978: Likert, 1961, 1967)—stress the importance of involving subordinates in decisions that affect them, goal setting by group participation, adequacy of training, and other characteristics that research has revealed are important to organizational functioning.[19]

The goal model is less exacting and expensive to use for research than the systems model. It requires that the researcher determine the goals the organization is pursuing—and no more. If official goals are chosen, this is comparatively easy. Operative goals—those the organization actually pursues—are more difficult to establish. To find out, it is sometimes necessary not only to gain the confidence of the organization's elite but also to analyze much of the organizational structure.

Research conducted on the basis of the system model requires more effort. Analysts must determine what is a highly effective allocation of means. This often entails gaining considerable knowledge of the way an organization of the type studied functions, which can be demanding work. However, the effort invested will not be wasted, since (1) the information collected in the process will be valuable for the study of most organizational problems, and (2) such knowledge will advance our basic theory about organizations. If the selected system variables turn out not to predict or co-vary with organizational success as judged by survival or other indicators, then clearly the theory needs modification.

We now turn our attention to organizational theory itself.

## NOTES

1. Some writers (e.g., Silverman, 1971, pp. 29ff) object to the application of the word *need* to organizations, claiming that only human beings have needs. We are keenly aware of the dangers of reification, but feel that it is quite proper to speak of groups or collectivities as having needs—for resources, leadership, rational achievable goals, and so forth.

2. In a study of the goals of American universities, Gross and Grambsch (1974) attacked the problem of distinguishing respondents' perceptions of university goals from their

conception of what those goals ought to be by asking them to rate a goal on *both* dimensions. For example, respondents were presented with a goal statement and asked to check their rating of its importance as follows:

| Goal Importance | | ABSOLUTELY TOP | GREAT | MEDIUM | LITTLE | NO | DON'T KNOW/ CAN'T SAY |
|---|---|---|---|---|---|---|---|
| Carry on Applied Research | *Is* | _____ | _√_ | _____ | _____ | __ | _____ |
| | *Should be* | _____ | _____ | _____ | _____ | _√_ | _____ |

If respondents answered in the way shown, they would be saying that applied research was of great importance at the university, but that it should be of no importance. This simple device helps people keep their own wishes or hopes from obscuring their perceptions of the way things actually are in their organization.

3. A related distinction is made by Corwin (1965, pp. 433–438) between "nonoperational goals" and "accumulated commitments." The latter may lead to goals that must be pursued. For example, a school that agrees to establish an adult education program for people who wish to upgrade their job skills may find itself committed to providing job placement facilities for its graduates. Hence it may "discover" that it has a job placement goal.

4. The researchers also examined firms in the container and packaged food industries, where there was less differentiation and fewer goal conflicts. But there, too, the successful firms developed techniques for conflict resolution.

5. The approach was actually laid out and described in detail by Max Weber. See Collins, 1975.

6. What we seem to have here is more a case of veto power than actual ability to influence organizational goals or policy. Without denying the importance of such power (see, e.g., Bacharach & Lawler, 1980), it would appear to be more relative to the study of how decisions are implemented or stalled.

7. Simon (1964) takes a somewhat different stance. Any organization, he points out, must operate in the face of a whole set of constraints—resource shortages or needs, expert advice, competitors, laws, and so on. Any one of these may, he suggests, be singled out and called a "goal" if it is currently problematic and requires special focusing of effort. All of these "requirements" may then constitute a "complex" goal—so one can see the organization as having many goals.

8. In one university under pressure to cut costs, a member of a musical quintet in residence suggested (tongue-in-cheek, obviously) that the quintet be converted to a quartet, for a 20 percent cost saving.

9. We discuss goal displacement as a separate topic here since a good deal of research has been done under that name. Later, when we turn to the compliance framework (Chapter 7), we shall show that the process may often be seen as a special case in which normative organizations find that utilitarian compliance pressures lead to ineffectiveness.

10. There have been criticisms of Michels' original statement, but most seem to be either misunderstandings or concerned with matters other than Michels' central point. For example, Gouldner (1955) attacks him for a "metaphysical pathos" (i.e., for pessimism), and Edelstein (1967) takes him to task for "a compelling mix of theory and evidence, value judgment and mood" (p. 20; see also Edelstein, 1976). It is true that Michels was strongly pessimistic about the chances of democracy in organizations, but that does not detract from his *theoretical* contributions. Each of Michels' arguments should be read as a statement of conditions necessary for democracy. For example: "Leaders must not have a monopoly of the means of communication"; "There must be ways that the rank and file can acquire political skills"; and "Leaving office must not constitute a serious drop in status." *If* such conditions are present, democracy will prevail, as Lipset, Trow, and Coleman (1956) show in the case of the printers' union. But the fact is—and herein lies Michels' pessimism—such conditions are very rare, so in most cases, oligarchies will prevail. It is, therefore, no disproof of Michels to find, as some researchers have, *a* case where democracy does prevail.

11. In a national survey of juvenile courts, Sosin (1981) finds that the pressure to serve the internal "maintenance" needs of staff (such as high salaries and comfortable working

conditions) does not necessarily mean that the goals of serving the client are neglected. The essential element is that the community's willingness to provide such maintenance should, in turn, be contingent on adequate attention to client needs.

12. Bachman and Blair (1976) argue that the establishment of an all-volunteer peacetime U.S. Army could result in a military ethos with different values from those held by the civilian population.

13. A distinction should be drawn between effectiveness and efficiency. *Effectiveness* focuses on goals and their achievement. *Efficiency* raises the question of costs. An organization may meet a production target, but only at high levels of waste of materials—which makes it effective but inefficient. So, too, a mental health clinic may report a high success rate in treating behavior problems, but only by restricting its attention to a small number of patients and giving each intensive treatment. The reverse can also be true: An organization can be highly efficient but not very effective, as when it gets maximum output from its employees but fails in the market because new competitors produce a new and better product.

14. Most of the issues are reviewed in Goodman, Pennings, and associates, 1979. Older but useful summaries of studies are Price, 1968, and the collection by Ghorpade, 1971. Critical discussions are found in Steers, 1977; Scott, 1981, Chap. 14; Hall, 1982, Chap. 13; and Keeley, 1984. The collection in Baugher, 1981, pays special attention to governmental organizations.

15. A good discussion is in Rossi, Freeman, and Wright, 1979. Scott, 1981, calls attention to the question of indicators: What shall you pay attention to? (1) Some measures use *outcomes* (products, services, profits). But shall you pay attention to short-term outcomes (profit this year) or longer-term outcomes (building a solid base of loyal customers)? Outputs may also be misleading unless inputs are held constant. For example, a university hospital that concentrates on rare or nonroutine diseases may show a low recovery rate, but one that is very high if compared to others like it. Elite schools can report a high success rate for graduates, partly by careful selection of students. (2) *Processes* may be employed, such as the proportion of X-rays reviewed by radiologists or the regularity of security checks. But this can lead to the old joke: The operation was a success but the patient died. (3) Another indicator is the presence or absence of *structures*. Does the government office have a unit that reviews client complaints and recommends changes? Does the business school being considered for accreditation have more than 50 percent of faculty with PhDs? These are measures of potential or of capacity, which may not be strongly related to outcomes or other desired features.

16. In the face of this problem, Hall (1982) offers what he calls a "contradiction model of effectiveness," with the paradoxical conclusion that "*no organization is effective*" (p. 302) (italics in original).

17. One could argue that there might not even be agreement on that point. If an organization is part of a larger structure (e.g., a supermarket in a national chain, or a division of the federal government), some executives might well decide that the organization should be phased out altogether, or some constituencies might decide to take their patronage elsewhere. We are therefore confining our attention to constituencies that continue to depend on the organization.

18. All systems, according to Parsons, must satisfy certain fundamental problems, which he summed up in his AGIL model: *adaptation* (obtaining resources from its environment and otherwise relating to that environment), *goal* attainment (mobilizing resources to attain its ends), *integration* (holding together and resolving conflicts), and *latency* (reaffirming its basic values and socializing persons to secure and retain their loyalty). These problems are examined in many of his works, for example, Parsons, 1951, and Parsons, Bales, and Shils, 1953. The application to organizations is in Parsons, 1956.

19. This group tends to be more research oriented than the previous group. We have already referred to one of their studies (Yuchtman & Seashore, 1967; Seashore & Yuchtman, 1967), and it might well be regarded as a system model study. However, their definition of effectiveness as the ability of an organization to acquire scarce and valued environmental resources would seem to limit the concept of system to resource acquisition. Such capacity is certainly part of the system, but, as Parsons has argued, it is only *one* part.

# CHAPTER THREE
# RATIONAL MODELS

The search for greater effectiveness and efficiency in organizations gave rise to the *Classical* theory of administration, perhaps more appropriately called *Scientific Management,* since the latter title expresses the claim of this organizational approach: Workers are motivated by economic rewards, and the organization is characterized by a clearly defined division of labor with a highly specialized personnel and by a distinct hierarchy of authority. Out of this tradition comes the characterization of the *formal organization* as a blueprint according to which organizations are to be constructed and to which they ought to adhere.

Arising partly in reaction to Scientific Management, another approach gained prominence in the United States—*Human Relations.* In contrast to Classical theory, Human Relations emphasized the emotional, unplanned, nonrational elements in organizational behavior. It stressed the significance for the organization of friendship and social groupings of workers, and it pointed out the importance of leadership and of emotional communication and participation. From these observations the concept of *informal organization* was developed. This is sometimes viewed as what there is to the organization beyond its formal structure; and sometimes as what the organization's life is really like, as distinct from its blueprint and charts.

It remained the task of a third tradition in organizational thinking to relate the two concepts of the formal and informal organization and to provide a more complete and integrated picture of the organization. This convergence of organizational theory, known as the *Structuralist* approach, was made considerably more sophisticated through comparative analysis.

Whereas the earlier schools focused largely on factories and, to some degree, on public administration, and were only later adapted to the study of other organizations, the scope of the Structuralist approach was much broader to begin with, in terms of both the kinds of organizations covered and the kinds of cultural backgrounds taken into account.

Not only do these three approaches differ in their views of the organization, but they also suggest quite different conceptions of human beings and of society. While none of the three approaches is exclusively concerned with serving either the organizational goals as viewed by management or the workers' goals, there are important differences among them as to the goals emphasized. The Classical approach recognized no conflict between humans and organization. It viewed the organization from a managerial standpoint and assumed that what was good for management was good for the workers. The Classical school argued that hard and efficient labor will in the end pay off for both groups by increasing the effectiveness of the organization: Higher productivity leads to higher profits, which in turn lead to higher pay and greater worker satisfaction.

The Human Relations theorists pointed out that the workers have many needs other than purely economic ones, and that the Classical approach benefits neither management nor the workers. They went on to suggest ways in which management could—by paying attention to the non-economic, social, and cultural needs of the workers—increase worker satisfaction *and* productivity. The Structuralists viewed some conflict and strain between humans and organization as inevitable, and by no means always undesirable.

Although the three approaches developed historically, the second two rising dialectically from a critique of the approach that preceded it, none has been demolished by the critiques. The Classical approach, profiting from the critiques, gave rise to theoretical approaches emphasizing costs and efficiency. We shall call them *rational models*. The Human Relations approach, emphasizing microtransactions, generated a strong social-psychological tradition, resulting in what we shall call *interactionist* models. The Structuralist approach has also grown in variety, leading to what we shall call *structural* models. Although each approach is distinct and has its enthusiasts, each has also much to offer the others. We consider *rational models* in this chapter, beginning with Classical theory.

## THE CLASSICAL MOTIVATIONAL THEORY

The Classical approach contained both a theory of motivation and one of organization. The central contribution to the motivational theory was made by Frederick W. Taylor (Taylor, 1911), in what became known as Scientific Management.[1] Scientific Management combines a study of the physical capabilities of workers, as is still done (primarily by engineers) in time-and-motion studies, with an economic approach that views people as driven by the fear of hunger and the search for profit. The central tenet of the approach is that if material rewards are closely related to work efforts, workers will respond with the maximum performance they are physically capable of.

Although Taylor originally set out to study the interaction between human characteristics and the characteristics of the machine—that is, the relationship between those two elements that make up the industrial work process—he ended up by focusing on a more limited subject: the physical characteristics of the human body in certain jobs, e.g., shoveling loose materials, picking up loads, and machining parts. Whereas Taylor started out considering human and machine resources as mutually adaptable, he eventually came to the view that people function as appendages to the industrial machine.

Taylor's students—the human engineers—searched for the physical limits of human performance, put in terms of loads, pace, and fatigue. For example, they studied how many hours and at what speed a worker could carry loads of 50 pounds. Fatigue was viewed as a muscular, physiological phenomenon. Efforts were made to find motions that were less fatiguing and hence allowed the same human body to carry out more work with the same degree of fatigue in a given time unit. The following are some typical propositions of Scientific Management:

1.  The two hands should begin and complete their motions simultaneously.
2.  Smooth, continuous motions of the hands are preferable to zigzag or straight-line motions involving sudden and sharp changes in direction.
3.  Proper illumination increases productivity.
4.  There should be a definite and fixed place for all tools and materials.

Workers, it was suggested, should receive payments in the closest possible association with output. Various methods of measuring worker output and ways of relating payment to it were devised. Many of these methods are highly complicated, and of interest mainly to specialists. However, the principles of the system are simple: (1) Pay should be based on merit of performance and no other criterion (e.g., seniority). (2) The time unit should be as small as possible—monthly salaries are highly undesirable, wages paid by the hour are better, but the ideal situation is piecework wages in which pay is directly dependent on the actual amount of work accomplished.

Taylor and his associates had little doubt that once the best working procedure was taught to workers (use both hands, etc.) and their pay was tied to their output, they could be induced to produce the maximum labor physically possible, as calculated by the time-and-motion engineers. In laying out these methods for increasing productivity, the central principle that

Taylor insisted upon was the separation of *decision* from *execution*. The manager (or engineer under the manager's direction) was to decide (on the basis of careful study) how a job was to be done; the worker was to carry out the procedure precisely as instructed. Taylor himself was merciless in castigating any suggestion of allowing the worker autonomy or initiative. His descendants softened the coercion behind his principle by calling it "cooperation," though there was never any question as to who was to cooperate with whom. Such cooperation was justified by the claim that the result would be a "bigger pie" for all to share in.

## THE CLASSICAL ORGANIZATIONAL THEORY

Adam Smith's description of the modern manufacture of pins in his *Wealth of Nations* (1791, pp. 7–9. Orig. pub. 1776) has become a classic illustration of the significance of the division of labor. This illustration also demonstrates a basic principle of the school of Scientific Management. Smith notes that a single worker alone could hardly produce 20 pins a day. But when the task of making pins was broken down into many simple operations (he estimated that there were about 18 different jobs, such as straightening the wire and cutting it), Smith stated that he had seen 10 workers produce 48,000 pins in a day. This represents 4,800 pins per worker, or 240 times what one could, at best, produce alone. The division of labor that Smith first noted in 1776 was to become the basis of a theory of organizational efficiency over a hundred years later.

The Classical administration theory, presented in works by Gulick and Urwick (1937), made the division of labor its central tenet. The Classical approach rests firmly on the assumption that the more a particular job can be broken down into its simplest components, the more specialized and consequently the more skilled workers can become in carrying out their part of the job. The more skilled workers become in fulfilling their particular job, the more efficient the whole production system will be.

The *division* of labor, the Classical approach pointed out, has to be balanced by a *unity* of control. The job has to be broken down into component tasks by a central authority, in line with a central plan of action; the efforts of each work unit need to be supervised; and the various tasks leading to the final product have to be coordinated. Since a supervisor can effectively control only a limited number of subordinates, it is necessary to appoint a number of first-line supervisors, and then a second-line supervisor to supervise the supervisors, and so on up. Each five workers, for instance, might need one first-line supervisor; every six first-line supervisors, and hence every 30 workers, need one second-line supervisor, and so on. The number of subordinates controlled by one superior defines that person's "span of control." What results is a *pyramid of control* leading up to one top executive. In this way, the whole organization can be controlled from one *center of authority*, without having any one supervisor control more than five to ten subordinates.

While all the Classical writers accepted the principles of need for supervision and need for a single center of authority and control in the organization, they differed on how these principles should be implemented. The disagreement centered on the most efficient way the work should be distributed among the elementary production units and how the organizational pyramid of control should be constructed. Most Classical writers, however, agreed that work in the organization should be specialized according to one or more of four basic principles.[2] By following these principles, the organization could achieve the optimal division of labor and authority.

The first principle stated that specialization should be by *purpose* of the task. Workers who serve similar goals or subgoals in the organization should be attached to the same organizational division. There should be as many divisions in the organization as there are goals or subgoals. The United States armed forces, for instance, share the general goal of protecting the country. But parts of the armed forces have different subgoals: The Navy is responsible for defense on the seas; the Air Force must guard against attack from the air; and the Army is responsible for land defense.

The second principle of specialization suggests that all work based on a particular *process* should be grouped together, since it must share a special fund of knowledge and requires the use of similar skills or procedures. For example, the three military branches all need intelligence information. The Central Intelligence Agency provides certain kinds of intelligence that are used by all three branches—an example of an organization divided according to process.

Specialization according to type of *clientele* is still another basis for division. All work directed to serve a specific group of clients is placed in one division. For example, teachers who instruct very young children are separated from teachers who instruct adolescents.

The fourth principle says that jobs performed in the same *geographical area* should be placed together. Here different types of jobs may fall in the same division as long as they are carried out in the same place. According to this principle, all the United States military units (Navy, Air Force, and Army) in Southeast Asia might be put under one command.

Such, in brief, were the major early contributions of Classical organization theory.

## THE FRIENDLY CRITICS

From its inception, Classical theory was heavily criticized, but those critics whom we can call "friendly" accepted the basic assumptions of both the motivation and the organization theory. They agreed that human beings were primarily driven by economic motives; they simply thought that the early attempts to devise incentive schemes were much too crude and could be greatly improved. They agreed that a division of labor was necessary for efficiency; but they thought that, too, should be improved in the light of experience and scientific research. On the other hand, the Human Relations critics questioned the very assumptions in a rather unfriendly manner. We will consider this group of critics in Chapter 4. Here let us look at the friendly critics. There were two kinds: those who urged and developed refinements and improvements in the *measurement* of performance; and those who felt that Classical ideas of motivation and organization took a far too *exaggerated view of human rationality*. This second critique came from economists.

## 1. Sharpening Measures of Performance

Almost from the start, analysts saw inadequacies in the Classical theory, but rather than rejecting the theory on this account, they saw those inadequacies as a challenge for improvement. The basic motivational theory was a form of what is now called behavior modification or reinforcement. Many sought to improve it by undertaking laboratory studies where the impact of suspected variables could be tested under controlled conditions. In seeking to apply those findings to real situations, sophisticated techniques of performance appraisal were developed. One used graphic rating methods whose criteria were spelled out (e.g., ratings were sought on the person's job knowledge, volume of work, and quality of work). Another technique employed behavioral methods (e.g., work methods or outputs were unobtrusively observed). Complex job evaluation schemes were devised in which points were assigned to various features of jobs (responsibility, skill, effort, working conditions) and periodic performance evaluation meetings were held between supervisors and subordinates, both to make decisions on pay or promotion and to plot improvement in performance. These methods are still widely used; one investigation reports that of 150 firms studied, 84 percent had some form of appraisal system for office employees and 54 percent had such a system for production employees (Bureau of National Affairs, 1975). They are mandatory in most federal agencies. Their most recent application has been to the question of "comparable worth," where attempts are made to equalize male and female earnings on different jobs.

In spite of all these efforts to improve and modernize the Classical motivational theory, it continues to present knotty problems in implementation. Here are the main issues:

1. Although you can measure precisely the effect of an economic motive in the laboratory, things rapidly get confused in the workaday world. For example, when a new incentive system is introduced, managers

usually make a careful study of the job and try to arrange things so that the worker has a fair chance to make a bonus. This often produces improvements in job design even before the new incentive scheme is introduced. Further, since the workers can only make a bonus if supplies are regularly forthcoming, management will take special pains to be sure there is a continual flow. Through such job and supply improvements, costs may indeed go down, making it difficult to measure the gain from the incentive system itself.

2. Introducing an incentive scheme in one department may impose costs on another department. For example, production department employees can only make a bonus if their machines are maintained in tip-top shape. So the production people may be happily making money while the maintenance staff are grumbling that they are responsible for the production people's good fortune. To take care of this problem, organizations may allow maintenance workers to share in the bonus, but the question of how it is to be divided leads to rancorous confrontations and much time spent in meetings.

3. Even where incentive systems do lead to improved productivity, they carry costs that are often not counted. These include the costs of job evaluation itself, of wage and salary administration, time-and-motion study, and accounting. Since managers, of course, want to pay bonuses only for products or services that come up to acceptable standards, to determine this they must institute many technically unnecessary inspections, which add still more costs.

4. When managers appeal to the *individual's* economic interests, research shows that they reduce the incentive for workers to help out fellow workers in trouble (since there is little payoff). A result is that the foreman has to step in to provide such help, or else management may have to offer an extra bonus for cooperative behavior (creating even more tricky measurement problems). Group bonus systems can overcome some of these problems.

There is another facet of this "individualistic" appeal that is even more troublesome. When you offer people an economic motive, you naturally encourage them to maximize their own best interests. One result that has been documented many times is that workers are pitted *against* management: they conceal "shortcuts" they may use in reaching work goals; they collude with accounting staffs to falsify records; or they try to "beat the system," as shown in the following excerpt (from the work diary of Donald Roy) in which an experienced machine shop worker named Starkey is explaining to a new worker named Tennessee how to outwit the time-study man (who sets rates on the job):

> "You got to use your noodle while you're working, and think your work out ahead as you go along! You got to add in movement you know you ain't going

to make when you're running the job! Remember, if you don't screw them, they're going to screw you! . . . Every movement counts!"

"The trouble with me [answers Tennessee] is I get nervous with that guy [the time-study man] standing in back of me, and I can't think."

"You just haven't had enough experience yet," said Starkey. . . . "Wait until you've been here a couple of years and you'll do your best thinking when those guys are standing behind you." (Quoted in Whyte, 1955, p. 15)[3]

Although management gets upset at such behavior, one can hardly fail to note how *rational* it is from the worker's point of view. Still, the unfortunate result is that management must add to its personnel a detective staff or force supervisors to spend valuable time watching for such deviant behavior. This, in turn, can lead to an ugly atmosphere of mutual suspiciousness and hostility, which may increase worker turnover, including supervisors who have grown weary and disgusted with the task of acting as policeman.

5. When one person has to pass judgment on another person's performance, as in the case in performance evaluation schemes, experience shows that supervisors are highly reluctant to give negative reports, and subordinates are often alienated by such reports when they are given. For example, one study at a large aircraft manufacturing company discovered that supervisors' ratings of their subordinates went up significantly when they found they had to discuss the ratings with their subordinates (there was a time lapse of 10 days between the two ratings).[4] Under such conditions, ratings are found to exhibit low reliability, and probably low validity as well.

Finally, there is the inevitable tendency of evaluators to focus on what is most visible or easiest to measure. For example, a study of policemen reported:

> Being where one is supposed to be, or showing up to roll call on time with an immaculate uniform and shiny shoes, may have little to do with a policeman's street sense, and how well he uses force, and with his ability to calm tempers in a dispute, or to aid a troubled family gain the outside help it needs. (Marx, 1975, p. 180)

Advocates of incentive systems and performance evaluation are aware of these problems[5] and see them as challenges that will lead to improvements. They have identified the conditions under which incentive systems and performance evaluation work best, namely:

1. When tasks are simple (as opposed to highly interdependent work situations).
2. When management and workers agree on criteria of evaluation and enjoy good relations with one another (which helps avoid the "deviance" problem).
3. When measurement is not too complex for the average worker to understand (people must be able to appreciate how their personal efforts will be rewarded).

4. When people feel secure in their jobs (for example, when they "identify" with management or share its goals, so that they are less inclined to be "individualistic").

In sum, economic motives *are* important, even though it is hard to measure them, and even though they can be appealed to best only under certain conditions. However small their contribution to productivity might be, it is a real one that must always be taken into account.

## 2. The Economists' Critique: Constraints on Rationality

The second "friendly" critique came from a group highly sympathetic to the idea of rationality and to the notion of managers as rational actors— that is, from economists.[5] The Classical approach assumes that managers will operate in a rational manner, selecting the best alternatives for achieving the goals of the unit of the organization they manage. Simon (1976), however, has argued that the very concept of rationality is too demanding if one insists (as Classical economic theory does insist) that the choice of alternatives must be optimal. Simon prefers to use the concept of "bounded rationality," which sees humans as "intendedly rational, but only limitedly so" in actuality, because of too little or too much information (Simon, 1976, p. xxviii).

Other critics go even further, pointing out that even when they have knowledge, people may be unable to articulate it in a teachable language, as when a group of rock musicians can produce strikingly original effects but cannot establish a notation so that other musicians can produce the same effects (Bennett, 1980). This situation is quite common, not only among skilled craftspersons in factories, but even among the unskilled (cf. Kusterer, 1978).[6] It is especially likely to be true as one ascends the managerial ladder, where uncertainty and complexity make teaching in any formal sense of dubious value. Instead, as Kanter (1977) points out, managerial selection usually involves attention to social background (education at elite schools, family, social origins), even though such criteria may not correlate highly with success. They are the most "rational" criteria anyone can think of, though cynics might call some of them, such as family and social origins, the very opposite of rational. Any attempts to establish objective criteria for performance appraisal (how many points to give for "breadth of vision"? how many for "loyalty"?) become very difficult to validate[7] (see also Perrow, 1983, p. 538; 1984).

An original way of looking at organizations is to see them not as carefully constructed rational structures at all, but rather as "*organized anarchies*" that follow "garbage can" models of decision making (Cohen, March, & Olsen, 1972). Instead of thinking of decision makers as examining a problem, considering alternatives, and then selecting the one with the lowest cost or best likelihood of succeeding, this view argues that all these elements get separated from one another. What you have instead are: (1) many problems, (2) many possible solutions known to the organization's members, (3) many possible occasions for considering what to do (meetings, informal conferences in the shop, accidental encounters at cocktail parties), and (4) many participants. It would be gratifying if just the right persons happened to be present when a particular problem they could handle best was being discussed, and when the company happened to be able to adopt their proposed solution because it had the money or proper equipment to do it. The reality, though, is far less rational. The organization has several "garbage cans," each piled high with a mishmash of problems, solutions, occasions, and participants. The company may call a meeting to discuss the problem of sales of a new product, but since the people who are able to attend the meeting happen not to know a lot about sales, that problem gets cursory attention. They do have other problems on their mind, however, and since the meeting gives them a platform, they bring them up. Unfortunately, the solutions suggested for some of these problems are simply not feasible (they might cost too much or require calling in experts). Further, some persons who might have better solutions have to leave the meeting early to attend another meeting, where the same process is repeated. This picture is not one of complete anarchy—there *is* organization. People at the meeting cannot bring up entirely irrelevant or personal matters, but they do their best to smuggle in whatever concerns they have. A university administration, facing budget cuts, asks the faculty to provide "guidelines" for the administration to follow. This the faculty does, happy to be a part of "collegial governance." Alas, although the guidelines they come up with are relatively objective ("Tenured persons are to be fired last;" "We must protect the 'core' functions"), it turns out that the faculty members have been very careful to think, for every guideline: "Now, let's see. How will that one affect me? Who among my colleagues is that going to ding, and how strong are my ties to those persons? Clearly, *my* department is a core function. But I think it can at least be argued that X Department is, shall we say, somewhat peripheral."). So here, too, whoever happens to be at the meeting, and whatever sorts of problems or solutions are available, will be dragged in and made relevant, or else another meeting may be proposed. There is rationality in all this, but you may have trouble modeling it in a rigorous manner.

The final friendly critique of the Classical theory revolves about the organization theory, the claim that the division of labor follows four principles—purpose, process, clientele, and geographical area. These principles turn out to be difficult to apply to a specific organization since they often overlap, are sometimes incompatible with one another, and are quite vague. Take, for example, building missiles for military use. Should the missile program be assigned to one branch of the armed forces or all three, since missiles can be used on land, sea, and air? Should we have a single missile force because all missile building requires a common fund of knowledge? Or should we have a number of different regional forces because some missiles are built for European defense and some for U.S. defense? It is difficult not to conclude that the four principles fail to provide a satisfactory guide to division of labor in the organization.

Furthermore, it has been pointed out that these principles are prescriptive rather than descriptive, that they state how work should be divided rather than how work actually is divided. The actual planning of the division of labor in a given organization is affected by many considerations not covered by the four principles. Organizations grow, develop, divide, and merge in patterns that are only partially predictable and controllable by management. Designing an organization is more like planning a forest than like designing a building. In short, the four traditional principles for dividing labor in the organization neither allow for a realistic analysis of existing organizations nor provide workable plans for improvement. The very terms themselves are ambiguous, as Simon (1976, pp. 30–31) shows with an example: "the Forest Service [may be seen] as a purpose (forest conservation), process (forest management), clientele (lumbermen and cattlemen utilizing public forests), or area (publicly owned forest lands) organization."

In reality, organizations are made up of various layers that differ in their degree of specialization. Often the tendency is for the lower layers to be organized according to area and/or clientele principles, and the higher ones by purpose and/or process. But even this statement should be viewed only as a probability that says effective organizations are *likely* to be this way, rather than as a certainty that they always or even usually are. Many of the problems we deal with in the following chapters arise from the fact that actual organizations often combine work units and divisions whose organizational principles are only partially compatible. We will see that not only is it possible to find contradictory principles operating simultaneously in the same organization, but also that such a "mix" may even provide the most effective organization.[8]

## CONCLUSION

We have seen how the Classical theory of motivation and organization laid out a vast set of ideas for controlling behavior in organizations. The leaders were convinced that organizations could be directed in a rational manner for the attainment of organizational goals. Coming as the theory did in the late 19th and early 20th centuries, it was hardly surprising that the ideas on motivation and organization were not research-based and tended to reflect the optimism and power of those who created the first organizational giants, such as the Ford Motor Company, General Electric, Standard Oil, and Dupont, not to speak of the architects of the burgeoning state governments that grew up after the Civil War in the United States and other wars in Europe.

When the principles and claims turned out to seriously diverge from reality, management researchers cheerfully bent themselves to the task of making their assumptions about rationality more realistic. They still felt that the principles were, although capable of improvement, basically sound. Economic motives *did* work. Organizations *could* be designed for maximum effectiveness and efficiency. But then came the first major research at one of the giants that was a centerpiece of Classical theory—the Western Electric Company, which manufactured the telephone equipment used by Ma Bell. And that research questioned the very foundations of Classical theory.

## NOTES

1. The term was coined by (later) U.S. Supreme Court Justice Louis Brandeis.

2. Many different kinds of "principles" were proposed; sometimes the number went beyond four to as many as seven (see, e.g., Dale, 1952, pp. 25–38).

3. Other examples can be found in Henry (1972) and Mars (1982).

4. Cited in French, 1982, p. 332.

5. The employment of rational models of behavior has recently begun to attract the attention of sociologists, particularly as exhibited in "exchange theory." (see Chapter 10). Much of that work has been social-psychological in perspective, but some researchers have begun to use "rational actor" models in explaining organizational phenomena as well (e.g., Hechter, 1983).

6. Kusterer (1978) describes the way in which workers who manufacture paper cones (for use as drinking cups and the like) perform inspections for defects on a stack of 100 cones by shifting the stack from one hand to the other:

> ". . . as the cones are arched over from one hand to the other, each is separated from the stack for a split second and rotated by a quick movement of the thumb. This bridging operation, combined with the operator's knowledge of what possible defects to look for and the acute visual sensitivity to minute differences in the cones which each operator develops, makes it possible to visually inspect a stack of a hundred cups in two or three seconds. Operators can spot deviations from the expected pattern created as each twirling cup emerges for an instant from within its predecessor" (p. 36). [Reprinted by permission from Westview Press, Boulder, Co.]

7. Doeringer and Piore (1971) have invented the concept of "internal labor market" to try to account for the fact that the wages and salaries of people working in organizations are determined not by market factors but by administrative rules and internal promotion ladders. The point is that once employers spend money on recruitment, screening, testing, and training, they have a stake in holding on to the worker. Workers also, finding that their skills are job-specific and thus not easily transferrable, have an incentive to remain. Because it is often not rational to go job hunting in the free external labor market, Freedman (1976) thinks of organizations as "labor market shelters," that is, forms of protection from the sharp cold winds of an uncertain future. We can see *individual* rationality in these cases (people looking out for their own interests), but it is far from clear that that adds up to organizationally

rational outcomes. Another concern is the study of the conditions under which it is rational to set up an organization when a market would involve transaction costs (e.g. costs of monitoring) that are excessive (Williamson, 1981).

8. Modern management experts are, however, increasingly drawing on the findings of social science research, and are therefore beginning to agree with that claim. See, for example, Mintzberg, 1979. Still, the search for "principles of management" goes on, as illustrated in Koontz and O'Donnell, 1972.

# CHAPTER FOUR
# INTERACTIONIST MODELS

While rational modelers were continuing their work, great changes were taking place in the working world in the first quarter of the 20th century. The age of the robber barons and industrial titans had passed, and governmental controls were now reaching into the marketplace. The tide of non-English-speaking, malleable immigrants had ebbed, and a new generation of more educated, more demanding workers was out on the shop floor. Labor unions were becoming powerful, and the market swings from depression (in 1913) to war, to inflation, as well as increasing foreign competition, began to shake the self-confidence of management. Managers, assisted by rational modelers, had always assumed they knew what they were doing (weren't they managers, after all?), but now they were not quite so sure. Then that self-confidence was dealt a telling blow by a set of experiments, the Hawthorne studies, carried out inside one of America's giant corporations. Management was never to be the same again.

The result was the birth of a new kind of theory, called Human Relations, which focused attention on interpersonal relations: how workers got on with their superiors, how they got on with one another on a face-to-face basis. This theory was soon subjected to heavy criticism, but, like Classical management, went on to spawn a whole set of new approaches, correcting its defects. We call these *interactionist* models.

First, we will look at the founding theory, Human Relations. Then we will consider the criticisms and how the defenders reacted. As improved models made their appearance, the effect was to turn the study of organizations in a social-psychological direction. What happened in organizations was felt to be understandable only if one looked closely at interaction and interpersonal communication.

## HUMAN RELATIONS

The Human Relations approach was born out of a reaction against the Classical formal approach. It focused on elements in the organization that were of small or no concern to the Classical theorists. Elton Mayo is generally recognized as the father of the Human Relations school; John Dewey (indirectly) and Kurt Lewin also contributed much to its initiation. The major findings were: (1) the amount of work carried out by workers (and hence the organizational level of efficiency and rationality) is not determined by their physical capacity alone but also by their "social capacity"; (2) noneconomic rewards play a central role in determining the motivation and happiness of workers; (3) the highest specialization is not necessarily the most efficient form of division of labor; and (4) workers do not react to management and its norms and rewards as individuals but as members of groups. Above all, the Human Relations approach emphasized the role of communication, participation, and leadership. Each of these insights was documented by one or more experiments or field studies, many of which have become "classics" widely referred to by social scientists.

## PHYSICAL VERSUS SOCIAL DETERMINANTS OF OUTPUT

The first of these studies was conducted at the Western Electric Company's Hawthorne Works in Chicago from 1927 to 1932; this series of studies (of which we discuss only a part) has become known as the Hawthorne studies. From the first, there were some highly unexpected findings. Roethlisberger and Dickson (1939) pointed out that in testing the effect of increased illumination on the level of production (the theories of Scientific Management predicted that better illumination would result in increased productivity), the investigators were amazed to find that no consistent relation existed between these two variables. In fact, in one of the later studies, when workers were placed in a control room, the results indicated that productivity continued to increase even after illumination was decreased! It only dropped off when the light became so dim that workers could not see properly.

This puzzling finding sparked a series of studies that, one by one, brought into question statements of Classical writers that there was a simple and direct relationship between physical working conditions and the rate of production. Following the research on illumination, the investigators tested the effect of rest breaks on the production of five relay assembly workers placed in a test room. A number of different combinations of five, ten, and fifteen minute rest periods were tried out to judge their differential effect on production rates. While the rate of production showed a fairly consistent and general increase, it was not related in any direct way to increases in the rest breaks and hence could not be attributed to them. This fact was surprisingly demonstrated when after the rest breaks were abolished at the end of the experiment and the longer "fatiguing" workday was restored, production continued to be higher among the experimental group than the general factory rate. The conclusion was that there was "no evidence in support of the hypothesis that the increased output rate . . . was due to relief from fatigue" (Roethlisberger & Dickson, 1939, p. 127). A suggestion about what factors were accountable for the increased production as well as for the general improvement in the attitude of the workers came from the investigators in the form of a hypothesis: Increased production was the result of the changed social situation of the workers, modifications in their level of psychological satisfaction, and new patterns of social interaction, brought about by putting them into the experiment room and giving them special attention. The discovery of the significance of "social factors" was to become the major finding of the Hawthorne studies.

The breakthrough in research came with an experiment involving the wiring of switchboards. This experiment called into question virtually all the assumptions of Scientific Management. When it was set up, the researchers were already aware that worker groups made ineffectual the individual and group piecework pay system that management had established. The workers were producing less than they were physically capable of; they were following a social norm enforced by their co-workers, which defined the proper amount of production, rather than trying to fill the quota management engineers thought they could achieve, even though this quota allowed them to earn more by doing as much work as they physically could. The phrase *restriction of output* was coined by the observers of this phenomenon, to contrast it with the output that was physically possible.

What actually caused the self-imposed quota restrictions? To find out, a group of 14 workers was set up as a work unit in a separate room in which they were closely observed for 6 months. Their job was to wire telephone switchboards (called "banks"), which required some individual work and some group cooperation. The payment system used was similar to that in the rest of the company. The workers were paid individual hourly rates, based on their individual average output, plus a bonus that was determined by the average group output. In addition, they were given individual allowances for work stoppages beyond their control, so that more efficient producers would not be penalized by work lags caused by the less efficient workers. In line with Taylor's theories on incentives, the managerial assumptions were that the men would work as hard as they could, since the harder they worked, the more hourly pay they would receive; that they would strive to cooperate and coordinate their efforts, since this would further increase their income by increasing group productivity; and that detailed and accurate records would be available on both output and the causes of stoppage, which would serve to set the amount of pay of the workers.

In practice, the men set a norm of a "proper day's work," which was for each man to wire two complete sets of equipment daily. Workers who produced more were ridiculed as "speed kings" and criticized as "rate busters." Those who produced considerably less were labeled "chiselers." The actual production averages were, over the months, day in and day out, surprisingly close to the group's norms. There was considerable pressure not to reveal to the foreman and other management personnel that the workers could produce much more. The workers firmly believed that if they produced a great deal more, their pay rate would be reduced or some of them would lose their jobs (the study took place during the Great Depression), and that if they produced considerably less, they would be unfair to management ("not provide a day's work for a day's pay") and this would also "get them into trouble." Neither belief had any basis in the practices of the company under study. Management was not dissatisfied; it thought that two boards a day was quite an acceptable output.

The major findings and conclusions of the Hawthorne experiments were:

1. *The level of production is set by social norms, not by physiological capacities alone,* a point illustrated by earlier studies of illumination and fatigue.

2. *Noneconomic rewards and sanctions significantly affect the behavior of the workers and largely limit the effect of economic incentive plans.* Two rewards and sanctions were particularly powerful, and both were "symbolic" rather than material.

First, workers who produced significantly more (or less) than the socially determined norm lost the *affection* and *respect* of their co-workers and friends. All the workers in the wiring room clearly preferred maintaining amicable relations with their friends to making more money. In a later study, Dalton (1948) showed that this is not always the case. He found that those who were "rate busters" were individuals whose education and social experience had taught them how to get along with less affection and respect, at least in the work context. The rate busters most often grew up on farms or in small towns, while the conformers came from big cities, where they had learned loyalty to their peers in street gangs. The rate busters were more interested in getting ahead and moving up in the organization than were other workers. Still, Dalton's findings do not contradict the Hawthorne ones: Most of the workers he studied did not break the group norms, and those who did were not integrated members of the work group.

The influence of another noneconomic factor on the production rate is best expressed by W. I. Thomas's famous statement: "If men define situations as real, they are real in their consequences." The workers *believed,* on the one hand, that if they worked harder, their pay rates would be reduced, and on the other hand, that if they did not produce a certain amount, they would be unfair to management and might be fired. The conceptions of what management expected, implicit in these beliefs, influenced the group norm that emerged. But the fact was that management, although it wanted the workers to produce as much as possible, did not have a specific "proper" level of production in mind. Thus, although the workers' beliefs had little objective basis, they influenced, if not determined, the level of production in the factory.

3. Often *workers do not act or react as individuals but as members of groups.* Each individual did not feel free to set up a personal production quota; it was set and enforced by the group. Workers who deviated significantly in either direction from the group norms were penalized by their co-workers. The individual worker's behavior is anchored in the group. Persons who will resist pressure to change their behavior as individuals will often change it quite readily if the group of which they are members changes its behavior. Lewin (1952) wrote:

> As long as group standards are unchanged, the individual will resist changes more strongly the farther he is to depart from group standards. If the group standard itself is changed, the resistance which is due to the relation between individual and group standards is eliminated. (p. 472)

Management, the Human Relations school concluded, manifestly cannot deal with individual workers as if they were isolated atoms; it must deal with them as members of work groups, subject to the influence of these groups.

4. The Human Relations approach came to emphasize the importance of *communication between the ranks,* of explaining to the lower participants the reasons why a particular course of action is being taken; and the importance of *leadership and participation* in decision making in which lower ranks share in the decisions made by higher ranks, particularly in matters that affect them directly. These emphases were to influence later work on the quality of work life, as we shall see. A more immediate consequence was the adoption at Hawthorne of an extensive interviewing program that encouraged employees to express gripes and complaints to a nonjudgmental interviewer. This form of interviewing was to lead to the development of new forms of therapy (and research) by Carl Rogers, which came to be known as "nondirective" counseling.

Two key related concepts that emerged from the Scientific Management and Human Relations schools have remained central to all organizational studies, whether they are guided by one of the organizational traditions or by none. These are the concepts of formal and informal organization. The former derives from the set of factors considered crucial by Scientific Management, and the latter from those stressed by Human Relations. *Formal organization* generally refers to the organizational pattern designed by management: the blueprint of division of labor and power or control, the rules and regulations about wages, fines, quality control, and so on. *Informal organization* refers either to the social relations that develop among the staff or workers above and beyond the formal ones determined by the organization (e.g., they not only work as a team on the same machine but are also friends); or to the actual organizational relations that evolve out of the interaction between the organizational design and the pressures of the interpersonal relations among participants (e.g., formally no worker should leave the plant before five o'clock, but it is informally accepted that on Fridays it is "all right" for the secretaries to leave at 4:45 since their bosses do). A discussion of formal organization brings to mind questions of relations between organizational divisions or ranks. Informal organization, on the other hand, suggests peer groups and their members, and relations within those groups.[1]

## Concluding Note

The Hawthorne experiments were attacked right from the outset, both for ideology (promanagement bias, as we shall see in the following chapter) and for substance and method. The attack continues to this day. Some have pointed out that control groups were rarely used (Carey, 1967), while others have claimed that the results can be explained by elementary principles of operant conditioning (e.g., when rest periods were introduced, output went up; when they were removed, it fell; also, learning occurred—see Parsons, 1974; Pitcher, 1981). Still others (Franke & Kaul, 1978), after applying rigorous statistical controls to the data, came to the conclusion that the results can be explained by tight managerial discipline, the economic adversity of the Great Depression, and the relief of fatigue during rest periods. One pair of critics (Acker & Van Houten, 1974) thinks the results may have been influenced by the fact that the relay assembly test subjects were women, whereas the bank wiring group were men. In particular, the women were drawn from traditional families where women were socialized to be subservient to male authority figures (and thus to the supervisors at the plant). As a result, it was perhaps not surprising that the relay assembly group (women) responded to the experiments with higher productivity, whereas the bank wiring group (men) exhibited restriction of output.

These criticisms have been met by defenders of the experiments (e.g., Shepard, 1971; Wardwell, 1979), who point out that the role of financial incentives (and other operant reinforcers) was not ignored but simply considered part of a broader package, and that the quantitative data advanced by some of the critics do not *ipso facto* wipe out the study's qualitative findings. Neither do sex differences between the groups cancel out the study's findings; more research would be needed to prove the critics' claims that they do.

Still, like many classic experiments that were later shown to be flawed, the basic insights of Hawthorne live on and continue to influence later generations. The terms *formal* and *informal* have become part of working jargon,[2] as has the phrase *Hawthorne effect.* The latter refers to the finding that the women in the relay assembly room responded less to the sheer fact that specific *changes* had been made in lighting, rest periods, and so forth than to their impression that these changes signified a serious concern on the part of management for workers' feelings. That is why today managers or others who introduce a new program in work situations are cautioned to wait until the "Hawthorne Effect" (the effect of change itself) has worn off before drawing any conclusions about the effect of the introduced program.[3]

Further, few social science studies have commanded the attention, both scientific and popular, that the Human Relations theory attracted. Many thousands of executives and lower-ranking supervisors have participated in Human Relations and encounter workshops, or have taken some type of instruction in which these materials were expounded. The early experiments, however problematic, soon produced a flood of further studies, which has shown no signs of abating.

We turn now to examine the more important of those studies, under the following headings: studies of job satisfaction, inquiries into what came to be called the "quality of work life," and new research on how workers construct conditions so they can pursue their own interests as they carry out their work tasks.

## JOB SATISFACTION AND PRODUCTIVITY

These studies took as their point of departure the Hawthorne conclusions that feelings and attitudes were at least as important as economic motives in explaining work behavior, especially productivity. One of the earliest and (still) most influential studies was carried out by Herzberg and various associates (Herzberg, Mausner, & Snyderman, 1959; Herzberg, 1966). Their method was simply to ask workers to recall times when they were satisfied with their work, and to assign reasons for that satisfaction. In addition, they were asked to do the same for times when they were dissatisfied. The finding (and it has been replicated by many others) is that *different* lists of factors turn up. For example, "dissatisfiers" included working conditions, supervision, and salary. "Satisfiers" included intrinsic work elements, a sense of achievement, and responsibility. This meant, said Herzberg, that even if you removed a dissatisfaction (say by paying workers more), workers would not feel any more satisfied unless you also changed their jobs to make them more fulfilling. Herzberg later changed the words, calling the dissatisfiers "hygienic" factors, and the satisfiers "motivators," thus implying that changing work content would not simply increase satisfaction, but would also motivate the worker to work harder.

The studies were heavily criticized (e.g., Athanasiou, 1969; Wall & Stephenson, 1970; Stollberg, 1977) both for their method (asking people to recall past feelings, ignoring how attitudes to work are affected by workers' overall life situation) and for their basic assumptions. Vroom (1964) comments that it is hardly surprising that when you ask people what they do not like about their work, they will refer to something they do not control, such as the money they get or their working conditions. As for what is good about their work, they are likely to say it is something *they* personally contribute or add to the job by their own initiative.

More generally, critics point out, there is a basic fallacy in the assumption that satisfied persons will put out more effort. Why should they? Perhaps some managers assume that workers ought to be grateful to them for the satisfaction the job provides and therefore work more. Yet being satisfied is almost a prescription for continuing to do what you are doing now. Further, would not the reverse assumption be more plausible? Only when persons are dissatisfied are they likely to try to do something to improve or change their condition. So perhaps motivation comes from dissatisfactions rather than from satisfactions (cf. Strauss, 1974).

These are not mere speculations, for many researchers have sought to test directly whether there is any relationship between attitudes to work and productivity, and the findings are inconclusive, not supporting any simple or direct relationship. A large part of the problem arises from the elementary fact that "satisfaction" is itself an elusive and highly complex phenomenon. If survey researchers ask workers how "satisfied" they are with their jobs (as they have been asking them for the last 50 years), the general reply (over 80 percent, on average) is "moderate" to highly satisfied (e.g., Robinson, 1969; Quinn & Shepard, 1974). But it is far from clear what aspect of their work lives they are reporting on. Are they simply telling us how they feel about working as such, or about work as compared to possible leisure? Are they reporting on the intrinsic features of their job, or about working conditions, pay, feelings about their supervisor, or other job or organizational features (cf. Seashore & Tabor, 1976)? Or are workers simply telling us what they think we want to hear?[4]

When the questions are asked in a more probing form, dissatisfaction begins to make itself visible (e.g., Quinn, Staines, & McCulloch, 1974). When asked whether they would choose the same job again if given a chance to start over, a high proportion of workers, especially those in blue-collar occupations, said they would choose a different line of work. Further, job satisfaction has been found to vary significantly (Blauner, 1960), depending on job prestige, closeness of supervision, extent to which the work allows for teamwork, and whether the worker is part of an occupational community (such as printers, railroad personnel, longshoremen, and musical performers.)[5]

The most recent research has turned up a newly identified form of dissatisfaction called *burnout,* a concept that took hold almost immediately after being named in 1974 and has already produced a burgeoning literature (Perlman & Hartman, 1982). The term is used mainly for those whose work involves dealing with other people's problems, and it refers to a condition in which workers are no longer able to perform as they feel they should, with accompanying feelings of helplessness, depersonalization, and emotional or physical exhaustion. Whether burnout is a new phenomenon or simply a newly uncovered one that perhaps formed part of the data in earlier studies, it smudges the picture of the happy worker, if not makes it totally unrecognizable.

Taking into account the measurement as well as the conceptual problems, the question becomes: Is the *variation* in job satisfaction that has now been found related to productivity? As studies have become more sophisticated in sample selection and methodological rigor, the relationship between these variables (if such complex factors may be called that) seems nonexistent, or extremely small. Looking over the findings up to the mid-1950s, Brayfield and Crockett (1955) reported no connection could be demonstrated, though satisfaction did seem to bear a relationship to turnover or absenteeism. Taking a careful look 20 years later, Locke (1976) could find little if any evidence for a causal connection, though Vroom (1964) had found an average of very small correlations.

But what about all the attempts to improve worker attitudes, many of which claim positive results? Katzell, Bienstock, and Faerstein (1977), reporting on over 100 "experiments" published between 1971 and 1975, tell us that, although 85 percent report success, the studies are so badly flawed methodologically (no control groups, sampling problems, analysis questionable) that little credence can be placed in them. Others have complained of the lack of follow-up (success in the early stages can be due to overenthusiasm or the "Hawthorne effect") and the likelihood that the published studies, bad as they are, probably include only the claimed successes: most journals are not prepared to publish reports of failures.

Some point out that the relationship between worker satisfaction and productivity, even when shown, may be spurious, that is, caused by a third variable.[6] Lawler and Porter (1967) actually report a reverse relationship: Job satisfaction does not increase productivity, but rather, becoming more productive (which may result in higher pay or other rewards) produces greater work satisfaction.

The difficulties in this research have led some researchers to point to personality (Macarov, 1982, Chap. 9; King, Murray, & Atkinson, 1982) either from a direct effect of job conditions on personality (Kohn and Schooler, 1982) or through the selection of workers who have the desired personality features for particular jobs. Such a matching process might produce a bitter fit between attempts to increase satisfaction and productivity since these workers might find such opportunities rewarding, given their personal needs or social makeup.

Clearly, studies of the relationship between job attitudes and productivity are leading to ever-more sophisticated research designs and the search for other intervening variables.

### Conclusions on Job Satisfaction and Productivity

What, then, has 50 years of such "ever-more sophisticated research" taught us? Four conclusions seem warranted:

1. Attitudes toward work and behavior on the job *are* related, though the connection is complex. The direct relationship appears to be small, but indirect relationships (through pay, changes in work conditions, etc.) may be important in many cases.
2. Job dissatisfaction *does* seem to increase absenteeism and turnover, a fact of great importance in many work settings.
3. The fact that this area has attracted and continues to attract some of the best researchers in the social sciences provides continued hope that more findings will be forthcoming. At the very least, the efforts of such skilled researchers have led to the invention of highly rigorous statistical and experimental methods. We are no longer dependent on anecdotal reports but have excellent tools for appraising results of future experiments and innovations.
4. Even if future studies should show that people's feelings about their work have little effect on productivity, we might still wish to improve those feelings for humane reasons. A happy worker may not produce more, but considerations of ethics and justice would nonetheless argue for increasing the sum of human happiness.

## THE QUALITY OF WORK LIFE MOVEMENT

In the Hawthorne experiments, it was repeatedly hinted that workers had ideas and resources that could be mobilized, if only ways could be found to unlock them. In addition, the "restriction of output" finding in the bank wiring study revealed that a strong adversary relationship existed between workers and management, which stood in the way of potential cooperative efforts. In the 1970s, a number of original writers and researchers took up this challenge under the banner of "quality of work life" (QWL for short). The key was felt to lie in providing real participation opportunities for workers at all levels, as well as an "open style" of management that would welcome and reward such participation.

The ideas on which the quality of work life principles rest come from the personality theory put forth by Maslow (1943, 1954)[7] and developed by Argyris (1960, 1973). Maslow advanced an unusual theory of human needs. He saw needs arranged in a hierarchy, with "lower" needs (such as hunger and thirst) having to be satisfied before attention could be given to "higher" needs, such as safety and security (e.g., a job that paid a living wage), belongingness, and, still higher, self-esteem and social approval Then when all those needs were met, human beings could turn to the "highest" need of all, what he called self-actualization:

> ... the desire to become more and more what one is, to become everything that one is capable of becoming. ... A musician must make music, an artist must paint, a poet must write, if he is to be ultimately happy. What a man *can* be, he *must* be. (Maslow, 1943, p. 372)

With those words, the first shot was fired in the battle for increased human potential.[8]

Argyris added the point that maturation means moving up the hierarchy, especially to the top, where people would be creative, autonomous, and independent. To do otherwise is to remain immature or in an unhealthy state. Yet when persons join organizations, said Argyris, they meet powerful forces that prevent such mature behavior. Organizations, by definition, seek to reduce discretion, to program and control behavior. They demand conformity and dependence, and these demands infantilize people. Some people choose to fight back by withdrawing: They regress into childish behavior and refuse to do more than the minimum. Others oppose the organization by restricting their work output, by committing sabotage, or by forming labor unions. So management finds it must impose still more restrictions just to keep the workers in line. This produces ever more withdrawal or rebellious behavior, and on and on in a vicious circle.

What is to be done? Perhaps the most influential early proposal came from McGregor (1960) in what he called Theory X and Theory Y. Theory X represented the sort of thinking suggested in Argyris's picture of organization. Managers assumed workers had to be "kept in line" by rules, that the only way they could be directed was by threats of punishment or by rewards. Such a view of the worker was wrong, said McGregor. In its place he urged Theory Y, which sees workers as passive and dependent only because management has made them that way. Actually, people are naturally interested in expressing themselves, in actively helping the organization attain its goals. Theory Y proposes that it is necessary to *redesign* the job so that workers can attain their own goals (whatever they are) by assisting management to attain the organization's goals. Similar ideas were expressed by Likert (1961, 1967), who developed them in considerably more sophisticated form and presented not two, but four models or systems of organization design, with worker participation clearly the most desirable model.

The quality of work life movement has broadened these efforts (e.g., *Work in America,* 1972; Davis & Cherns, 1975). Some examples will illustrate the basic procedures.

A widely cited instance is the attempt to enrich an otherwise dull assembly job at the Motorola Company. Workers had to assemble a Pageboy unit (used by persons who wish to be "on-call") of some 80 parts. As assembled in the traditional way, each worker had to make a small change and pass parts onto the next worker. As the job was redesigned, each worker assembled an entire unit, and that worker's name appeared on the completed Pageboy. Although the costs of assembly were higher, it was claimed that product quality was also higher and absenteeism and turnover rates were lower.

Another example involved white-collar workers who had the tedious task of updating telephone books for Indiana Bell Telephone. Originally the job was designed so that each worker performed a different task: One crossed out or corrected numbers, a second person checked the first person's work, a third added new numbers, and so on. Workers were asked if they would be able to turn out "error-free" work (that is, correct their own work). Those who thought they could were then given entire responsibility for a small town. The claim was that this gave each person a greater sense of responsibility and a pride in possession (some spoke of "my turf").[9]

Other examples are modifications in the auto assembly line at the Saab-Scandia works in Sweden, which enables workers to pull a car section completely off the line to one side, where a group of workers then surrounds it and allocates tasks as it sees fit; quality circles, in which employees get together to offer suggestions on how to improve their work; and worker participation in long-range planning and market strategy at the board room level.[10]

It is impossible to draw final conclusions about the long-range effects of these experiments since they are so recent and since we often have only journalistic reports on which to base judgment. Problems have surfaced already, but we can learn from them how to make QWL work better. The Maslow-Argyris theory of human needs in organizations, for example, has been shown to require amendment. The picture of organizations as inhuman monsters that chew people up in a Chaplinesque manner[11] is greatly exaggerated, if it is accurate at all. In any case, there are fewer mass production jobs now than ever, as robots take over many of the dullest, most programmable jobs. While a strong case can be made that there are basic human needs (Etzioni, 1968) and that self-actualization may well be one of them, that need is probably differentially distributed in the population (Strauss, 1963). Research by Goldthorpe and others (1968) suggests that many workers have quite limited expectations of self-fulfillment at work, preferring to see the job in strictly economic terms while they seek fulfillment (if they do) outside of work in hobbies, family association, or other interests. Yankelovich (1982), drawing on national survey data, claims that "Maslowism" led to an overemphasis on need satisfaction, which proved impossible to realize in the light of economic problems, or else involved conflicts when the needs of one person contradicted those of others. He finds indications that people are now turning to an "ethic of commitment" in which self-fulfillment is sought in more realistic terms, as in enhanced personal relationships and a switch from instrumental to more expressive values. In sum, the need for self-fulfillment remains potent, but rather than simply being assumed, its forms and locations are now being more carefully researched.

One writer (Alvesson, 1982), for example, calls attention to the importance of technology and hierarchy in organizations. Many experiments have focused on highly routine forms of work performed by employees often at the bottom of the work hierarchy. Yet if schemes to increase human potential are to work, there must be at least the opportunity for such humanistic effects to occur. Routine work, by its very nature, presents few opportunities for allowing or encouraging employees to use their own discretion and participate in job change. Also, those at the bottom may have little motivation to participate because they do not have a long-range interest in the organization, or because they have chaotic work histories and therefore lack self-confidence. Schemes for worker participation are more successful if the technology is complex, if the workers have sufficient education and training to make intelligent suggestions for change, and if those suggestions reach someone with enough influence in the organization to actually follow through on them. QWL also works better with persons higher up in the chain of command, whose jobs are more complex and allow for discretion, especially if they are expected to make original contributions and are rewarded for doing so. Identification of these conditions helps us to do a more fine-grained analysis of QWL and to apply it with greater sophistication.

Another criticism has revolved about just how much participation workers are actually allowed in such programs. Some researchers (Hackman, 1975; Lytle, 1975) have found that worker participation is sought only in minor decisions, or that the boss reserves veto power. If real participation has rarely been given a fair chance, that may explain why some experiments have not worked well.

Still other problems are methodological in character, raising the question of whether the positive claims are actually valid. For example, we seem to have many "Hawthorne effects" (reports of success based on change itself), since most of the reports are of early successes (Berg, Freedman, & Freeman, 1978). Other QWL studies rarely use control groups, or they refer to situations in which many changes were put through at once, which makes it difficult to single out the effect of any particular variable.

For instance, changing the pay scheme is usually not a planned part of QWL studies. Yet when managers set up a plan—say involving joint participation and planning—they have to train workers in the new methods, and the work is often on a higher technical level. The worker then must be given a higher pay grade. How does one separate out the effect of that change, which is not unlike what happened at Hawthorne? In the case of the Motorola Pageboy, Glaser (1976, p. 111) tells us that having one person assemble a whole unit was "made possible by a new design technique that resulted in a dramatic reduction in the number of components in the new paging device, from 210 to 80." Surely the claimed benefits (including increased efficiency and better use of facilities layout in that case) may be at least partly attributed to the improved work design.

Yet all of these problems offer challenges for solution as well as hope for the future. For example, one carefully examined study of the introduction of worker participation in planning councils at the highest level at a large manufacturer of hi-fi equipment in Los Angeles (Witte, 1980) showed that even the Hawthorne effect was not inevitable. The firm was favored with a management that had positive views about worker participation, and the planning councils (eight elected workers, five elected managers) were given wide discretion over major policy matters.

Results, over time, are shown in Table 4-1.

The lower the figure, the higher the worker participation as compared to that of managers. (For example, reading down the first column, managers participated 1.59 times as often as workers, absorbed 2.09 times as much time (talking) at meetings as did workers, and so on. It is not surprising that almost all figures are above 1.00, meaning that managers participate more than workers. After all, they have more experience, more sources of information, and are more self-confident. But the key finding lies in the trend of the figures from left to right, that is, over time.

In most cases, the figures start out relatively low, but then show a jump in the second time period. This reflects early enthusiasm, and perhaps a natural tendency of managers (who were supportive of QWL) to hang back and allow workers to express their ideas, at least at first. If the report had stopped at the end of the *first* period, we would have a standard Hawthorne effect (initial success). If we stopped at the *second* period, we might report another "failure." What actually happened was that workers started out making many suggestions, but their lack of experience and ignorance soon led managers to intervene, whereupon the workers withdrew—but did not give up. Then a *period of learning* occurred, during which workers began to recover and ended up participating even more than they did at the start (with some exceptions, to be sure). In sum, when

TABLE 4-1 Changes Over Time (by Quarters) in the Ratios of Management Participation to Worker Participation in Planning Councils

| MEASURE | FIRST COUNCIL, 1975–1976 | | | | SECOND COUNCIL, 1976–1977 | | | |
|---|---|---|---|---|---|---|---|---|
| | 1ST | 2D | 3D | 4TH | 1ST | 2D | 3D | 4TH |
| Frequency of participation | 1.59 | 2.02 | 1.87 | 1.46 | 1.42 | 2.58 | 1.75 | 1.36 |
| Time of participation | 2.09 | 2.82 | 2.53 | 1.86 | 2.39 | 3.21 | 2.67 | 2.11 |
| N proposals | 1.66 | 2.05 | 1.85 | 1.40 | 1.49 | 3.58 | 2.33 | 1.49 |
| Acceptance of proposals* | 2.96 | 1.83 | 1.84 | 1.71 | 1.61 | 1.17 | .75 | .82 |
| Supplying information | 9.84 | 5.83 | 5.25 | 5.91 | 6.03 | 9.40 | 4.37 | 4.25 |

NOTE: With the exception noted below, all entries represent per-person ratios; i.e., the averages per manager divided by the averages per worker. E.g., in the first quarter of 1975, each manager supplied information 9.84 times more often than each worker.
*Entries for "Acceptance of proposals" are the ratio of the percentages of proposals accepted by managers divided by the percentage accepted by workers.
From Witte (1980, p. 80, Table 16). Councils were composed of elected representatives of management and workers, who made joint policy and other decisions at Sound, Incorporated, a large manufacturer of hi-fi equipment. Reprinted by permission of the University of Chicago Press.

given a real chance to participate, and allowed sufficient time to learn by a sympathetic management, workers' response can be strongly positive.

Clearly the QWL movement will continue, for it seems to be responding to strong public desires. Workers, even the most unskilled, have been taught to expect challenging work, to want to "work smarter," not harder. With a change in managerial attitudes, as well as a reduction in traditional worker antagonism to management, more experiments in this direction will be carried out, providing further data to evaluate the impact of the QWL movement.

## THE SOCIAL CONSTRUCTION OF ORGANIZATIONS

The approach that we shall call "social constructionist"[12] follows a different tradition than approaches based on early Human Relations findings. Some using this approach base their work on pragmatic theory, whereas others are based on phenomenological perspectives. But still, some of its findings parallel those of Human Relations researchers, and researchers favoring this approach go even further in the role they assign to workers' potential.

The social constructionists see organizations as *temporary* coalitions of people who together try to do their jobs in such a way as to satisfy their own needs while doing the work necessary to keep the organization functioning. On the question of "participation," as the QWL people might call it, social constructionists insist that workers inevitably do participate in attaining organizational goals—such participation cannot be avoided, and attempts to frustrate it will lead to dysfunctional consequences.

Perhaps the best illustration of the work of this group of thinkers is their treatment of that archetypical form of formal behavior, the rules. In a sense, "rules" can be seen as the most explicit form of managerial control. Yet sometimes it may be necessary to bend or even break the rules in order to uphold them. For example, Turner (1947) examined the Navy disbursing officer and what he is exposed to by those who want him to break the rules. Superior officers will sometimes pressure him for an advance on their pay or to commit other irregularities. What is he to do? The rules are quite clear: If directly ordered, the disbursing officer is to seek a ruling from higher headquarters or have the commanding officer order him to make the payment "under protest." Neither of these actions is much used, however, either because of the time delays involved or the disbursing officer's fear of personal consequences for asking the commanding officer to intervene. While some disbursing officers agonize over the matter or invent devices to avoid making the payments, the most common reaction is that of a social type called a "realist." To this person, writes Turner (1947):

> Regulations are seen as illogical concatenations of procedures, restrictions and interpretations, frequently ambiguous, sometimes contradictory, and often, when strictly applied, defeating the purpose for which they were constructed. Rules specify chiefly the papers which must be filed in support of expenditures, and these may be correct without the payment being correct. (p. 347)

The realist finds ways around the rules, or rather ways of satisfying the intent of the rules, so that the Navy can continue to do the job it is supposed to do.

A classic study of the management of rules in what are the most repressive and rigid of organizations—namely, prisons, mental hospitals, prisoner-of-war camps, army barracks, and monasteries—was carried out by Goffman (1961).[13] After his vivid description of how inmates are torn loose from their previous identities and mortified to "fit" them into the organization, it would seem there are few alternatives other than simply to obey. Some do, even to the point of "conversion," so that they take over the official or staff view of themselves and seek to act as they think the staff act, even to carrying out punishments against fellow inmates for rule violations. Many, however, engage in what Goffman calls "secondary adjustments" to deal with the awful deprivations of their restricted life. The most extreme form is situational withdrawal into a world of one's own, so the inmate has as little to do with the organization as possible. Some inmates become intransigent, disobeying all rules in an assertion of independence and taking a defiant attitude toward punishment. Still others engage in "colonization"—finding a "home" in the organization, even to the point of refusing to leave it (in the case of prisons or mental hospitals) when the time for release comes, or hanging on in what is sometimes called "old soldieritis" in the armed services. Most inmates, however, "play it cool," using any secondary adjustment that comes to hand, keeping out of harm's way, volunteering for nothing, and adopting minimal strategies for keeping their sanity or for standing up to the rigid requirements.[14]

Goffman's treatment of "secondary adjustments" clearly reminds us of the famous "restriction of output" that we described at Hawthorne, but his approach has affected subsequent treatment of that form of behavior. It has been found widely—almost universally—in organizations, but social constructionists treat it as a set of techniques that workers employ to manage their managers. In one of the most carefully executed microstudies of workers, Lupton (1963) compared two British firms, one making waterproof garments in an unstable market of heavily competitive firms, the other manufacturing transformers in a controlled market of large firms, where costs could be passed on to consumers. Both firms employed piecework systems, yet Lupton found worker controls on output only in the transformer company. His interpretation casts doubt on the Hawthorne claims that workers are simply intent on "resisting" management, or that their own norms are more coercive than managerial controls. Instead, he says, the makers of waterproof garments *had* to go all out, producing at top speed, because their jobs were in jeopardy and they needed to build up a savings reserve for times when they would be out of work. Since the transformer workers had few such concerns, they were free to engage in what the workers called "the fiddle" (systematic manipulation of the incentive scheme). Both sets of workers were behaving rationally, given the work situation they were confronted with. For the garment workers, it was only rational to "look out for Number 1" by "getting it while you can"; for the transformer workers, even a benign management (which they had) was no excuse for not protecting themselves against inevitable breaks in production or the realistic possibility of rate cutting (which was, after all, quite rational for management).

Such studies suggest that worker cooperation in the attainment of organizational goals is not simply something that would unlock "potential," as the QWL thinkers might put it, but is necessary to the very attainment of those goals. A set of rules can never be any more than a guideline; organizational functioning requires that each participant use his or her discretion in the application of the rules. A rigid insistence on the rules can frustrate goal attainment (as we saw in Chapter 2). The voluntary commitment of employees, from top to bottom, is not simply desirable, but essential.

Social constructionists go a good deal further than merely examining rules. Zimmerman (1970), for example, in a study of intake workers in a government welfare office, shows how workers make up "rules" when they encounter difficult or "unusual" cases, until it is not clear whether the case follows the rule or the rule follows the case. The employees are seen as constructing a meaningful and practical reality, without which work would hardly go on at all. Other studies have been made of how nurses transform the handling of dead bodies into routine work, of how telephone calls are interpreted and reinterpreted so as to make workaday sense, and of how "turn-taking" in conversations among organizational members reflects "deep structures" hardly imagined in traditional studies.

Many of the social constructionist researchers have dealt with organizations that "process" people (Hasenfeld, 1972), such as mental hospitals, diagnostic facilities, rehabilitation agencies, schools, and police courts. In addition to the humane concern with how such organizations "bureaucratize" people in the process of dealing with them, these studies make clear that agents must pick up cues and act quickly on what is often fragmentary evidence. For cases of alleged rape, for example, Bennett and Feldman (1981) and Rose and Randall (1982) present evidence that public prosecutors as well as juries make commonsensical assumptions about the reasonableness of a presumed rape victim's claims, placing the burden of proof on her to put forward a believable story. Promptness in reporting and seeking a medical examination, willingness to cooperate with police, and external evidence such as torn clothing and actual proof of physical injury are felt to be indicative of a believable story. In one case, a rape victim's claims were dismissed by a jury since the trial brought out the fact that she had spent time after the rape straightening up her apartment, such behavior being viewed by the jurors as inconsistent with emotional upset. In a new trial, however, she had a better defense, which showed that traumatized persons often engage in seemingly mindless or routinized behavior under shock conditions.

All "boundary personnel" in organizations—those who must deal routinely with the public—develop commonsensical categories (cf. Goffman, 1974) into which they place their "clients," partly to enable them to deal with the cases, but partly to express their moral view of the client. Roth (1972) shows how staff in hospital emergency wards decide quickly whether those who come in or are brought in are "deserving" (the young are considered more deserving than the old; the sober more than the drunk; high-status persons more than welfare cases) or "legitimate" (beatings and stabbings are more legitimate than gynecological problems; an overdose of pills—especially if accidental and therefore "deserving"—is preferred over muscle spasms and digestive upsets). If a patient wants rapid treatment, it would seem best to arrange to be both legitimate and deserving. The staff makes such decisions, Roth shows in many cases, on only sketchy evidence.[15]

Particularly intriguing are studies of situations in which boundary personnel and clients negotiate with one another as to which category the client is to be placed in.[16] The best-known instance of this kind of negotiating is plea bargaining in courtrooms: Charges are reduced or changed in exchange for a guilty plea, when the accused may not even have committed the altered charge (cf. Sudnow, 1965; Rosett & Cressey, 1976). Such negotiation is believed to be a fundamental part of interaction in all organizational situations: Workers negotiate with superiors, not only for salary increases and promotions, but also for definitions of their work world; colleagues negotiate among themselves in exchanges that are felt to be just and rewarding (we say more about this process in Chapter 10), as well as deal with customers and persons in other organizations (O'Toole and O'Toole, 1981).

As a result of these studies, complex theories of negotiation and bargaining (Strauss, 1978) have been developed to make sense of this process, as well as to account for how people construct the sort of "realities" that make their work, if not an interesting, fulfilling experience, at least somewhat meaningful in terms of their own view of the world.

Beyond that, these studies provide a paradoxical twist to the Classical view of worker behavior as "rational." Rational motives—or at least claims to rational motives—are held to be one kind of justification or excuse that people advance for their behavior. This does not mean that their accounts (Scott & Lyman, 1968; Staw, McKechnie, & Puffer, 1983) of their actions are to be dismissed as "mere" rationalizations. These accounts reveal the ways in which typical members of any work organization (Silverman & Jones, 1976) explain to others why puzzling or disconcerting behavior makes sense (Atkinson & Heritage, 1979) from the speaker's point of view and, more generally, from that of members of a subculture or work community (cf. Bruce & Wallis, 1983).[17] In this light, the "rules"—the commands of superiors, the "blueprint" of the organization's formal structure, and the reward structure—are not so much "fixed realities" as material to draw on to explain what goes on in organizations. Intensive close study of the organization's members in action is necessary to pick up the subtle kinds of conduct that reveal how the organization really works—something that, the social constructionists claim, is missed by those who use more "structural" or macro approaches.[18]

## CONCLUSION

Human Relations theory, studies of job satisfaction, the quality of work life movement, and social constructionist approaches have earned a permanent place in the study of organizations. Yet from the very beginning, and in the teeth of improvements and responses to criticisms, there remain two issues they leave unresolved—one ideological, the other analytic.

The ideological issue is as follows: Although some of these theories began as an attack on the smug "principles" of Classical managers, and although they were, not surprisingly, resisted by those managers as dangerous, even revolutionary, the new findings slowly took hold among managers, who realized that they could turn them to their own use. If workers really do have other than economic motives for working (such as desires for friendship, good treatment, self-fulfillment), well, why not provide for them? If such gestures might result in higher productivity or lower turnover, then they are surely worth it. A large part of the explosion of research on the relationship between job satisfaction and productivity was done under managerial auspices and tried out in realistic work situations for a simple reason—the findings might well provide managers with new weapons to control and manage work more efficiently. Much of the research, then, has suffered from a strong managerial bias, and therefore its scientific objectivity is questionable.

The analytic question arises because the strong social-psychological tone of all these models results in their telling us very little about organizations as such, little about how they are set up, little about their overall structure. In rejecting Classical principles of organization (division of labor, unity of control, staff, and line), these models risk throwing the baby out with the bath. There *are* departments, some persons *are* charged with the authority to control whole divisions and make decisions, goals *are* set. In short, there *is* structure, and no amount of studies of what one person says to another will, alone, describe that structure. Some organizations are larger than others, and some dominate their markets while others hardly survive past one season. In some, relationships are formalistic and bureaucratic; in others, they are casual and spontaneous. Some industries enjoy harmonious labor-management relations; others are strike-prone in spite of skilled leadership. Even the social constructionists must grapple with the fact that however much employees may bend the rules or adapt the organization to their own needs, the rules *are* real and the organization imposes constraints that must be examined in their own right. It was the Structuralists who early recognized these problems and offered new approaches for dealing with them.

## NOTES

1. The question of how the formal and informal are related to each other was left for the Structuralists to deal with, as we shall see in the next chapter.

2. In a survey of employees in organizations in three U.S. cities, Hollinger and Clark (1982) report that informal sanctions were perceived as more salient than formal sanctions (those originating from management).

3. Although critics are now prone to reject claims of the effectiveness of some deliberately-introduced change on the grounds that the change is a "mere" Hawthorne Effect (meaning it is temporary, or merely due to a perception of employees that they are receiving attention), Pasmore and Friedlander (1982) argue that just such a change in perception, however temporary, may be necessary before other more basic changes can be made. They describe a "contagion" situation in which beliefs about muscle stress led to increased absenteeism, resulting in still more stress and absenteeism for those who showed up for work. New

work materials were introduced to help reduce muscle stress, and, by chance, a supervisor who was perceived as putting on too much pressure was transferred (for other, unrelated reasons). There followed a change in perception on the part of the employees that management was doing something about their problems, leading later to a reduction in injury rates and absenteeism (for a variety of reasons). This is no argument for deliberately introducing a Hawthorne Effect (which would be manipulative and would probably be perceived as such), but rather that researchers should consider the Hawthorne Effect as a separate variable in its own right. A large number of studies of the Hawthorne Effect are critically reviewed in Adair, 1984.

4. For example, the United States is supposed to be an action-oriented, problem-solving, optimistic country. How, then, can a citizen of such a country reply, "I'm dissatisfied," without risking facing the raised eyebrows of the interviewer, whose unspoken question is: "Well, if you are unhappy with your work, and you are a red-blooded American, why don't you do something about it?" Even if the interviewer is not suspected of framing such an unspoken question, the workers are likely to ask it of themselves. Since people tend to resist unpleasant thoughts, especially those involving their self-esteem, they are likely to convince themselves that although their job has negative features, it is acceptable, especially considering their education, experience, and alternative job opportunities.

5. Caution in interpreting these findings is suggested by Weaver's (1977a, b) analysis of National Opinion Research Center data. Some of these variables, including prestige, have not been found to be associated with job satisfaction when other variables are held constant. Interestingly, neither has race or sex.

6. For example, many experiments involve changes in the system of payment. It may be believed that this change makes workers happier, and they respond with increased production. But if the relationship is spurious, then what might actually be happening is that pay does make workers happier, and (independently) also leads them to raise production so as to make more money. The result is that worker satisfaction (with pay) and productivity do go up, not because one causes the other, but because both are caused by increased pay. Similar methodological as well as conceptual problems are carefully described by Campbell and Pritchard (1976).

7. It is interesting that in later years Maslow became somewhat alarmed at the misuse of his ideas. He said: "My work on motivations came from the clinic, from a study of neurotic people. . . . I'm a little worried about this stuff which I consider to be tentative being swallowed whole by all sorts of enthusiastic people who really should be a little more tentative, in the way that I am" (quoted in Tausky, 1978, p. 61). Alas, he cannot get off the hook so easily, nor is he the first to express alarm at what his followers have done. Karl Marx once protested, "I am not a Marxist."

8. Actually, the first shot should probably be credited to Rousseau, since the basic idea of self-expression is at least that old. But Maslow expressed it in modern psychological language, though even there he was anticipated by the large-scale nondirective interviewing program that was the final upshot of the Hawthorne experiments. That kind of interviewing seeks to encourage employees to freely express their gripes and complaints, without censure or moralizing. See Rogers, 1942.

9. For larger cities, such as Indianapolis, a worker was assigned one or more letters of the alphabet, again with total responsibility.

10. Other examples are described by Cummings and Molloy (1977), who examine 78 different experiments in work organizations, from autonomous work groups (where workers are permitted to decide their own division of labor) to job restructuring (which allows for worker initiative, participative decision making, and other changes). Glaser (1976) summarizes about 30 attempts to introduce such changes in industry, both in the United States and abroad.

11. In the classic movie *Modern Times*, Charlie Chaplin satirizes the attempts of time-study engineers to mechanize the eating of lunch. In the same movie, he literally gets caught up in a machine, which swallows him and discharges him at the other end, like any "raw material input."

12. We include here those who call themselves ethnomethodologists (though they might object), as well as those who go by various other names, such as symbolic interactionists,

action theorists (a term preferred in England), phenomenological sociologists, and interpretive (or "hermeneutic") sociologists and psychologists.

13. Goffman (1961) calls these, collectively, "total institutions," since they are all-encompassing and have strong barriers to contact with the outside world.

14. In monasteries, convents, and exclusive military units or schools, people do not look forward to "getting out" but rather to the transformation of their identities into something "higher." Even so, secondary adjustments can assist them to make that transformation with less personal trauma.

15. A special situation is one in which what starts as personal troubles of clients becomes public problems of an agency dealing with such clients. The troubles of the clients are reinterpreted, and their uncooperativeness (or resistance to the interpretation) now turns into an agency or public problem. Conciliation may then become as much a matter of controlling the client as it is a process of dealing with the personal troubles which brought the client to the agency in the first place. See Emerson and Messinger, 1977; Emerson, 1981, and Miller, 1983.

16. Although bureaucratic agents are supposed to respond only in terms of the rules and merits of the case (which we discuss in Chapter 5), researchers have found that interactions with clients are subject to considerable negotiation. For example, Weimann (1982) finds that the weaker a client's bargaining power (as in dealing with the police), the more successful is an altruistic appeal (e.g., "Please help me. I really need it."). On the other hand, if the client has some bargaining power by being able to make use of an alternative organization, then a normative appeal ("I deserve this service.") is more likely to be effective. Other studies of this interactive process are brought together in Katz and Danet, 1973.

17. A form of accounts is what has come to be known as "attribution," of which a large literature exists that we cannot consider here. As illustration, Bettman and Weitz (1983) find that letters to shareholders from large corporations sought, as do individuals, to account for less successful activities by reference to external causes (free market prices, general slowdown), whereas successful activities were attributed to internal causes (management's programs, internal cost controls).

18. Social constructionists have also begun to apply their approach to the study of organizations directly, even to whole industries. Weiss and Faulkner (1983), for example, show how free-lancing in the Hollywood film industry turns out to have a tight social structure whereby a few free-lancers dominate, while more than half of all craft workers fail to be employed on a regular basis. Other macro studies are Vaughan, 1980; Farberman, 1975; and Denzin, 1978. Some of these researchers are concerned with defending this approach against the criticism that it is "astructural."

# CHAPTER FIVE
# STRUCTURALIST MODELS
## *Origins and Assumptions*

The term *structure* is used in sociology to refer to enduring social relationships. Just as the physical structure of a building is expected to endure through the many uses of the building, and the biological structure of animals and humans to be subject to only minor alteration in basic respects, so, too, the social structure includes those kinds of relationships that last, such as parent-child bonds of affection, widely held societal values, ties between speakers of a common language, and relationships among interdependent occupations.[1] These can change, of course, just as a building may be redesigned, but normally the change is slow and betokens fundamental shifts when it does occur.

Structuralist models of organization call attention to the fact that though choices do exist when an organization is set up, once it is established, the structure endures and even seems to possess a life of its own. It is the special view of Structuralists that we had better understand just what this structure consists of, especially if we wish to change it. Otherwise we will only delude ourselves, tilt at windmills, and become ever more pessimistic about the chance of improvement. That pessimism will lead to cynicism, so that we do not even try to change what *can* be changed. The Structuralist approach injects a powerful note of realism into discussions of change, leading to more practical programs than those that have so often been offered by researchers whose enthusiasm beclouds their judgment.

The Structuralist models of organizations developed from the work of one of the giants of sociology, Max Weber, as well as, to a degree, from that of Karl Marx. Basically, these scholars pointed to fundamental dilemmas in the very nature—that is, the structure—of organizations, such matters as conflict of interest between owners and workers, the shape of markets in which organizations operate, the way in which technology shapes relationships, and the ceaseless power struggle among interest groups.

But as a distinct position among organizational theorists, the Structuralist view arose dialectically from a critique of the Human Relations approach and, by implication, interactionist models generally. Hence its foundations are best understood through examination of the criticisms it raised against the Human Relations approach. As we pointed out in the conclusion of the last chapter, the Human Relations findings were turned to management's advantage, offering new tools to increase worker productivity. The Structuralists saw such attempts as fated to meet fundamental organizational dilemmas: the inevitable strains—which can be reduced but not eliminated—between organization needs and personal needs; between discipline and autonomy; between formal and informal relations. They saw other structural elements to consider, which the interactionists leave out altogether, including environmental changes; wars; swings of the business cycle; the recent declines in U.S. productivity in the face of new competition from abroad; the growth of entitlement programs such as Social Security, Medicare, and veterans' benefits; and shifts in values and demographic changes, including the growth in female employment, the decline in male participation in the labor force, and high unemployment among blacks and Hispanics. Finally, the Structuralists broadened the scope of studies from business and governmental organizations to hospitals, prisons, churches, social-work agencies, and schools. All of these critical elements added up to an enrichment of studies and of theory as well.

In this chapter, we first consider Structuralist criticisms of the Human Relations and interactionist models. Then we move on to discuss the contributions of the greatest of the Structuralist writers, Max Weber, since much subsequent research has started where he left off. In the next chapters, we consider various kinds of structure, drawing on more recent studies, many of which make use of advanced quantitative techniques. These lead us to the compliance structural model, a model that will occupy us in subsequent chapters.

## THE CRITIQUE OF HUMAN RELATIONS APPROACHES

The Structuralists early saw that the battle between Human Relations and Scientific Management concealed a fundamental consensus: they were not as far apart as appeared. That consensus made it easy for managers to "co-opt" the researchers, and, as we saw in the last chapter, many studies sought to show a relationship between a happy worker and higher productivity. The Structuralists then accused managers of manipulating workers by engineering incentive schemes that only *seemed* to be based on concern for worker welfare. In contrast, they advanced the claim that there was a basic conflict of interest between managers and workers, as well as many other conflicts, all of which added up to a case for the inevitability, sometimes even the desirability, of organizational conflict. That argument, in turn, led to a questioning of the separation of the formal and informal, with research showing that these kinds of behavior were actually related, if one only appreciated the total structure of the organization as well as its setting. We shall deal with each of these criticisms and contributions in turn.[2]

### Questioning the Assumption of a Basic Harmony Between Management and Workers

Scientific Management and Human Relations were in many ways diametrically opposed. The factors one school saw as critical and crucial, the other hardly considered, and the variables one viewed as central, the other largely ignored. The two schools, however, had one element in common: Neither saw any basic contradiction or insoluble dilemma in the relationship between the organization's quest for rationality and the human search for happiness. Scientific Management assumed that the most efficient organization would also be the most satisfying one, since it would maximize both productivity and the workers' pay. Since workers were viewed as seeking to maximize their income, and since it was assumed that they were satisfied with their share of the corporate income, the implicit belief was maintained that what is best for the organization is best for the workers and vice versa.

The Human Relations approach assumed that the most satisfying organization would be the most efficient. It suggested that the workers would not be happy in a cold, formal, "rational" organization that satisfied only their economic needs. The Human Relations school did not believe that management would be able to establish an organization that would keep the workers satisfied by simply allocating labor and authority in the most efficient way, as determined by the intrinsic nature of the task. But, like the Scientific Management school, it did not view the problem of worker satisfaction and productivity as inherently unsolvable. True, management had to become enlightened and take certain steps, such as encouraging the development of social groups on the job and providing them with participating, and communicative, leadership. But once the real nature of the workers' needs and their informal group life and organizations were understood, nothing would prevent management from making the organizational life a happy one.

Moreover, the Human Relations school taught that it is necessary to relate work and the organizational structure to the social needs of employees, for by making the employees happy in this way, the organization would obtain their full cooperation and effort and thus increase its own efficiency. Thus the path to a fully rational organization lay in making deliberate efforts to increase the happiness of the workers. There are many almost lyrical pages in Human Relations writing depicting the worker as anxious not to miss a day at the factory or to come in late, lest he forgo spending time with his friends on the job and disappoint his foreperson, who is like a warm and understanding parent. The work team itself is often seen as a family, and workers should feel trust in management and a sense of pride in organizational membership (Gardner, 1945, p. 283).

In short, the Human Relations school held out the promise of a perfect balance between the organization's goals and the workers' needs. In this respect, it differed from the Scientific Management school only in the substance of that balance. Whereas Scientific Managers saw the balance as natural if restraints were removed, the Human Relations researchers believed the ideal state had to be deliberately constructed. Implicit in many Human Relations writings is the suggestion that the task of the social scientist is to show management how to engage in the art of social engineering to the benefit of all concerned. Considering the basic agreement between the two schools, it remained for the Structuralists to point out that alienation and conflict are both inevitable and occasionally desirable, and to emphasize that social science is not a vehicle to serve the needs of either worker or organization. It is no more concerned with improving the organization of management than it is with improving the organization of employees.

Quite apart from the fact that later research showed that there was no direct or simple relationship between how "happy" or satisfied workers were and their productivity or work behavior, the Structuralists pointed out that searching for such a relationship concealed a manipulative intent. Management was accused of not really seeking such a harmony, but rather new weapons to force worker conformity. Let us look at this manipulative charge, and at the attempts to refute it.

### The Manipulative Charge

An anthropologist recorded the following conversation in a mental hospital. It involved the medical director, the administrative director, and a nurse, and it concerned sessions in which patients were encouraged to express their dissatisfactions with hospital routines.

MISS NUGENT (*nurse*): Are you going to have a gripe session?

DR. SCOTT: I'm personally against these gripe sessions.

DR. SHAW: So am I, particularly if the patients feel that they are legislating at these sessions, and find out later that they are not.

DR. SCOTT: The only good that these gripe sessions do is that if you can get the patients as a group to scrutinize what is going on in their behavior. . . . (Caudill, 1958, p. 78)*

Here conferences (gripe sessions), which patients were led to believe were being held to provide an opportunity for upward communication, were actually used for purposes of downward communication and direction. Such "manipulation" is objectionable to many Structuralists, although in this case their opposition might be somewhat less intense since the manipulation had therapeutic intent, and this was, after all, a hospital. But they believe that in most other organizations, and especially in industrial organizations, such manipulation is unethical;[3] for Human Relations and other interactionist techniques are being used to help those higher in rank manipulate those lower in rank.

Those lower in rank might be invited to participate in "democratic" discussions leading to joint decision making, when in fact the decisions have already been made and the real purpose of the conference is to get the lower in rank to accept them.[4] Or the lower in rank might be allowed to decide on relatively unimportant matters whose outcome is of indifference to top management. What is created here is a false sense of participation and autonomy, deliberately induced in order to elicit the workers' cooperation in and commitment to organizational enterprise. Providing workers with "gripe sessions" and suggestion boxes,[5] with social workers and psychiatric interviews, as is done in some Human Relations programs, may reduce their dissatisfaction without improving their lot.

Interactionist proponents counter that they do not favor one group over another; that their findings are public and hence anyone—including both workers and management—may have access to them (indeed, some union leaders have taken Human Relations courses in order to improve their control of their membership). Then, too, workers and management have always tried to manipulate each other; the study of manipulation did not create it. Moreover, most social science studies are open to use by "manipulators" since they provide readers with insights into the structure and dynamics of social processes that might be used to the disadvantage (or advantage) of others. Furthermore, only the most biased observer would deny that increased communication and participation and the granting of social rewards—even without wage increases—have improved the workers' life and job. Finally, one must recognize that many of the plants that have Human Relations programs are among those in which pay is highest, working conditions best, and unions most accepted. The use of such social

*Reprinted by permission of Harvard University Press.

approaches may improve the workers' social situation without sacrificing their economic interests.[6]

## The Inevitability of Conflict

In spite of the defense of the basically humane values of managers who practice Human Relations leadership, and in spite of the often benign effects of manipulation, it remains true that the end result favors management and often misleads the workers (Bendix & Fisher, 1961). This is true because Human Relations views present, at best, a partial view of the organization.

In contrast, the Structuralist sees the organization as a large, complex social unit in which many social groups interact. While these groups share some interests (e.g., in the economic viability of the corporation), they have other, incompatible interests (e.g., in how the gross profits of the organization are to be distributed). They share some values, especially national ones, whose influence becomes evident in periods of international crisis; but they disagree on many others, for example, in their evaluations of the place of labor in society. The various groups might cooperate in some spheres and compete in others, but they hardly are or can become one big happy family.

Two groups within the organization whose interests frequently come into conflict are management and the workers. This is largely because management's effort to get the workers to work is basically alienating. There are many ways to make labor more pleasant, but none to make it satisfying in any absolute sense. The Structuralists accepted this viewpoint and, following the analyses of Marx and Weber, they sought in the contrast between the medieval artisan or farmer and the modern worker some clues to the source of the latter's dissatisfaction.

According to Marx, the modern factory hand is alienated from his work since he owns neither the means of production nor the product of his labor. Specialization has fragmented production so that each worker's labor is repetitious, monotonous, and without opportunity for creativity and self-expression. The worker has little conception of the whole work process or of his contribution to it; his work is therefore meaningless to him. He has little control over the time at which his work starts and stops, or over the pace at which it is carried out. To this Marxian analysis, Weber added that this basic estrangement exists not only between the worker and the means of production, but also between the soldier and the means of warfare, the scientist and the means of inquiry, and so on. Thus the issue is not really one of legal ownership (e.g., that the gun belongs to the army and not to the soldier), but rather that with ownership goes the right to control, and that those who provide the means also define their use. The worker, soldier, and researcher—and, by implication, all employees of all organizations—are frustrated and unhappy because they cannot determine what use their efforts will be put to since they do not own the instruments necessary to carry out independently the work that needs to be done. *Alienation* is a concept that stands for these sentiments and the analysis of their source in the Marxian-Weberian terms.

The claim that management-worker conflict is built into that relationship (and is, therefore, structural) receives support from historical researchers, who return us to Adam Smith's famous defense of the efficiency of the division of labor in pin manufacturing.[7] Marglin (1974) points out that even if it is true that productivity will go up if separate specialties are made of straightening the wire, making the head of the pin, and sticking the completed pin on a piece of paper, it does not follow that separate *persons* have to spend a whole lifetime doing one of those tasks. Why not instead have one person (or several) do each of those operations in sequence; say, spending a half day at a time at each? The same savings would be generated, and the work would be a little less destructive of human integrity. As for the argument that specializing such work in one person's hands increases dexterity, the work is so simplified that entirely new workers, with no experience, can be taught the job and reach top efficiency in very short times. A similar case is made by Chinoy for modern-day assembly-line autoworkers in the United States, for whom "maximum hourly rates [are] ten cents above the minimum and [are] automatically reached ninety days after a worker [is] hired" (Chinoy, 1955, p. 38).[8]

If, then, the gains of efficiency could be secured by task specialization *without* requiring person specialization, why were factories set up that way? The answer, suggests Marglin, is that such narrow person specialization made it easier for the entrepreneur to control the work and to fire workers he thought were indolent or who resisted his authority, because the individual could hardly claim possession of a "skill" that he could use to get the job elsewhere. Anyone could be replaced easily since the learning time was so short.[9]

In recent times, the same tendency has been described in detail by Braverman (1974), who points out that the heart of Taylorism was the separation of the planning function from that of execution, with planning reserved to management.[10] The goal was to negate any possibility of worker initiative so that management would be less dependent on workers and could easily replace them (cf. Wallace and Kalleberg, 1982). This division prevails not only in factories, where there is a separation between "mental" (planning, which is carried out by the office) and "manual" work, but also in offices, where the process of deskilling has been increasing because of the use of computer-assisted clerical functions, as well as microprocessors, which have rendered obsolete what little autonomy or judgment the clerical worker once possessed. As Glenn and Feldberg (1979) show, even the "secretary" may be on her way out. This last bastion of executive personal privilege is proving too costly to maintain and is being replaced by three departments: word processing (which accepts dictation from all managers, even those in distant cities, by electronic hookup), administrative support (for telephone answering, supply ordering, and record keeping), and a reproduction center (for all reproduction work). The office then becomes segregated into two parts: a small number of high-level decision makers, and a larger group of operatives who can be replaced as easily as they can be prepared. It is no wonder then that there is a problem of "motivation." Obviously it is difficult to create involvement or excitement when a job has been deliberately stripped of all possible exercise of worker judgment and independent contribution.[11] The problem becomes even more serious as the level of education in the general population rises, and as what survey researcher Yankelovich (1982) calls a "new breed" of Americans begins to reject the way in which work depersonalizes the worker and to demand a greater degree of individual fulfillment from the job.[12]

To be sure, Human Relations researchers and others using social models have offered many ways in which some of these worker needs may be met, but, the Structuralists insist, there are sharp limits on the degree to which their suggestions can be achieved. The development of social groups on the job might make the worker's day more pleasant, but it will not make his task any less repetitious or uncreative. Similarly, rotation eases monotony, but not much, because all the alternative jobs are dull, routine, and of a meaningless nature. Workers, it is suggested, spend much of their working day in a semiconscious delirium, dreaming about their major source of satisfaction—the post-workday.

By providing an unrealistic "happy" picture, by viewing the factory as a family gathering place rather than as the scene of a power struggle among groups with some conflicting values and interests as well as some shared ones, and by seeing the organization as a major source of human satisfaction rather than alienation, the Human Relations school glosses over the realities of work life. Its view of worker dissatisfaction and how to alleviate it stems from a misunderstanding of the real situation, which involves an underlying conflict of interests. Although Warner and Low (1947), for example, in their classic study of a strike in a shoe factory, were aware of the workers' desire for higher wages in a situation where wages had been severely reduced, they located the really important factors behind the strike in the workers' loss of a sense of community, the decline in primary relations, and communication blocks between management and workers.

It is to this partial approach, with its underplaying of the importance of material rewards, that the Structuralists objected. The Structuralists did accept, although with some lessening of emphasis, the Human Relations insights into the significance of social rewards in industry, but they criticized the use to which these insights were put in those instances where management sought to placate workers by granting them inexpensive symbols of prestige and affection instead of an increase in wages.

Nor do the Structuralists believe that fundamental differences of interest can be made to vanish by better communications, or by pointing to the fact that although management and workers may differ in how the pie should be divided, all have a common interest in increasing the size of the pie. As any parent who has ever had to cut up a birthday cake for distribution among eagerly waiting children knows, the size of the cake has nothing to do with the problem. No matter how big it is, the question remains of who gets how much.

Structuralists have even seen conflict as having desirable elements (Coser, 1956; Collins, 1975). It allows genuine differences of interests and beliefs to emerge, whose confrontation may lead to a test of power and adjustment of the organizational system to the real situation, and ultimately to real organizational peace. If repressed, conflict and its concomitant, latent alienation, will seek other outlets, such as worker withdrawal or accidents, which in the end are disadvantageous to both the workers and the organization.[13]

## Formal and Informal Relationships

After Hawthorne, no one can ignore the role of informal relationships and their possible effect on attitudes and behavior. But the Structuralists point out that the emphasis on such informal relations has been exaggerated, that the pendulum has swung too far. Without denying their presence, we must still ask (1) how they are related to formal relationships, and (2) how widespread they are. After all, the Western Electric researchers told us only about *two* groups. Are such informal relationships widespread or a rarity? Do they (if they exist) affect only work behavior, or do they have a wider influence outside of work?

1. On the first question, research findings have shown that informal relationships cannot be seen merely as a rebellion against management, as is suggested by the phrase *restriction of output*. Instead, formal structure provides the *conditions* under which informal relationships exist, sometimes facilitating such relationships, sometimes frustrating or even preventing them. For example, a classic study by Roy (1954) of piecework production in a machine shop showed that restriction of output required the *collaboration* of set-up men and inspectors (who would agree to allow machinists to get a head start on production while still officially on set-up, or inspection, which paid a fixed hourly rate), tool crib men and stockmen (who would allow the machinists free access to tools and materials), and time checkers (who would see to it that the machinists' time records satisfied cost-accounting controls).

Bensman and Gerver (1963) describe how aircraft manufacturing workers routinely made use of a tap, a device that enabled them to re-thread a nut in the wing section when holes did not line up properly, a forbidden (and dangerous) practice. Yet use of the tap was structured, workers being socialized to its proper utilization, even by foremen, since often it was the only way that *formal production goals* could be met.

Bigus (1972) reports that suburbanization and the spread of the su-permarket in the San Francisco Bay area threatened the survival of the home-delivery milk business, particularly since there was a *legal* require-ment that home-delivered milk prices be higher. The delivery firms met this severe environmental constraint by encouraging their drivers to devel-op informal ways of handing the problem (since any formal endorsement would constitute encouragement of criminal behavior). Besides resorting to such perfectly legal devices as cultivating customer loyalty and per-forming personal services like putting milk directly into customers' re-frigerators, drivers would offer customers "deals," such as a "free quart of milk as a reward for loyalty or an actual reduction in price, and then cover the deal by "dumping"—that is, claiming the product had gone sour or been damaged in transit. The company carried "dumpings" as business losses, and the customer got home delivery at competitive prices, as well as the satisfaction of specialized attention, in contrast to the cold, impersonal treatment of the supermarket.

A final example of the interrelationship of formal and informal sys-tems is brought out in a careful study of reward systems in British hotel-restaurants (Mars & Nicod, 1981). Workers were able to supplement their very low income by tips, as well as by "knockoffs" (taking food home) and by selling customers their own products (e.g., wine that they had purchased outside, or saving wine left over and selling it as "house wine"). The point is that this behavior was not universal, but depended on the formal structure of the hotel. It was practically nonexistent in chain or larger bureaucratic hotels, for there the workers' major reward was promotion or permanent employment, so they did not need informal rewards. In the small hotels, such behavior was common since it provided the *major* way in which *man-agement* could supplement—or rather, allow the workers to supplement—near-starvation wages. Managers not only allowed such behavior but even facilitated it by active connivance, since otherwise workers could hardly have carried extra wine or other products in and out undetected. In some cases, managers (as well as head waiters or other staff) had to be given a share to ensure their collaboration, especially in controlling the record keeping so that everything balanced out. In even the simplest kind of cases, managers were able *differentially* to reward certain workers by giving them preferred stations (say near the window with a view, where customers known to tip well would be seated) or by simply allowing certain workers a "knockoff" but not allowing others. In this way, desired behavior, such as loyalty and trustworthiness in all other respects, punctuality, and discipline could be ensured, resulting in the provision of a career for even lowly workers in a small organization.[14]

2. The second question about informal groups and relationships asks how widespread they are and how much of the workers' life they pervade. The focus of the early Hawthorne studies on small experimental groups, particularly the intensive observation of the men in the bank wiring observation room, led to an assumption that such groups must be important. Yet Structuralists have found informal groups to be rather uncommon and not necessarily important to workers. Dubin (1956), in a survey of "the central life interests" of 1,200 industrial workers, found that "only 9 per cent of the industrial workers in the sample preferred the informal group life that is centered in the job" (p. 136). He added that "In particular, work is not a central life interest for industrial workers when we studied the informal group experiences and the general social experiences that have some affective value for them" (p. 140). Walker and Guest (1952) found virtually no social work groups in their study of 179 assembly-line workers, and Vollmer (1960) reported that 53 percent of male skilled workers had "no coworkers as close friends outside work" (p. 75). However, Orzack (1959) did find work to be more central to the lives of nurses, and further studies (summarized in Dubin et al., 1975) report that the role of informal group life is a variable, being more significant in some settings than in others.[15]

In a careful case study of 47 relatively skilled workers, Zaleznik, Christensen, and Roethlisberger (1958) identified eight groups whose work life revolved around such nonwork activities as number pools, savings and merchandise clubs, games, and having coffee together. Some continued their association after working hours, but many did not. The single most important factor accounting for such group formation, particularly acceptance in what were considered the most desirable groups, was ethnicity—being of Irish origin. Here, then, where groups were found, they had only an indirect relationship to work activities.

But another extensive study in 30 plants turned up approximately 300 work groups,[16] which the author (Sayles, 1958) classifies into four types: apathetic (rarely acting together, but showing evidence of suppressed discontent), erratic (capable of unity, but often over trivial issues), strategic (rational, calculating groups, engaging in militancy only when clearly justified), and conservative (high-status groups who acted together only when they felt their high status or position was threatened). The major finding was that type of group was strongly associated with technology, in particular such factors as similarity of jobs, degree to which the work was indispensable, precision with which management could measure work load and pace and other work factors. Here, then, small-group relationships *were* associated with work activities, but the impact hardly matched that of the famous Hawthorne groups.

In sum, no simple case can be made that workers are "cliqued" in a solid phalanx against management, or that peer pressure is the single or even the most powerful determinant of worker behavior. Nor are groups, even when found, peculiar to lower-level workers. Dalton (1959) found that managers formed a variety of cliques, some in defense of their interests against *other* managers, and some as expressions of alienation.

Such findings only appear surprising in view of the expectation of the early Human Relationists, especially Mayo, that industrialization would lead to the atomization of society. Industrialization, they thought, would cause the disintegration of traditional social groups such as the family, the village community, and religious units. They predicted the disappearance of the intermediary bodies between the state and the individual as mass society evolved. Hence they saw it as the mission of the new social unit, the factory, to provide a new home, a place of emotional security for the atomized individual. Management was expected to furnish the needed social and emotional shelters, and in return it would be rewarded with a devoted, hardworking, satisfied labor force. In fact, the traditional social groups did decline in importance, scope, and degree of integration. The typical modern family is smaller in size, less stable, and socially less prominent than the traditional one. Many rural communities and religious groups have similarly declined. But most of these groups have not disappeared. After a long period of descent, their decline stopped and has even been partially reversed. While experimentation with different intimate life-styles goes on, and though the proportion of single-person households is growing, there is no evidence that people value intimacy and social relationships any less than they ever did. Although the straightforward Maslowian thesis that we discussed in the last chapter does not seem to be universally applicable, still, there does seem to be a shift to values more in conformity with the *general* thrust of the theory. Rokeach (1974) found that most values remained unchanged between 1968 and 1972, but those that did change included a concern for world peace, equality, and mature love, with declining emphasis on a sense of accomplishment. Other studies have also provided evidence for some decline in acquisitive values and a greater concern for more satisfying life-styles (see Etzioni, 1975). Similarly, whatever may be happening to the established religious denominations, there seems to be no letup in interest in ethical and moral values, nor any decline in the formation of religious sects and utopian communities (cf. Zablocki, 1980).

Moreover, new bases of social relations have developed, especially in urban and even more in suburban ecological units. The women's movement has led to a massive return of older women to colleges and universities, partly for vocational reasons, partly for intrinsic satisfaction. People may become alienated from national politics out of a sense of powerlessness, but then they may turn to local public affairs, founding alternative schools or influencing the direction of health services through membership on voluntary boards. There has been a revival (if there ever was a decline) of informal institutions (Henry, 1981), including nonmarket transactions (where people exchange services rather than paying money); informal caring institutions, such as those for alcoholics, disabled persons, and self-help networks for older people; and even informal judicial procedures, as overloaded court systems encourage the growth of private tribunals, marital conciliation centers, do-it-yourself divorce, and other "mediating structures" (Berger & Neuhaus, 1977). Thus the average modern worker does not come to the work situation starved for affection and affiliation, which a beneficent management must supply. This is not to deny that *some* workers do indeed find their major satisfactions and even fulfillment at work, but perhaps that is most true of top executives who are "married" to their work. Whether such attachment is strong or modest is an empirical question that must be settled by research.

### Conclusion

To a considerable extent, then, the Structuralists may be said to be offering a synthesis of the Classical and Human Relations contributions by focusing on the social structure of organizations. That focus leads us to study the differing and often conflicting interests of management and workers, to examine other groups with special interests (such as professionals and craftspersons), to show the ways in which conflict is built into the makeup of organizations, and to demonstrate how formal and informal relationships are interdependent. But Structuralism does more than simply synthesize—it offers a distinct point of view, to which we now turn.

## BUREAUCRATIC STRUCTURE AND LEGITIMACY: THE WEBERIAN LEGACY

Up to this point, we have seen the Structuralists mainly as a group on the attack—showing up the deficiencies of Human Relations and other interactionist approaches. Yet that critique uncovered vast areas that called for research: social conflict and its structural sources, the importance of environmental forces and social change, the relationships between formal and informal structures. The awareness of such factors did not spring directly from the study of the deficiencies in other approaches. Rather, Structuralists were sensitized to their presence by being schooled in the sociology of Max Weber (1968) and his followers.

Weber was concerned with the distribution of power among the organizational positions in the bureaucratic structure, and this represents the "formal" element of his work. At the same time, in his exploration of legitimation, he opened up a whole new perspective on the study of satisfaction derived from participation in the organization. His insights on the interplay between the power to control and the ability to justify ("legitimize") that power set the context for a great deal of subsequent work on the central organizational question: how to control the participants so as to maximize effectiveness and efficiency and minimize the unhappiness this very need to control produces.

To what extent can the organization expect its participants to accept its rulings because "they always were so," to what extent because the rulings agree with a law the participants acknowledge, and to what degree must the person who issues an order be highly persuasive? What characterizes the more rational power structures? What services do nonrational elements perform for the rational ones? And what effects does the departure of the "charismatic leader," the focus of the nonrational commitments and the ultimate source of legitimation, have on the participants, and hence on the organization's ability to control them? These were some of the questions that Weber sought to answer.

### Legitimation and Authority

Organizations, which Weber referred to as bureaucracies, set norms and need to enforce them; they have rules and regulations and issue orders, which must be obeyed if the organization is to function effectively. To a degree, an organization can rely on its power to make the participant obey. That is, it can use some of its resources to reward those who follow its rulings and to penalize those who do not. Such discipline does not require that the recipient of the order agree with it, and certainly not that he accept it as morally justified. He may follow an order to avoid loss of money or prestige and to increase his income or status. To some extent, the organization can maintain discipline by manipulating various rewards and sanctions in order to ensure maximum contentment and minimize disappointment.

The exercise of power, however, has a major limitation: It keeps the subject, as he conforms, alienated. He conforms because of ulterior motives. His conformity is likely to be limited to the matters explicitly backed by power. He will be unlikely to volunteer information, show initiative, or cooperate, except when he is explicitly forced to. Moreover, in moments of crisis, when the power structure of the organization is weakened, he will tend to prefer whatever other norms he subscribes to rather than the organization's.

On the other hand, when the exercise of power is seen as legitimate by those subject to it—that is, when the orders issued or rules set conform to the values to which the subjects are committed—compliance will be much deeper and more effective. The subject will "internalize" the rules. He will find the discipline less alienating, and he will continue to follow rules and orders when the organization's power is weakened or even absent.

It is crucial to realize the nature of the power increment that legitimation bestows. It does not increase the material interest of the subordinate in compliance. It does not make the order or rule necessarily pleasant—i.e., gratifying to the subject. But it fulfills a third kind of need, the need to follow norms that match rather than conflict with one's values. In order to emphasize the difference between normative satisfaction of the need for justice (or legitimacy) and the gratification of other needs, it is important to realize that whereas some legitimate orders are gratifying, many other orders may be legitimate and not gratifying, and still others may be illegitimate and yet gratifying. Thus Weber's study of legitimation introduces a whole new dimension to the study of organizational discipline. He used *power* to refer to the ability to induce acceptance of orders; *legitimation* to refer to the acceptance of the exercise of power because it is in line with values held by the subjects; and *authority* to refer to the combination of the two—i.e., to power that is viewed as legitimate.

## Weber's Typology of Authority

Weber's typology of authority is based on the sources and kinds of legitimation employed rather than on the types of power applied. He referred to authority as *traditional* when the subjects accept the orders of superiors as justified on the grounds that this is the way things are always done; and as rational-legal, or *bureaucratic*, when the subjects accept a ruling as justified because it agrees with a set of more abstract rules that they consider legitimate, and from which the ruling is "derived" (and, in this sense, is rational). (The work of the Roman courts is a fine example of bureaucratic authority.) Finally, Weber pointed to *charismatic* authority, in which the subjects accept a superior's orders as justified because of the influence of his personality, with which they identify.

Weber's classification of authority may be applied on at least three levels:

1. One might apply it on the societal level, comparing traditional, bureaucratic, and charismatic societies. The medieval society is often viewed as traditional, the modern democratic as bureaucratic, and societies in revolutionary periods—such as Russia after 1917 and Nazi Germany in the years following 1933—as charismatic.
2. One might compare different kinds of social units according to type of authority base. Here the family is seen as traditional (even in a bureaucratic society), complex organizations as bureaucratic (even in a charismatic period), and revolutionary political parties as charismatic (even in a traditional society).
3. Finally, one might use the breakdown to characterize relations between individual subjects and their superiors within a given organization.

Moreover, different authority relations tend to arise in different social structures. Traditional authority relations are typically found in a diffuse status structure where a superior in one realm is a superior in others, as, for example, in an aristocracy. Authority relations in bureaucratic structures are limited in scope; superiority is not transferred from one social realm to another. In the case of pure charismatic relations, not only is there no differentiation between the organization and other social units, but there is little internal differentiation between the leader and the followers.

Weber suggested that to be effective and efficient as an organizational instrument, a modern organizational structure requires bureaucratic authority. Charismatic relations lack any systematic division of labor, specialization, or stability. Organizational activities in traditional social units are not sufficiently immune from nonrelevant political, stratification, and kinship considerations to allow the rationality of the productive or administrative process to exert itself. Only where the scope of the organization is low do immunity from irrelevant factors, freedom to structure relations according to the requirements of a task, and acceptance of the rules on permanent grounds—all of which are essential to modern organization— emerge. Hence bureaucracies are the social units most suited for rational, modern organizations.

Yet Weber was aware of the fragility of the rational structure. Not only are there constant pressures from outside forces to encourage the bureaucrat to follow norms other than those of the organization, but the subject's commitment to the bureaucratic rules tends itself to decline. Here is a typical organizational dilemma: For the organization to be effective, it requires a special kind of legitimation, rationality, and narrowness of scope. But the ability to accept orders and rules as legitimate, particularly when they are repugnant to one's desires (frequently the case in bureaucracies), requires a level of self-denial that is difficult to maintain. Hence bureaucratic organizations tend to break either in the charismatic or the traditional direction, so that disciplinary relations are less separated from other, more "natural" or "warmer" ones. Moreover, the capacity for self-denial that the rational organization requires cannot be developed within it; it depends upon the more encompassing social relationships that exist in the traditional family or in a charismatic movement. Weber traced the origin of bureaucracies to earlier social units of these types, a point to which we will return once the nature of the bureaucratic structure is spelled out.

### The Bureaucratic Structure

Weber spelled out in considerable detail the features of the bureaucratic structure. They all specify what makes a highly rational structure.[17]

1. "A continuous organization of official functions bound by *rules*." Rational organization is the antithesis of ad hoc, temporary, unstable relations; hence the stress on continuity. Rules save effort by obviating the

need for deriving a new solution for every problem and case; they facilitate standardization and equality in the treatment of many cases. These advantages are impossible if each client is treated as a unique case, as an individual.

2. "A specific sphere of competence. This involves (a) a sphere of obligations to perform functions which have been marked off as part of a systematic division of labor; (b) the provision of the incumbent with the necessary authority to carry out these functions; and (c) that the necessary means of compulsion are clearly defined and their use is subject to definite conditions." Thus a systematic division of labor, rights, and power is essential for rational organization. Not only must each participant know his job and have the means to carry it out—which includes first of all the ability to command others—but he must also know the limits of his job, rights, and power so as not to overstep the boundaries between his role and those of others and thus undermine the whole structure.

3. "The organization of offices follows the principle of hierarchy; that is, each lower office is under the control and supervision of a higher one." In this way, no office is uncontrolled. Compliance cannot be left to chance; it has to be systematically checked and reinforced.

4. "The rules which regulate the conduct of an office may be *technical* rules or norms. In both cases, if their application is to be fully rational, specialized training is necessary. It is thus normally true that only a person who has demonstrated an adequate technical training is qualified to be a member of the administrative staff. . . ." We examine below the full import of this statement by Weber. It suffices to say here that he thought that the root of the bureaucrat's authority was his knowledge and training. Not that these replace legitimation, but the bureaucrat's command of technical skill and knowledge is the basis on which legitimation is granted to him.

5. "It is a matter of principle that the members of the administrative staff should be completely separated from ownership of the means of production or administration. . . . There exists, furthermore, in principle, complete separation of the property belonging to the organization, which is controlled within the spheres of the office, and the personal property of the official. . . ." This segregation, which Weber applied to other elements of the official's status, such as the segregation of his personal residence from the organization, keeps the official's bureaucratic status from being infringed by the demands of his nonorganizational statuses.

6. In order to enhance this organizational freedom, the resources of the organization have to be free of any outside control and the positions cannot be monopolized by any incumbent. They must be free to be allocated and reallocated according to the needs of the organization. "A complete *absence* of appropriation of his official positions by the incumbent" is required.

7. "Administrative acts, decisions, and rules are formulated and re-

corded in writing. . . ." Most observers might view this requirement as less essential or basic to rational organization than the preceding ones, and many will point to the irrationality of keeping excessive records, files, and the like, often referred to as "red tape." Weber, however, stressed the need to maintain a systematic interpretation of norms and enforcement of rules, which cannot be maintained through oral communication.

Weber pointed out that officials should be compensated by salaries and not receive payments from clients in order to ensure that their primary orientation will be to the organization, to its norms and representatives. Moreover, by promoting officials systematically, thus channeling their ambitions by providing them with careers, and by rewarding those loyal to it, the corporation reinforces this commitment.

Underlying the whole analysis is a set of principles that follows from the central organizational problem as Weber saw it: The high rationality of the bureaucratic structure is fragile; it needs to be constantly protected against external pressures to safeguard the autonomy required if it is to remain closely geared to its goals and not others.

### The Nonbureaucratic Head

The rules Weber specified are concerned with relationships between bureaucrats—i.e., those who make up the administrative body of the organizational hierarchy and structure. But, Weber indicated, organizations have nonbureaucratic heads. Although the bureaucrats follow the rules, the head sets them; although the administrative body serves the organization's goals, the head decides which goals are to be served; although the bureaucrats are appointed, the head is often elected or inherits his position. Presidents, cabinets, boards of trustees, and kings are typical nonbureaucratic heads of bureaucratic organizations.

These organization heads fulfill an important function in helping to preserve the emotional (and in this sense, nonrational) commitment to rationality. Most mortals find it difficult to maintain a commitment to an abstract set of norms and rules, especially when these run counter to the extraorganizational relations that pressure the bureaucrat to express irrelevant (to the organization) preferences, such as acting on kinship, local, political, racial, religious, or ethnic considerations rather than on the criteria set by the organization. Identification with a person, a leader, or the head of the organization provides the psychological leverage of a concrete and "warm" image that reinforces abstract commitment to the rules of the organization.

Through a process that he called "the routinization of charisma," Weber viewed some bureaucracies as emerging historically from charismatic movements—e.g., the Church from the early Christian communities, and the Soviet state from the Communist movement. The founder of the movement, the great charismatic, is also the spiritual father of the new structure. He bestows his light on it and, by blessing the new structure, transfers to it some of the commitment of his followers. Weber saw the successors to the charismatic head being like the moon which reflects the light of the sun. They have little or no charisma of their own, but retain the commitment of the lower ranks by acquiring charisma from the office they occupy. Thus the popes are viewed as representing Jesus, and are endowed with some of his charismatic power.

These secondary leaders, according to Weber, never match the founder in charisma. On the contrary, they gradually use up the stock of charisma that the top office acquired from the founder, until it is exhausted and the structure loses its legitimacy. Then, according to Weber's theory of history, the unit—whether a society or a bureaucracy—disintegrates, the final blow being dealt by a new charismatic leader who emerges from the old structure and topples it by means of a revolutionary movement, from which a new structure develops, built on the ruins of the old one.

## The Succession Crisis

According to Weber's model, the rational commitment of the lower in rank to those higher in rank, and to the organization in general, makes most higher-ranking individual participants "dispensable." As long as the individual who leaves or dies is replaced by someone with similar technical qualifications, the organization's effectiveness should not be impaired. Commitments are to the position, not to the incumbent, and hence should be easy to transfer. Only the departure or death of a nonbureaucratic head of an organization—the one person to whom commitments are personal rather than bureaucratic—precipitates a major organizational crisis. The succession crisis is particularly evident in totalitarian states, and there almost invariably leads to a period of instability. But corporations, churches, armies, and other organizations are also subject to succession crises.

Gouldner (1954), for instance, studied a succession crisis in a gypsum plant in which a beloved paternalistic head was replaced by a new executive who had a mandate to increase efficiency. Unable to depend on the group of informal associates who had fed the previous head vital work information, the new head was forced to institute paperwork communication to get such information. The previous head had ensured compliance by an "indulgency pattern": He had allowed workers to use company property for their personal needs and had tolerated absenteeism. The new head, unaware of just how that system had worked and unable to automatically shift it to comply with his own mandate, had to institute new rules and insist on their enforcement. When subordinates resisted, he brought in his own lieutenants to supervise the changes, which led to further resistance and withholding of information. In turn, he had to demand tighter rule obedience, make up new rules, and emphasize formal communication even more. In this way, bureaucratization was shown to be a consequence of succession, as Weber himself had demonstrated in the process of "the routinization of charisma."

Some structural factors, however, may routinize the succession process so that disruption to the organization is minimized. In contrast to the Gouldner case, Guest (1962) reported a smooth succession in an automobile plant—a result explainable by the fact that labor was in short supply and the economic situation was less severe, so that the new head was under less pressure to increase efficiency. Grusky (1964), comparing a business corporation and a military installation, found that the latter had a higher succession rate, a result attributable to a military policy of reducing dependence on particular officers so as to make rapid replacement less disruptive when necessary, as during wartime.[18] Other studies have shown that larger organizations are better able to tolerate high succession rates with little disruption (Grusky, 1961; Kriesberg, 1962; but see the disagreement by Gordon and Becker, 1964) than are smaller organizations, a difference attributable to the fact that large organizations are more diverse and formalized, meaning that any one person can do little to change things within them. Another factor that reduces disruption is the degree of "paradigm[19] development." In a study of academic departments, Pfeffer and Moore (1980) report that those with high paradigm development exhibited longer tenure of the department head, but that such departments were also able to handle a change when it did occur because of the basic consensus that prevailed within them.

These studies should not lead to the conclusion that avoidance of a succession crisis is always desirable. Actually, the succession period can be a stage in which needed innovations are introduced to counteract earlier deterioration of the organization.[20] A considerable literature has grown up examining this phenomenon for the case of sports teams. The question asked is: What happens when the manager of a baseball or basketball team is replaced? Since professional sports teams generate voluminous statistics on performance, researchers can readily examine the relationship between executive turnover and subsequent team performance. The findings are, unfortunately, inconclusive. Some show a deterioration because of the change itself, others show little change, and one even offers a "Hopi rain dance" explanation. The last points out that the Hopi employ the rain dance only when there has been a long drought, meaning that, eventually, the dance *has* to be followed by rain. Similarly, a baseball team will fire its field manager only when the team is in a slump, not necessarily because a change in managers will help, but simply because the fans are unhappy and are demanding that the team leadership *do* something. The manager is offered as a "sacrifice" to placate the fans. (The evidence that this action has little to do with his competence is that he is often snapped up immediately by another team.) Since the team is basically a good one, eventually it pulls out of its slump. Like the Hopi rain dance, the sacrifice has "produced results." (See Grusky, 1963; Gamson & Scotch, 1964; and Allen, Panian, & Lotz, 1979; see also Eitzen and Yetman, 1972.)[21]

It is difficult to say whether Weber would have been pleased with this research that his work on charismatic succession has stimulated. Still, it is not too farfetched to consider baseball managers charismatic (their fans certainly shower them with adulation—when the team is winning), and, after all, turning away from charismatic figures when they are believed to have lost their unique charisma is far from rare in history.

## Some Critical Observations

As Weber's work was translated, it came under criticism, like any good theory. Some of these criticisms derive from the simple failure to read Weber (e.g., the claim that Weber did not "understand" informal organization, when much of his work deals with the way in which power is used by subordinates to further their own interests), others from a failure to understand his use of the "ideal type" (e.g., in discussing bureaucracy, he presents an obviously exaggerated model to show more clearly the features he wishes to highlight). But certain critical observations[22] are valid.

1. Genuine charismatic leaders may succeed the original head and endow the organization with legitimacy, so that their reign increases rather than depreciates its stock. In other words, a society or an organization might be rejuvenated without being disbanded. For example, the most distinguished American universities have known periods of deterioration following the deaths of their original founders, but very few have been disbanded, and many have at a later state been revived by another charismatic leader who has restored them to prominence.

2. The sharp distinction among the three modes of authority and social structure is exaggerated. Indeed, there are many "mixed" types.[23] For instance, there were semitraditional and semibureaucratic organizations in ancient Egypt, Imperial China, and medieval Byzantium, in which hierarchical structures and adherence to rules and regulations were combined with a fairly diffuse, totalistic status structure, such as seems to characterize modern totalitarian regimes.

3. An organization might shift from a more bureaucratic to a more charismatic structure, and then back to a more bureaucratic one. Peacetime armies are highly bureaucratic. In time of war, especially in combat, they lose many of their bureaucratic qualities. Rules and regulations are waived or disregarded; personal leadership counts more than formal power positions; oral communications replace many written ones; separation of pri-

vate and organizational life is largely abolished. Although novelists like to draw on the strains these transitions cause, as a rule they are carried out rather smoothly. After the war, though not without crisis, the organization again shifts gears and returns to a bureaucratic structure. Labor unions have similarly shifted from bureaucratic relations in periods of "business as usual" to charismatic relations as the tensions mount on the eve of and during the "combat" period of collective bargaining and strike. The conclusion we draw from the frequency of such shifts is that there is no inevitable movement toward increasing bureaucratization at any given time, though there may be a long-range tendency in that direction.[24]

4. Lastly, the appearance of leaders with charismatic qualities is not limited to the top organizational position. Lower-ranking combat officers, low-ranking priests, and university professors occasionally exhibit a great deal of personal charisma.

Having considered some of the antecedents and components of the Structuralist approach, we turn now to apply its insights to understanding how organizations function, capitalizing on the work of Weber and building on the foundation he provided. In the next chapter, we examine research that has explored the relationships among the variables Weber identified, such as formalization, and complexity, but also others that have been found to be important.

### NOTES

1. Examples of less enduring relationships might include brief encounters on an elevator and crowd gatherings at a public spectacle. These occasions also have a structure, but it quickly materializes and then quickly vanishes.

2. Another criticism, as we have already pointed out, is that interactionists tend to see only the relationships internal to the organization, ignoring environmental and broader societal influences. We deal with that complex question in Chapter 10.

3. How far such control can go is well brought out in Hochschild's (1983) study of the manipulation of feelings by corporations, in particular the complex process by which the airline stewardess's smile is taught.

4. The situation in which the underlying structure is unresponsive to human needs, but a front of seeming responsiveness is projected, characterizes *inauthenticity* (as opposed to *alienation,* which describes a situation in which both are unresponsive). Cf. Etzioni, 1968.

5. Whyte (1955, pp. 169–188) offers an excellent critique of the use of suggestion systems, as well as a description of how they can be improved.

6. The dogged persistence with which Human Relationists defend their position, even in the face of evidence to the contrary, suggests to Kaplan and Tausky (1977) that there are powerful ideological or even political elements involved, which are felt to be worthy in their own right. We saw this in the case of quality of work life advocacy in Chapter 4.

7. We discussed Adam Smith's examples of pin making on p. 33.

8. Actually, the case was clear even in Adam Smith's day from the fact that such work was commonly carried on by women and children, with the man (as husband and father) serving as a sort of foreman over the work of his family. During wartime, many kinds of weaving were quickly taken over by women and children, with no apparent difficulty.

9. Even the coming of the modern factory was associated as much with the advantages it provided in controlling workers as it offered in efficiency. Although most people assume the factory came into existence because of the superior efficiency of steam power and mechanical inventions, Marglin (1974) shows that the first factories *preceded* the use of steam power and mechanical inventions. The first weaving sheds, for example, were simply aggregations under one roof of weavers who continued to use the hand shuttles they had used in their homes under the putting-out system. So the impetus for the first factories was to make the workers easier to control. However, once workers were brought together under one roof, it proved easier to introduce power tools and other inventions, since they could be applied to large-scale production. If further evidence is needed, the historian Marc Bloch (1967) shows how the watermill in the Middle Ages was not a reflection of greater efficiency in grain production, but rather a device to collect taxes more easily by forcing peasants to bring their grain to the lord's mill instead of grinding it themselves in their own homes.

10. Braverman (1974, p. 99) reminds us that Taylor himself never doubted for a moment that the workers who engaged in what he called "systematic soldiering" (deliberate restriction of output to group-agreed levels) were behaving rationally, from their point of view. When he became a foreman and was approached by his old colleagues, he even admitted that he would do exactly as they were doing if he were a lower-level employee. He was clearly at the opposite pole from the Human Relations researchers, who sought the explanation of restriction of output in "irrational" or "emotional" sources.

11. The reduction in worker contributions cannot be explained solely as a result of technical improvements or "labor-saving" inventions; it is intimately tied up with society-wide shifts in economic and cultural structures, requiring the kind of historical or comparative perspective provided by Burawoy (1983), Edwards (1979) or Clegg and Dunkerley (1980). We discuss some of these questions in Chapter 10, where we turn our attention to societal environments.

12. In a study of these changes in machine design (lathes, and milling machines to make tools or machines that must grind aircraft surfaces to tolerances of a 1000th of an inch), Noble (1979) describes a continual battle: Management and engineers try to bypass the machinist by creating electronic, computer-programmed instructions for running the machine, but the machinist remains irreplaceable because someone has to monitor the machine and correct it when it shows signs of breakdown or when the material used shows flaws. Noble quotes a manager: "We want absolutely no decision made on the floor." But a moment later, when the same manager looked out at all the expensive machinery that could go wrong, he said, "with equal conviction, that 'We need guys out there who can think . . .'" (Noble, 1979, p. 44. Copyright © 1979 by Andrew Zimbalist. Reprinted by permission of Monthly Review Press). See also Wood, 1982.

13. In an analysis of self-management in Yugoslavian organizations, Radmondt (1979) sees wildcat strikes as an expression of the failure of workers' councils to articulate worker grievances and disagreement effectively, even to the point of hiding the extent of such disagreement.

14. Unofficial reward systems seem to be a part of formal structures everywhere since managers are always allowed some discretion as to which workers they recommend for promotions and which they do not, whom they give preferred jobs to and whom they allot the dirty work to, and so on. This is described in detail in Dalton, 1959.

15. Some of the variability in findings may be attributable to the central-life-interest scale itself, since one study (Maurer, Vredenburgh, & Smith, 1981) reports low statistical reliability as well as low discriminatory ability of the scale items.

16. We cannot make a direct calculation of number of groups per plant since the author tells us that he and a colleague (George Strauss) interviewed a "minimum" of 25 percent of the work force in each plant. In any case, since the 300 groups were distributed among 30 plants, we can hardly draw the inference that each plant was packed with work groups. The firms were mostly in metal processing, but some were producers of fiber cartons, breakfast foods, and other products.

17. There have been many translations of various portions of Weber's works, the most comprehensive being that of Roth and Wittich (1968, especially Vol. 3), which should be

consulted in order to place the discussion of bureaucracy in the historical context in which Weber treated it. The features of bureaucracy that we discuss can be found in Merton, Gray, Hockey, and Selvin, 1952, pp. 18–20. One of the best summaries of Weber's ideas is by Bendix (1960).

18.  Saroff (1974), exploring the claim that "temporary" organizations are more flexible than bureaucracies, describes an experiment in which the headship of a federal government executive training institute was deliberately rotated. He found that the shortness of tenure led to heads spending all their time learning procedures, with the result that the structure was not modified but was just as rigid as that of any bureaucracy. Also, since they had little stake in the organization, the succeeding heads did as little as they could get away with. The lesson is that there are limits to the value of succession as a deliberate organizational policy.

19.  The concept of *paradigm* was used in a widely received study by Kuhn (1970) to refer to the extent to which members of a scholarly community share a theory, preferred methods of research, and a tacit understanding of the problems needing study. Mathematics and physics are found to have strong agreement on a paradigm, whereas political science, sociology, and the Romance languages are found not to (or else have many paradigms).

20.  Actually, several studies (e.g., Carlson, 1961; Helmich & Brown, 1972) show that outside replacements are often *deliberately* brought in when there has been poor performance or when a large-scale change is contemplated. It is felt that such persons will not be bound by attachment to existing practices or by obligations to favored subordinates.

21.  In a careful examination of large corporations, Lieberson and O'Connor (1972) report that various leadership variables account for only a small part of the variance of the performance of those corporations, finding instead that environmental variables have larger effects. This study thus indirectly supports the argument that managers are likely only to have a moderate effect, at best, on the performance of their organizations. Lieberson and O'Connor are, of course, dealing with large organizations, whereas baseball teams are much smaller. But Carroll (1984), in a critique of baseball succession studies, even questions whether they should be regarded as organizations, suggesting they might be better conceived of as work groups. Still, the finding that managers have such small effects even on work groups is all the more striking.

22.  We draw here on Etzioni, 1975, Chaps. XII and XIII.

23.  Or even different types. For example Rothschild-Whitt (1979) calls attention to the continued viability and even growth of "collectivist" organizations—such as alternative institutions and collectives—which should not be disposed of as "failures" for not having become bureaucratized, but rather should be seen as genuine alternatives based on different organizational principles. In such organizations authority is dispersed, there are minimal rules, and there is much use made of normative and solidarity incentives. Although such organizations have their survival problems and are subject to pressures to bureaucratize (as we saw above, p. 19), such is the case for any organization.

24.  DiMaggio and Powell (1983) advance the intriguing hypothesis that organizations may become rationalized and bureaucratic not necessarily because these forms are most efficient (or proven to be most efficient) but rather because of the operation of "isomorphic" influences. These include coercion (as when state law requires that there be formal accounting records), "mimetic" processes (as when organizations, in doubt as to what to do when goals are ambiguous, settle questions by simply imitating other organizations which are themselves often bureaucratic), and normative pressures (especially those created by professionals in organizations, people who employ similar criteria of judgment and practice which they then insist be instituted in the organizations that employ them).

# CHAPTER SIX
# THE USES OF STRUCTURE
*Post-Weberian and Beyond*

In this chapter, we examine several forms of structure that shed light on behavior in organizations. Some structural variables, such as complexity and formalization, came directly from Weber, but were subjected to careful quantitative treatment, as well as attempts to show their relationship to other variables such as size and technology. Although the latter variables are not structural in the strict sense, they were found to affect structure quite closely. Other research focused on ecological and demographic forms of structure, such as physical layout and age distribution in organizations. Each of these approaches offered impressive evidence of the power of structural analysis.

After reviewing those approaches, we turn to the compliance model in the next chapter, which will then occupy us for much of the rest of the book.

## THE WEBERIAN LEGACY: MEASURING BUREAUCRACY

Once Weber's work became available in English (beginning in the late 1940s), attention was focused on the "ideal-type" characteristics that we discussed in Chapter 5: rules, keeping of records, specific fields of competence, hierarchy, and so forth. Students began to ask: Are these characteristics related to one another? For example, does the keeping of records lead to the institution of rules, and vice versa? Does hierarchy grow with the proliferation of specific fields of competence so as to coordinate such fields?

In order to answer such questions, we had to develop ways of measuring these characteristics. That has proved to be no small task. How, for example, do you measure "record keeping"? Count the number of filing cabinets? Count the number of staff assigned to record keeping? Or how do you get at "rules"? Count the number of regulations listed in a codebook? Ask supervisors how important they estimate "rule adherence" to be? Observe instances where employees are discharged (or fined) for rule violations? At the same time that students wrestled with such questions, there was an explosion in quantitative analysis techniques leading to highly sophisticated ways of "controlling" variables and measuring causation. We are still in the midst of all these changes, so all we can do here is offer a brief illustration of the spirit and excitement of these developments.

Although students began with the features suggested by Weber, they came to focus attention on a limited set of factors (treated as variables). We discuss them together, since those who study them typically treat them as a group and spend much of their time examining the relationships among them, holding some constant while examining the covariance of others. The variables are: *centralization* (control from the top, as opposed to more dispersed control), *complexity* (the division of labor or specialization), *formalization* (the degree to which behavior is specified or rule governed), *size*, and *technology*. Although Weber gave little attention to some of these variables (such as size and technology),[1] the importance of all taken together can hardly be denied.

To illustrate, consider the question: Does organization stifle original ideas? Popular writers often assume that large organizations inevitably create a barrier to creativity, and insist that only the isolated individual— the Eli Whitney, James Watt, or Madame Curie—can actually originate ideas. (Whether such geniuses were really isolated is seldom examined.) However, the great economist Joseph Schumpeter (and his celebrated student John K. Galbraith) insisted that only large organizations could afford the risks of innovation.

Actually, the evidence is quite mixed (e.g., Blumberg, 1975, pp. 54–55) because it turns out that there is no simple relationship between size and creativity. Instead, structure is found to be critical. Hage and Aiken (1970) used program change as an index of how much social agencies were oriented to change and new ideas. They concluded that, apart from size, program change is associated with a high degree of complexity and low levels of centralization and formalization.[2] High complexity means persons with different occupations and kinds of knowledge interact, generating both pressures to promote their own collective interests and the dynamics that are associated with advancing knowledge in the professions. On the other hand, high centralization means new ideas have to be accepted by those at the top, who may be conservative or feel that innovators threaten their own entrenched position. Besides, if new ideas have to take a tortuous route to the top before they can be implemented, there is a high likelihood they will be sidetracked. When Hage and Aiken measured the *attitudes* to change held by individuals in the organization, they found that positive attitudes either correlated very poorly with program change or produced contradictory results. This does not mean that individuals are unimportant to change, but rather that they need to operate in situations or structures that allow for or are hospitable to their new ideas.[3]

Despite the promise suggested by these arguments, those researchers who have limited their studies to analysis of these structural variables have thus far run into many problems. We will present a brief survey of major findings, and some of the problems encountered.

*Centralization* has turned out to be more difficult to measure than it might at first seem. In the abstract, it is possible to ask whether key decisions are made by an elite or by a more widely dispersed group of participants. In practice, it proves difficult to decide what are "key" decisions, and to relate the many kinds of control and power to one another. For example, the top policymakers or elite may exercise effective control without giving direct orders merely by requiring that subordinates follow a rulebook closely. If an output measure is used to gauge conformity, people may be hardly aware that the controls are very tight. Many controls are unobtrusive, coming directly from the technology (as in an assembly line), and people may be so thoroughly socialized (or brainwashed) that they do not notice they are conforming, thinking instead that they are behaving spontaneously. In a study of retail department stores, Ouchi and Maguire (1975); and Ouchi (1977) find that two modes of organizational control— personal surveillance and the measurement of outputs—are employed in quite different organizational settings. In small units, for example, or those in which the job is sufficiently simple for a supervisor to be able to judge whether it is being done correctly (or according to requirements), personal surveillance is appropriate and is found. But when stores are large and highly complex, it is simply impossible to observe and directly evaluate behavior, so output measures are the *only* way of appraising organizational performance. An elite still maintains a degree of control by deciding which outputs shall be measured and what the requirements are, but the measurement itself has to be left in the hands of lower units.

As we have noted, the current managerial mood encourages more employee autonomy, and thus less centralization. However, in a study of human service organizations (for drug abuse, family counseling, welfare services, etc.), Glisson and Martin (1980) report that centralization is positively associated with higher *productivity* (as measured by number of clients served) as well as by higher efficiency (though not so strongly), but the staff appear to be unhappy with the centralization. The result, then, is a dilemma, with unpleasant trade-offs.

*Complexity* is measured by the number of occupational specialties, length of required training, and participation in professional activities (Hage & Aiken, 1967), or by the number of different positions or subunits (Blau & Schoenherr, 1971; Pugh, Hickson, Hinings, & Turner, 1968). Complexity is found to be associated with size (though the causal direction is unclear), as well as with spatial dispersion (having few or many sites), which itself is sometimes also considered a form of complexity (Mileti, Gillespie, & Haas, 1977). Organizational complexity clearly creates problems of coordination, therefore inducing decentralization, which is not surprising, but also influencing the organization's degree of competitiveness, which *is* surprising. To show this, Aiken and Hage (1968) reported that the more complex a social agency was, the more likely it was to be involved in interdependent relationships with other agencies, a relationship they attribute to the search on the part of specialists for resources to support innovations they would like to introduce, or which their own specialization requires for effective performance. That, in turn, forces the organization into competitive relationships with other organizations that are bidding for the same resources. The result, then, is a quite nonintuitive finding: The more complex the organization, the more competitive it is.

*Formalization* has been measured by ascertaining how job procedures are codified and how much tolerance for variation is permitted (Hage & Aiken, 1967), or by estimating how much standardization there is (the extent to which rules or definitions are invariable, illustrated in work by the "Aston group"[4]—see Pugh, Hickson, Hinings, & Turner, 1968).

On the one hand, as Weber pointed out, formalization acts as a control on the tendency of officials to be arbitrary and arrogant, as they often were in traditional societies. If rules clearly specify how agents should be rewarded and clients should be treated, then there is greater likelihood that people will be dealt with on their merits. On the other hand, actual studies of formalization as a variable show that as it increases, there is also an increasing inhibition of innovative behavior and greater alienation (Aiken & Hage, 1966). Perhaps, then, the benefits Weber noted are bought at a cost to the employees who must work in such formalized work settings. When people bring into the organization high expectations of autonomy and discretion, as highly educated and specialized engineers and scientists usually do, the degree of alienation may be especially high (as Miller, 1967, found in a study of an aerospace firm).

*Size* (measured variously by number of persons employed or quantity of resources) is generally assumed to be causal; Blau and others (e.g., Blau & Schoenherr, 1971; Klatzky, 1970; Meyer, 1972) generally report that increased size is associated with greater internal differentiation (e.g., greater specialization) as well as with economies of scale. These two factors have different effects on the size of the administrative component—specialization increases it and economies of scale reduce it. But the latter effect is stronger, resulting in a net reduction in the proportion of administrators (thus disproving "Parkinson's Law").[5] However, Hall and Tittle (1966) and Hall, Haas, and Johnson (1967) report findings that suggest size has little relationship to complexity or formalization, or to other variables. Along with Aldrich (1972), they doubt that size "causes" other changes, suggesting that perhaps it is better regarded as a consequence of growth in specialization or formalization that gives rise to a need for more monitoring and personnel. In other words, size may be an *indicator* of other aspects of the organization rather than a structural factor in its own right.[6]

Perhaps because of the research focus on how size is related to other structural variables (such as formalization and centralization), the relationship between size and individual experience has been neglected. Fragmentary studies show that both satisfaction and productivity seem to be highest neither in large nor small, but in medium-sized firms (Meltzer & Salter, 1962; Smyth, 1982). However, Kahn et al. (1964) report that "stress" seems to increase monotonically with size, at least up to a point, after which it levels off.[7] Size does seem to be related directly to pay, with smaller firms paying, on average, about 70 percent of what larger firms pay (Lester, 1967; Stolzenberg, 1978). No clear explanation of the differential has been offered, though there is some evidence that larger firms, being more subject to financial as well as general accountability, make a point of hiring persons with visible credentials, such as college degrees. The competition for such people tends to bid up the price of labor.[8]

*Technology* is obviously worth examining but has proved difficult to operationalize. Much of the interest in technology was stimulated by a pioneering study made in England by Woodward (1965; replicated in the United States by Zwerman, 1970), in which she compared unit production (one or a few at a time, as in "made to order" clothing or scientific instrument engineering), mass production (as in the automobile assembly line), and continuous production (as in pharmaceutical drug or chemical manufacturing, where machinery does most of the actual work, with workers monitoring dials and switches). Some of Woodward's findings are presented in Figures 6-1 and 6-2, which show the relationship between technology and structure in her easy-to-understand form. For example, in Figure 6-1, the proportion of staff (including maintenance) rises steadily as we move from unit through mass production to process. In Figure 6-2, the span of control of first-line supervisors is highest in mass production (one person supervising an average of 50 persons) and lowest in process (one person supervising about 11 persons). Many of Woodward's other findings deal with levels of management, relative size of the management group, size of the clerical and administrative staff, proportion of skilled workers, as well as finer organizational distinctions, which she discusses in case studies.

Blauner (1964) follows Woodward's lead by examining the relationship of such technologies to alienation, but found that there were few simple or direct relationships. For example, textile workers, who might be

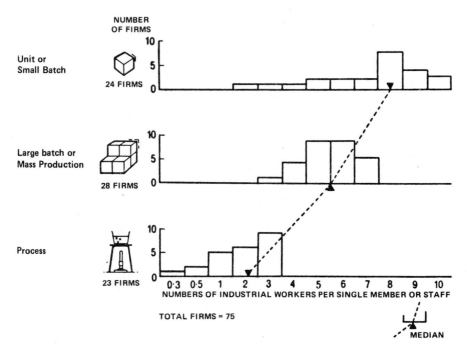

**FIGURE 6-1    Ratio of staff to industrial workers.** (From Woodward, 1965, Figure 18, p. 60)

assumed to be most alienated by the character of their work, were, in fact, strongly integrated into community networks of family and friends, a consequence facilitated by the location of the mills in small southern towns. Thompson (1967) distinguished among "long-linked technologies" (where parts move from one person or department to another in serial form), mediating technologies (where the organization links clients or members of the public to one another, as in employment agencies, telephone companies, and post offices), and intensive technologies (in which procedures are adapted to the case at hand, as in filling prescriptions in a drugstore, or in hospitals that have elaborate technology and equipment, which are adapted to different patient needs). These technologies, in turn, were thought to require different forms of coordinative structures.

The most influential model of the relationship between technology and structure is the one offered by Perrow (1970), who takes the view that *all* organizations can be looked at, on the one hand, in terms of the kind of "raw material" they deal with (whether iron ore, money, or people), and on the other, according to how they handle that raw material. If, for example, the inmates of a prison (a people-changing organization), are believed to be much alike (at least the guards make no important distinctions among them), and if the staff believe they know how to treat the inmates ("treat 'em rough so they show respect"), one has the kind of organization shown

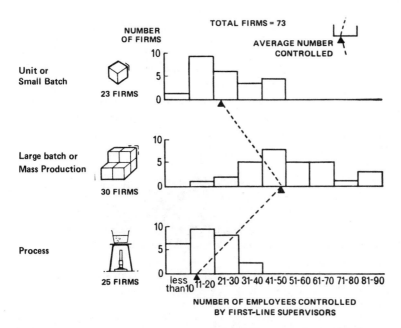

FIGURE 6-2   **Size of the span of control of first-line supervisors.** This figure and Figure 6-1 (p. 94) come from Joan Woodward, *Industrial Organization* (New York: Oxford University Press, 1965), pp. 60 and 62. Both are reprinted by permission of Oxford University Press.

|  | UNIFORM AND STABLE | NONUNIFORM AND UNSTABLE |
|---|---|---|
| **NOT WELL UNDERSTOOD** | Socializing institutions (e.g., some schools)  1 | Elite psychiatric agency  2 |
| **WELL UNDERSTOOD** | Custodial institutions, vocational training  4 | Programmed learning school  3 |

FIGURE 6-3   **Raw material variables (people-changing examples).** (From *Organizational Analysis,* p. 79 by C. Perrow. Copyright © 1970 by Wadsworth Publishing Company, Inc. Reprinted by permission of Brooks/Cole Publish Company, Monterey, California.)

in Cell 4 of Figure 6-3. At the other extreme of a people-changing organization is an elite psychiatric agency (Cell 2 of Figure 6-3), where each case is felt to be unique and to present special problems of therapeutic intervention, requiring new or experimental approaches. These two might simply be called "routine" and "nonroutine" types.

But it is possible for cases to fall into the other two cells of Figure 6-3. In Cell 1 are found many (perhaps most) public schools, in which children are treated in a uniform manner and all follow the same lesson plan, with allowance made for difficult cases, who are sent to the school counselor (or expelled). In Cell 3 fall schools that are staffed by enthusiasts (often parents) who feel certain they know what education should consist of (e.g., programmed learning), and who also insist that every child must be dealt with differently, following a program to match the child's own potential. In both these cells, the technology is not routine, but it is not completely nonroutine either, since procedures may be quite clearly specified, even following a precise ritual.

Generally, the more routine the technology, the more bureaucratic the organization. On the other hand, as exceptional or unusual cases show up, and as the technology must be adapted to suit the unusual case (special kinds of aluminum for airplane parts, or a special school for "exceptional" children), there will be many more meetings to measure progress and decide on next steps, and failures will occur more often (wasted material on aircraft, dropouts in schools). The resulting frustration may mean more professionals will be hired, adding to costs and perhaps leading to even greater complications in technology.[9]

The studies we have examined have attracted wide attention, partly because of the use of rigorous quantitative methods (usually regression and path analysis), thus leading, some hope, to the beginnings of a cumulative science. At the moment, this work is in ferment, with many unsolved conceptual and measurement problems. But though there is frequent disagreement, the end result is usually better studies. For example, early studies employed number of workers as their measure of size. Later it was found that results differed if researchers used other measures (e.g., number of clients, scope of operations). This is especially true with human service organizations (such as social agencies; see Martin, 1979), whose work requires them to be more sensitive to their clientele.

Another example is the finding, to which we alluded earlier, that larger organizations have a smaller proportion of administrators than do smaller ones. While many studies have confirmed that generalization, it has been found that it cannot be applied directly to growing or declining organizations (Freeman & Hannan, 1975). A growing organization might continue to add administrators until, perhaps, it is merged with another organization, when there might be a sudden firing of many administrators. In turn, declining organizations have been found to be reluctant to drop administrators, perhaps because it is more difficult to manage decline than it is to manage growth. In this way, we are developing more sophistication in learning how structures operate in dynamic situations.[10]

We turn next to two other types of structure—ecological and distributional. They shed a rather different light than those considered thus far.

## ECOLOGICAL STRUCTURE

Here we are calling attention to the social effects of physical and temporal work arrangements. What differences does it make if everyone is on the same floor, on different floors, in different buildings, in different cities? What if everyone is in one large room (the favorite situation of those who criticize large organizations for oppressing workers),[11] or if separate offices or partitions cluster people into smaller groupings? For example, Nigel Walker (1961), in a study of a large division of the British Treasury Department, found an inverse relationship between average days of yearly sick leave and the rank of the staff member: the lower the rank, the more days taken off, a finding that held when sex, marital status, and age were all controlled. Some part of the relationship may be attributed to social class differences, though the availability of socialized medicine attenuates that effect (but, of course, there are still class differences in diet, home heating, and the like). When respiratory infections were held constant, the differences vanished, leading the writer to speculate that the main causal factor was simple exposure to fellow workers. Top officials have private or semiprivate offices. The further down you go in the organization, the more likely you are to find multiple-person offices, until at the bottom you may find large numbers in one big room, all exposed to the sneezes and sniffles of fellow workers.[12] In sum, working—at least at bottom levels—can be dangerous to health.

More direct evidence of the effects of physical structure are presented in the most famous and frequently cited prototype of the factory—the assembly line. In a classic study, Walker and Guest (1952) found three interaction patterns, each corresponding to the physical requirements of the line: isolated workers (such as a paint sprayer of wheels and small parts who worked independently in a shed located some distance from other paint operations), workers in close proximity on the assembly line (Figure 6-4A), and team workers (Figure 6-4B). Although the sheer amount of noise (another physical factor) interfered with interaction, the physical layout was critical: Team workers could more easily talk to one another. As one worker put it (p. 68), "If it weren't for talking and fooling, you'd go nuts."

Right at the outset, we underline a key point that will come up repeatedly as we go along: *We make no assumption of structural determinism.* It is easy

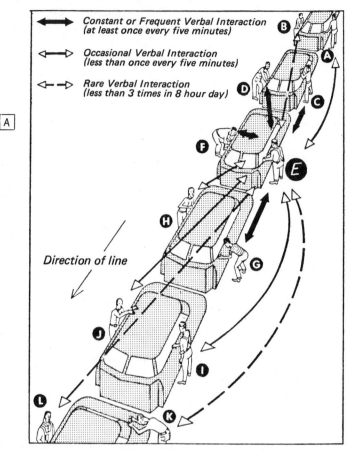

Social Interaction Pattern of Typical Main Assembly-Line Worker—Polisher, Paint Department.

Panel A (above) and B (upper right, facing page) from Charles R. Walker and R. H. Guest, *The Man on the Assembly Line,* 1952, pp. 71 and 75. Reprinted by permission of Harvard University Press. Panel C (lower right, facing page) from Jan-Peder Norstedt and Stefan Aguren, *The Saab-Scania Report* (Stockholm, Sweden: Swedish Employers Confederation, 1973). Reprinted with permission from the Swedish Employers Confederation.

**FIGURE 6-4    Physical patterns on automobile assembly lines.**

to fall into this trap, especially since, when observing great complex machinery, many despair of any change, seeing the worker as a tragic victim of "progress." But even on assembly-line operations, there are usually at least two options: (1) robots can take over many of the dullest and most degrading of operations; (2) the assembly line itself was designed by humans and can be designed differently.

An example of the second option is provided in Figure 6-4C, which

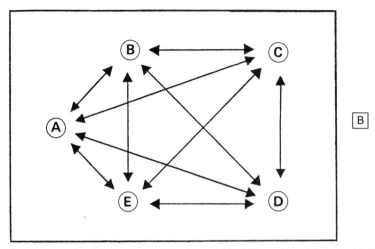

Social Interaction Pattern among Members of the Grille and Fender Assembly Team. All members of the unit interact with all other members. The group remains the same for all five individuals.

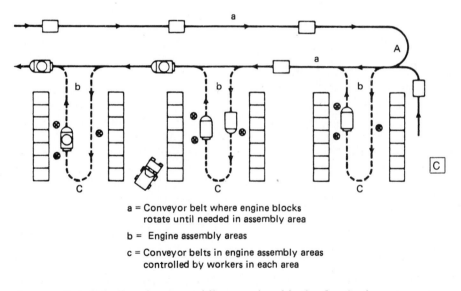

a = Conveyor belt where engine blocks
     rotate until needed in assembly area

b =  Engine assembly areas

c = Conveyor belts in engine assembly areas
     controlled by workers in each area

shows a Swedish line for assembling engine blocks for Saab motor cars. Engine blocks circulate around the line labeled *a* until the workers are ready to work on one. It can then be *removed* entirely from the line, and workers can cluster about it (in Area *b*), assigning jobs to suit themselves, and then return the block to the line. The jobs are no less monotonous, but at least conversation and informal interaction are possible.

Other assembly-line operations, such as packing Ping-Pong paddles into boxes or cleaning tuna, may not yield to either mechanization or redesign. A journalistic report (Garson, 1975) quotes one worker in a tuna cannery as follows:

> I clean tuna. The loins come past me on a belt. [Loins are the skinned, headless, tailless, halved or quartered pieces of fish—*Ed*]. I bone the loin and take out the dark meat—the cat food. I put the clean loins on the second belt, the cat food on the third belt and I save my bones. You're not allowed to dump any garbage till the line lady okays it. Because that's how they check your work. They count your bones and see if they're clean. (p. 23)

When asked how she gets through the day, the operator replied that she daydreamed. Mechanization of such an operation may be theoretically possible, but is often too costly.

Interaction patterns may also be influenced by the temporal organization of work. Several studies (Mott et al., 1975; Finn, 1981) have documented the effects of shift work. Although some workers, especially mothers of small children, find that night work or a split shift enables them to discharge family responsibilities, most studies show interference with family activities, problems in biological rhythms (appetite, bodily functions, and sleep), as well as more serious health problems. Some part of these problems are attributable not to shift work as such, but to the fact that people often seek to carry on other activities at the same pace as before they went on shift work. For example, women who prefer to work the night shift because their children are then asleep, still try to carry on a full round of daytime activities with young children.[13] Some part of the difficulties are related to too-frequent changes from one shift to another.

When people remain on one shift, such as the night shift, for a long time and adjust their lives accordingly, many of these problems decline. Melbin (1978) for example, offers a picture of "night as frontier," comparable to the settlement of the United States in the middle decades of the 19th century. He points out that census figures show that in 1976, 12 million out of 75 million in the work force were on the job mainly after dark. Of course, those persons (working in restaurants, hospitals, public transportation, all-night cinemas, radio and television broadcasting, as well as in three-shift factories, public utilities, and funeral homes) served a much larger body of nighttime clients. He argues for the positive features of such work, such as "welcome solitude, fewer social constraints and less persecution [of deviants]." Experiments he conducted found more helpfulness and friendliness at night. Organizations with night shifts often experience a change of climate. After supervisors and high-status persons depart, the organization as a whole shifts to a slower, more relaxed pace, even to what one researcher (Millman, 1977) calls a "revolt of the nightworkers." In a hospital study, Millman found that night staff tolerated a relaxation of status lines (e.g., between nurses and cleanup help), as well as a relaxation of rules (policemen, after delivering an emergency case, might stay around to flirt with the female staff or to share in a midnight supper).[14]

In contrast to Millman's picture of a relaxed atmosphere, a study of an adolescent inpatient unit in a large residential mental health facility (Joy, 1981) reported greater use of physical confrontation by the evening shift than by the day shift. Joy explains the difference by pointing out that while daytime was defined as "therapy time," evening was considered simply maintenance time (feeding patients, making sure they took their pills, getting them to bed). The evening staff, resenting this demeaning view of their role, and not permitted to participate in therapy, turned to rougher physical tactics and restraints to demonstrate their competence as "crisis managers."

To sum up, the evening or night shifts are different from the day shift, though sometimes they may be more, rather than less tense.

Going beyond the concept of shift, a number of studies have examined the effects of organizational and occupational work in which people are caught in wholly encompassing life patterns, resulting in the growth of what have been called "occupational communities" (Salaman, 1974). Examples include fishermen, musicians, the police, railwaymen, and printers, whose work is of such a nature that it is carried out on a schedule different from the 9-to-5 routine found in most urban organizations. For example, a study of the printers' union (International Typographical Union) by Lipset, Trow, and Coleman (1956), which we referred to earlier in another context, calls attention to the fact that printers "put the paper to bed" late at night, when they are under no pressure to rush home to dinner or to other engagements. Some participate in late-night club activities, while others engage in recreational activities *before* going to work, after getting up and eating the kind of leisurely breakfast seldom enjoyed by 9-to-5 workers. Various writers (Salaman, 1974; Gerstl, 1961; Goode, 1957) have suggested that these kinds of organizations or occupations create a special involvement with the work so that people value it highly and find their friends among work associates. In fact, the work is so pervasive that it absorbs the whole of their lives[15]—hence the idea of a "community."

The role of such a community is illustrated in a classic international study of strikes by Kerr and Siegel (1954). In all comparable industrialized countries, they found certain industries to be more "strike-prone" (e.g., mining, maritime and longshore, textile) than others (e.g., railroad, trade, clerical). The variations cannot be explained by the presence of certain dominant personalities or certain dispute settlement tactics, for these kinds of explanation simply raise the further question of why such features are found in some industries and not in others. Kerr and Siegel ended up with a structural explanation in terms of the location of the worker in society. Miners, longshoremen, loggers, and textile workers form isolated masses living in separate communities (the coal patch, the waterfront district, the logging camp, the textile town) where there are few neutrals to mediate disputes. A disturbance or grievance can therefore easily become aggravated, until collective action is taken. By contrast, those in railroad work, trade, the services, or clerical work are better integrated into the total society. They are more likely to live in multiindustry communities and to associate with a heterogeneous assortment of others who do not share the same set of grievances. Such living and working conditions dampen disputes,[16] and so reduce the likelihood of strikes.

Although ecological factors are usually seen as causal, we must repeat our earlier caveat: What comes first is seldom clear, suggesting the usefulness of a system approach. Even without any physical or temporal constraints, interaction can be influenced by ecological factors that are voluntarily introduced. Mack (1954), in a study of a railroad repair shop, found light repair to be monopolized by Italians and heavy repair by Finns and Swedes. The two kinds of repairs took place in different locations in the repair yard. Segregation was so complete that neither group would approach the other for a crane when needed, even though the crane was idle, preferring to wait until one of its own cranes was available. The two groups similarly segregated themselves while eating and lived in different parts of the town. In other words, the separation was just as complete as if physical barriers had been erected between them. Historical and social-psychological factors had produced the segregation, which had, as one of its functions, the prevention of intergroup conflict. In any case, whatever the causal order, we can say that physical (and temporal) factors are related to interaction patterns, and their easy visibility makes it useful to watch out for such factors.

## DISTRIBUTIONAL STRUCTURE

By *distributional structure* we mean the social makeup of an organization or work group. For example, are most persons young (or old), or is there an even distribution of ages? Are top positions monopolized by the aged, or by younger persons? Are blacks or Hispanics a majority, a minority, or present only in token numbers? What is the educational distribution, and did persons of high education receive their degrees recently or a generation ago? In certain countries, some universities have established quota systems for foreign-born students, allowing a maximum of some group or requiring a minimum of students born in the host country.

Such distributional facts about an organization can have key effects on careers, productivity, and psychological attitudes. Like the physical structure, these distributions are structural in the basic sense that they are part of the "social facts" for newcomers and cannot be easily changed in the short run. Very little research has been done on this kind of structure, but what little there is suggests the subject deserves more attention. We shall not concern ourselves with how such distributions came into existence (historical factors such as immigration, social movements like the women's movement, and growth and technological change, may all be important—see Pfeffer, 1983) but rather provide examples of the possible effects of distributional structures.

Kanter (1977) examines the effects of being a token woman (less than 15 percent) in a large corporation among women in sales and managerial positions. Being in this position had three major types of effect:

1. The women were highly visible, which had both positive and negative effects. Any achievements might immediately be noticed, but the women had little privacy, and they had to put up with being paraded around by top management as symbols of how progressive the company was in encouraging women to move up to managerial positions. At the same time, their technical abilities were obscured by the fact of their being women, so they had to exert more effort to earn recognition for achievement. Such performance pressure was stressful.
2. Men subjected the women to continual tests of competence, as well as to reminders of the fact that they were women (e.g., pointedly telling off-color jokes in their presence, or arguing that they were being protected by being given easy assignments).
3. The women were encapsulated in their roles, or stereotyped, so that it was assumed that their female identity was their only identity (e.g., on trips with male associates, it was assumed by others that they must be wives, secretaries, or girlfriends, or else they were assigned to traditional female jobs such as serving coffee, or to the "female slots" such as affirmative action officer).

Some of these women gave up struggling for career advancement and accepted their role as feminists, fighting for women's rights (but usually forfeiting promotional opportunities by such tactics). Others withdrew and tried to be simply "one of the boys," earning bitter criticism from other women as renegades and traitors. Few were able to maintain an even balance and manage effectively in the face of the differential treatment they suffered.[17] One possibility is to avoid such individualistic efforts and try to change the structure itself by encouraging more women to enter the company. Even a small shift upward from a token position toward that of a minority (say as many as 20 percent) can have a strong effect, since it would provide women with allies with whom they could make common cause.

There is some evidence for the "new blood" assumptions of those who are concerned that organizations resist change. Since organizations remain the major places in society where innovation takes place, this approach suggests that the makeup of organizations be changed to encourage such innovation. Actually, organizations that are in the process of change are likely to experience more turnover, and to be attractive to outsiders who will bring in new ideas or capabilities. In contrast, organizations where the average length of service is long are less attractive to outsiders; and insiders, having more at stake, are less likely to leave (Katz, 1981; Stewman & Konda, 1982). But it is also true that newcomers do not innovate until they have been with the organization for some time and "learned the ropes." In universities, this does not occur until *after* persons have attained tenure (6 to 7 years), as well as enough eminence to attract research grants.

The concept of cohorts (Ryder, 1965)—drawn from basic ideas originally offered by Mannheim (1952)—may have useful applications in research. Mannheim (who used the term *generation* rather than *cohort*) called attention to the impact of a common experience on persons of a given age. Growing up during a period of war, large-scale immigration, continued inflation, or depression has long-range effects on people, leading to what Bird (1966) described as an "invisible scar." For example, those who grew up in the Great Depression of the 1930s may remain anxious throughout their lives, wondering whether it can happen again, which leads to a continuing concern for security and a predictable future (cf. Elder, 1974). When such a cohort is replaced (or gives birth to) a new one, the stage is set for the classic conflict between generations. In a study of the Women's Christian Temperance Union, Gusfield (1963) describes how the repeal of Prohibition changed the organization's tactics. The older generation, who had fought the original fight to legislate repressive measures such as restriction on the sale of liquor, wanted to continue that approach. But a younger cohort who came into the organization favored the use of educational approaches, feeling that they were both more practical and more in tune with the times. The split in the organization led to a gradual withdrawal of younger members, further entrenching the older group, which, however, found itself increasingly ineffective in pursuing organizational goals in the face of changes in public life-styles and morals. It would be a mistake, though, to conclude that cohorts in place must always give way to newly entering cohorts. If technology is changing slowly or markets are being gradually transformed, then the experience and contacts of older cohorts may be critical for organizational survival, as well as for socialization of the newer members.[18]

Distributional structure—whether of race, sex, age, or lifestyle—is particularly worth examining, not only because of its potential importance, but also because of its high visibility. Consequently, by looking over the distribution in the organization by age, for example, newcomers can estimate their own chances for advancement or for attaining other career goals. Thus distributional structure suggests not only research hypotheses, but also strategies for the individual who seeks a career in organizations.

## CONCLUSION

This chapter has taken us on a "tour" of recent studies, showing the usefulness of examining different kinds of structure.[19] How complex, or formal, or centralized an organization is has predictable effects on innovation, managerial control, and interdependency among organizations. Parkinson's Law has been shown to be false, and technology, when treated as a "variable" (degree of routineness), is seen to affect the span of control and degree of professionalization. Worker isolation has been shown to be related to strike proneness, and the conflict of generations has been found to be an important element in explaining the shifts in fortunes and goals of organizations.

Yet each of the findings, however valid, leaves us with a lack of sense of closure. We begin to wonder whether "structure" is just a catchall for any "variable" that someone might think of. What is lacking is a coherent theory that will knit together disparate findings and enable us to generate understanding of what is happening in and to organizations. Weber clearly had such a theory, stated in historical form, of shifts over vast time periods from charismatic and traditional forms of organizations to bureaucratic forms. But as researchers singled out "formalization" or "centralization" for measurement and treatment as "variables," they failed to deal with their place in the total Weberian theory. This is not to deny the utility of measurement, but rather to deplore the treatment of variables in separation from a more general theory.

The compliance model, in contrast, begins with a general theory of organization, built on the one that Weber provided, particularly in his emphasis on power and authority. The value of the theory can be shown by the testable hypotheses, as well as the insights, that it provides. We now turn to the compliance model.

### NOTES

1. Weber presented his studies in a historical context, concluding that there was an inexorable trend toward increasing rationalization. Consequently, it seemed reasonable to assume that since the modern era is characterized by increasing dominance of large organizations, size is probably an important determinant of other organizational characteristics. Technology has obviously grown in importance since Weber's times.

2. They also report that a *low* level of program change is associated with high degrees of stratification (high reward differences), emphasis on quantity of production and efficiency, and low job satisfaction.

3. This finding is confirmed by a study of program change carried out in California and Illinois schools (Baldridge & Burnham, 1975), and a report on technological and administrative innovations in hospitals (Kimberly & Evanisko, 1981).

4. This group of researchers (and others) took their name from the British university with which many of them were affiliated. They preferred to employ official records to esti-

mate degree of formalization, whereas Hage and Aiken, as well as others, use workers' or officials' perceptions.

5. This "law" was announced (tongue-in-cheek) by a British historian of that name to explain figures he presented that showed, for example, that the administrative staff of the British Colonial Office quadrupled between 1935 and 1954, a time when the Empire was shrinking. Parkinson then drew the conclusion that bureaucratic staff had an inherent tendency to increase, irrespective of the work load, because officials seek to enhance the importance of their own office by multiplying the number of their subordinates.

The "law" became an immediate favorite of drawing-room critics of government, who would point out, for example, that employment in the U.S. Department of Agriculture was 19,500 in the year 1920, when the farm population was 31 million. By 1975, when the farm population had *declined* to under 9 million, employment in the Department of Agriculture had *increased* to 121,000.

6. These considerations provide further reasons to doubt Parkinson's Law. Bertram Gross (1964, p. 42) points out that a shrinking Empire requires greater staff to handle the complex transition to independence. In addition, the Colonial Office took over massive increases in administration of welfare payments. As for the U.S. Department of Agriculture, although the farm population declined between 1920 and 1975, agricultural output doubled during that time. In addition, the department assumed new responsibilities involving acreage controls and subsidies, and took over new activities such as the food stamp program. So the work load did increase. Whether the increase was exactly what it should have been is another, and far more complex, question requiring careful research. A good discussion is offered by Porter, 1980, and Child, 1973.

7. But see Zeitz (1983) who reports a complex relationship of size to morale (of a group or organizational property) but not to satisfaction, which seems to be more a response to such factors as task variability and perceived openness to information.

8. Worth noting are studies which are less addressed to the causes or consequences of size than they are with taking research advantage of the giant size of organizations themselves to study factors which are usually only considered in historical treatments of whole societies. A good example is provided by Zald and Berger (1978) who call attention to the existence, *within* organizations, of *coups d'etat,* insurgencies, and mass movements.

9. Other questions about the relationship between technology and structure are addressed in a collection of research-based studies focusing mainly on educational and hospital organizations—Meyer and Scott, 1983. These studies are especially useful for the way they illuminate the role of environmental variables at the local and national levels.

10. But the problems of disetangling complex relationships still present many puzzles. In light of those studies we have just referred to, it is worth noting that Hage and Aiken (1967) report a positive relationship between centralization and formalization, while the Aston researchers (Pugh et al., 1968) find no necessary relationship. Another researcher (Child, 1972) concludes that both variables are alternative ways of controlling work behavior, centralization being capable of "substituting" for formalization, and vice versa. To further complicate matters, Hsu, Marsh and Mannari (1983) find limited support for all three findings, since rather different processes seem to be at work. In their study of Japanese managers, they report that those managers employ *both* centralization and formalization. Some of this difference may be related to cultural and other variations, but Hsu, Marsh and Mannari offer a good case for substantial structural similarities which are at least as important as the cultural differences.

11. Reports of the effects of introducing "open-plan" offices are mixed in their claims (cf. Oldham and Brass, 1979; and Canty, 1977). Part of the problem is that such changes may mask the reasons behind them, such as the desire to reduce the square footage of space per employee. But careful statistical controls as utilized in a study by Oldham and Rotchford (1983) do show a relationship between office density and such attempts to establish privacy (by workers)—like the use of "spatial markers (plants, etc. etc.); their study suggests that employees are sensitive to crowding, provoking them to employ resources for self-defense, including their own originality and imaginativeness.

12. A colleague expressed skepticism at his explanation on the grounds that current medical thinking attributes infection with the sniffles more to direct skin contact than to

sneezing. But perhaps there is more of that too at lower levels, as when people split crumpets at tea or share work tools. Still another colleague, who had had experience in civil service bureaucracies, argued that it was more a matter of whether your work waits for you. When a low-level clerk is absent, someone else does the work. At the top, your work sits there till you return—which is a strong incentive to keep your absences to the absolute minimum. This explanation might account for differences between the extremes, but not for differences between adjacent ranks in sick leave.

13. The increased use of home computers had led to a movement dubbed *flexiplace*, in which it is assumed that people will be able to work at home on many tasks, so saving the time spent traveling to and from work, as well as enabling them to continue normal home duties. One observer (*World of Work Report*, May 1982) even suggests that children can "help" parents working at home (by stuffing envelopes, checking figures, etc.). The response, as of this writing, has not been enthusiastic. As stated, this proposal underestimates the time and energy that child care requires (it does not suffice to be merely physically present), and it resurrects the specter of child labor and exploitation. Further, many women go to work to *get away* from precisely those home duties this movement sees them doing between work tasks.

14. A nice touch is added by a report of the use of a surgeon's scalpel to cut up a pizza. In addition, a high-status manager, coming in in the morning, was disconcerted to find a banana peel left inadvertently on top of a computer console.

15. We discuss the concepts of pervasiveness and scope in Chapter 8.

16. Criticisms of the Kerr-Siegel study are offered by Shorter and Tilly (1974) who report on strikes in France, and by Snyder and Kelly (1976) who studied strikes in Italy. Findings offer little support for industry as a structural factor, though other structural factors, such as size and duration of strikes (in the Italian study), are associated with the militancy of the strike. Tilly (1978, p. 68) urges that attention be paid especially to mobilization and opportunity.

17. When Spangler, Gordon, and Pipkin (1978) tested Kanter's arguments in a questionnaire survey of two law schools, they provided some support—token women were found to overcompensate, speak up less in class, and enter public law (as opposed to corporate law, for example) or the "feminine" specialties (e.g., probate, family, and mental health law).

18. We take up socialization as a general topic in Chapter 8.

19. By no means, have we sought to treat all the forms of structure to which organizational researchers have given attention, since, as noted, the whole area is in ferment at the present time (cf. Hachen, 1982). There are two kinds of structure that seem to be attracting research attention. The first, which looks outside of organizations to the labor market or to whole industries, is a kind of research which some have called "the new structuralism." A careful study from that perspective is Baron and Bielby, 1980. The second kind of structure is coming to be called "organizational culture"; this approach is "new" only to the extent that it uses new analytical tools in its studies. Although the subject of considerable enthusiasm (cf. the whole of the September 1983, issue of *Administrative Science Quarterly*), it is important to bear in mind that "culture" is almost certainly a variable (and a highly complex one at that), as Wilkins and Ouchi (1983) argue. Insofar as the concept of culture implies some degree of uniformity or consensus, we should expect that it will exhibit greater applicability in some organizations than it will in others.

# CHAPTER SEVEN
# THE COMPLIANCE MODEL
*Organizational Control
and Leadership*

The compliance model of organizational structure directs our attention to the ways in which power is used in organizations and to the kinds of involvement that are associated with different forms of power. It suggests that throwing together organizations with different kinds of compliance in the same research design may lead to misleading or inconclusive results. For example, Chapter 6 referred to studies of the effects of formalization on conformity. But we would argue that before one can seriously study such effects, one must first ask how that formalization is achieved: by coercion (as in a prison), by paying persons to obey rules (as in a business), or by enlisting their wholehearted devotion to a ritual (as in a church)? We would expect different findings in different types of organizations, even though the amount of formalization achieved might be the same in each case.

We are not arguing for the utility of typologies as such (cf. Scott, 1981, Chap. 2; Hall, 1982, Chap. 2), although they can be very useful. For underlying any typology is an implicit theory of organizations, and we think it essential that the theory be explicitly considered. Those who think organizations can be typed by, for example, whether they affect a *lot* of a client's personality or only *one segment,* and whether the client is *dealt with briefly* or over a *long period* (Lefton & Rosengren, 1966), are making the assumption that organizations so classified will be found to differ in many *other* features as well. Those who would use such a typology, then, have the obligation to show or propose that such differences do exist and what they might be. In our judgment, the compliance model does indeed offer a theory of organizational structure, to which we now turn.[1]

## THE NEED FOR CONTROL

Nowhere is the strain between the organization's needs and the participant's needs—between effectiveness and efficiency, and satisfaction—more evident than in the area of organizational control. In part, the two sets of needs support each other. An increase in the income of a corporation might allow it to raise wages and salaries; an increase in the prestige of a school might enhance the prestige of the teachers who work there. To the degree that the two sets of needs are compatible, little control is necessary. The participants will tend to do what is best for the organization in order to gratify their own needs; and the organization, in seeking to serve its needs, will serve theirs. But such meshing of needs is never complete; in fact, it is usually quite incomplete. The corporation's profit might grow, for instance, but the wages it pays might not be increased. Hence the organization has to make deliberate efforts to reward those who conform to its regulations and orders and to penalize those who do not. Thus the success of an organization is largely dependent on its ability to maintain control over its participants.

All social units control their members, but the problem of control in organizations is especially acute. Organizations are artificial social units: They are planned, deliberately structured; they constantly and self-consciously review their performances and restructure themselves accordingly. In this sense, they are unlike natural social units such as the family, ethnic groups, or community. The artificial quality of organizations, their high concern with performance, their tendency to be far more complex than natural units—all make informal control inadequate and reliance on identification with the job impossible. Most organizations most of the time cannot rely on most of their participants to internalize their obligations, to carry out their assignments voluntarily, without additional incentives. Hence organizations require a formally structured distribution of rewards and sanctions to support compliance with their norms, regulations, and orders.

To fulfill its control function, the organization must distribute its rewards and sanctions according to performance, so that those whose performance is in line with the organizational norms will be rewarded and those whose performance deviates from it will be penalized. We are not, of course, implying a return to Taylorism nor to a simple behaviorist model of rewards and punishment. Instead, we are pointing out that the control structure of any organization will have to be designed in such a way that desired behavior will become more probable or predictable than the reverse. This is the essence of control.[2]

## CLASSIFICATION OF MEANS OF CONTROL

The means of control applied by an organization can be classified into three analytical categories: physical, material, and symbolic. The use of a gun, a whip, or a lock is physical since it affects the body; the threat to use physical sanctions is viewed as physical because the effect on the subject is similar in kind, though not in intensity, to actual use. Control based on application of physical means is described as *coercive power*.

Material rewards consist of goods and services. The granting of symbols (e.g., money) that allow one to acquire goods and services is classified as material because the effect on the recipient is similar to that of material means. The use of material means for control purposes constitutes *utilitarian power*.

Pure symbols are those whose use does not constitute a physical threat or a claim on material rewards. These include normative symbols, those of prestige and esteem; and social symbols, those of love and acceptance. When physical contact is used to symbolize love, or material objects to symbolize prestige, such contacts or objects are viewed as symbols because their effect on the recipient is similar to that of "pure" symbols. The use of symbols for control purposes is referred to as *normative power*. Normative power is exercised by those in higher ranks to control the lower ranks directly, as when an officer gives a pep talk to his men, or indirectly, as when the higher in rank appeals to the peer group of a subordinate to control that person (e.g., a teacher calling on a class to ignore the distractions of an exhibitionist child).[3]

The use of various classes of means for control purposes—for power, in short—has different consequences in terms of the nature of the discipline elicited. All other things being equal, in most cultures at least, the use of coercive power is more alienating to those subject to it than is the use of utilitarian power, and the use of utilitarian power is more alienating than the use of normative power. Or, to put it the other way around, normative power tends to generate more commitment than utilitarian, and utilitarian more than coercive. In other words, the application of symbolic means of control tends to convince people, that of material means tends to build up their self-oriented interest in conforming, and that of physical means tends to force them to comply.

The powers organizations use differ largely according to the ranks of the participants that are controlled. Most organizations use less alienating means to control their higher ranks than they do to control their lower ranks. For instance, coercive power—if used at all—is applied to lower participants; e.g., prisoners are put in solitary confinement if they try to escape. Higher participants, e.g., guards, are more often rewarded or sanctioned materially to ensure good performances (e.g., tardiness is fined). Hence, in making comparative observations, it is essential to compare participants of the same rank in different kinds of organizations or different ranks within the same organization. If this precaution is not observed, it is difficult to tell if the findings differ because of differences in rank or in the nature of the organizations, or both.

Comparing the controls applied to the lower ranks of different organizations is a fruitful way of classifying organizations, since differences in the nature of controls is indicative of, and in this sense predicts, many other differences among organizations. Most organizations most of the time use more than one kind of power, but control is *predominantly* coercive, utilitarian, or normative. Among organizations in which the same mode of control predominates, there are still differences in the degree to which the predominant control is stressed. Ordering organizations from high to low according to the degree to which coercion is stressed, we find concentration camps, prisons, traditional correctional institutions, custodial mental hospitals, and prisoner-of-war camps. Ordering organizations from high to low according to the degree to which utilitarian power is predominant, we find blue-collar organizations such as factories, white-collar organizations such as insurance companies, banks, and the civil service, and peacetime military organizations. Normative power is predominant in religious organizations, ideological-political organizations, colleges and universities, voluntary associations, schools, and therapeutic mental hospitals.

Not every organizational type has one predominant pattern of control. Labor unions, for instance, can fall into any of the three analytical categories. There are labor unions that rely heavily on coercive power to check deviant members; for instance, those that border on being "underworld" organizations. There are "business unions," in which control is largely built on the ability of the union representatives to "deliver the goods," i.e., to secure wage increases and other material improvements. Finally, there are unions in which control is based on manipulation of ideological symbols, such as commitment to a Socialist ideology ("Those who do not pay their dues retard the service of the union to the cause of the laboring classes"), or in which the community of workers is recruited to exert informal pressures on members to follow the norms and orders of the organization ("Strikebreakers are poor friends"). More complicated combinations need not be discussed here.[4] (See Etzioni, 1975, Chap. III.)

The response of the participants to a particular use of power or combination of powers is determined not only by that use of power but also by the participants' social and cultural personalities. For instance, the same exercise of coercive power—a foreman slapping a worker—would elicit a more alienated response in working-class persons than it would in those from "Skid Row"; in contemporary Britain than in the Britain of three generations ago; in an aggressive than in a subservient person. If, however, the effect of all these factors is "checked," when the effect of various means of control on the same group of workers is compared, the more normative the means of control used, the less alienating the exercise of power, and the more coercive the means, the more alienating the use of power. Utilitarian power rarely elicits as alienating a response as coercive power, nor does it as a rule generate as much commitment as normative power. To state it more concretely, most factory workers rarely feel as alienated as prisoners or as committed as church members. This correspondence of type of power to type of commitment (or alienation) is a fundamental assumption of the theory and is referred to as the *congruence thesis.*

## TESTS OF THE THEORY

The real worth of a theory lies not in its plausibility but in how well it stands up to criticism and testing. A sample of the voluminous literature is now offered. First we consider general evaluations of the theory, then three empirical tests in the three major types of organization—coercive, utilitarian, and normative.

One way of appraising a theory in general terms is to assess its relationship to other theories that have proved fruitful. If this is done empirically, and if the theory is shown to relate to but not duplicate the other theories, then we can feel greater confidence that a theoretical advance is being made. Such an effort in intertheory bridge building was attempted by Hall, Haas, and Johnson (1967). They related the compliance typology to another typology, that of Blau and Scott (1962), using data from 75 organizations of many types. The two typologies were found to be correlated, providing support for a common scientific goal by giving us greater confidence that the compliance typology enables us to predict the distribution of types in a rather different typology. Commonwealth organizations (those serving the public at large) tend to be coercive, business organizations to be utilitarian, and both service and mutual benefit organizations to be normative.[5] That businesses turn out to be utilitarian is not surprising, but still it constitutes a test of the face validity of the concept of utilitarian compliance. It is somewhat surprising that commonwealth organizations are so predominantly coercive, but this finding perhaps underlines the view of the state as having a monopoly on the use of force in organizations. That service organizations turn out to be so strongly normative is somewhat surprising, but provides impressive evidence of their use of symbolic means of control, as the theory would predict. Since the decision to place organizations in the type categories was made by researchers who had no bias toward the compliance theory, such findings are promising.

One critic of the general theory (Heiskanen, 1967) questions whether it derives its claims by logical deduction only, and whether its basic hypothesis that there is congruence between means of control and forms of commitment (the congruence thesis) is testable. Such questions cannot be answered in the abstract, but only by reference to actual studies, three of which we take up next.

Julian (1966, 1968) examined the compliance structure of five hospi-

**TABLE 7-1  Commitments of Lower Participants to Support Goals and Norms and to Remain, in Less and More Utilitarian Organizations (in Percentages)**

| INDICATOR | LESS UTILITARIAN (N = 120) | | | MORE UTILITARIAN (N = 145) | | |
|---|---|---|---|---|---|---|
| | NOT COMMITTED % | MODERATELY COMMITTED % | HIGHLY COMMITTED % | NOT COMMITTED % | MODERATELY COMMITTED % | HIGHLY COMMITTED % |
| CO1(Norms)* | 5.0 | 15.8 | 79.2 | 13.8 | 11.7 | 74.5 |
| CO2(Goals)† | 27.5 | 44.2 | 28.3 | 49.7 | 31.7 | 18.6 |
| CO3(Remain)‡ | 10.0 | 45.0 | 45.0 | 28.2 | 42.8 | 29.0 |

*The difference between levels of commitment in more and less utilitarian organizations is significant at a probability greater than .02, less than .05.
†The difference is significant at a probability greater than .001, less than .01.
‡The difference is significant at a probability greater than .001, less than .01.

CO1 = willingness to uphold the norms of the organization.
CO2 = willingness to support the organizational goals.
CO3 = desire to remain in the organization.

SOURCE: From Franklin, 1972; Reprinted in A COMPARATIVE ANALYSIS OF COMPLEX ORGANIZATIONS, Revised Edition, by Amitai Etzioni. p. 74. Copyright © 1975 by Amitai Etzioni. Reprinted by permission of the Free Press, A division of Macmillan, Inc.

tals (a university hospital, two general hospitals, a tuberculosis sanatorium, and a veteran's hospital). As expected of normative organizations, they all showed high patient involvement. However, the two hospitals that ranked highest in *frequency* of reported coercive sanctions also had the highest degree of negative involvement. In turn, the hospitals with the lowest degree of coercive sanctions also exhibited the highest degree of positive involvement.

Franklin (1972) set out to test the congruence thesis in utilitarian settings, choosing for that purpose a small manufacturing plant, a creamery, a public service company, and (surprisingly) two newspapers and a general hospital. Leaving aside names, which can be misleading,[6] when Franklin classified organizations by the actual kind of power that was employed, he came up with the findings shown in Table 7-1. As can be seen, willingness to uphold the norms, to support the goals, and to remain in the organization were all significantly lower in the more utilitarian organizations. Turnover scores were also higher in those organizations. The findings add up to evidence that as organizations demand more utilitarian compliance, employees become increasingly less committed.

A third test of the congruence thesis was carried out in a federal correction center by Bigelow and Driscoll (1973). Although it would be easy to make the same mistake here of being misled by the name of the center and therefore dismissing it as simply "coercive" (see Note 6), the researchers took advantage of the fact that there was variation in coerciveness within the center (a dormitory group was subject to more coercion than a workshop group). A measure of commitment showed that there were both more cooperative attitudes and more subscription to cooperative norms in the workshop than in the dormitory.

In sum, whether we look at normative, utilitarian, or coercive organizations, careful studies reveal support for the congruence thesis.[7]

## LEADERSHIP AND ORGANIZATIONAL CONTROL

The power of an organization to control its members rests either in a specific position (department head), a person (a persuasive individual), or a combination of both (a persuasive department head). Personal power is always normative power; it is based on the manipulation of symbols and it serves to generate commitment to the person who commands it. Positional power, on the other hand, may be normative, coercive, or utilitarian. An individual whose power is chiefly derived from his organization position is referred to as an *official*. An individual whose ability to control others is chiefly personal is referred to as an *informal leader*. One who commands both positional and personal power is a *formal leader*.

A person who is a leader in one field is not necessarily a leader in another; the football captain is not necessarily the politically most influential student. If we say that X is a leader, we must also specify the field in which he leads. There are many ways to distinguish among various kinds of activities. Two main spheres of activity an organization might wish to control are distinguished here: instrumental and expressive. *Instrumental* activities deal with the input of means into the organization and their distribution within it. Seeing to it that soldiers have properly functioning equipment or that workers are paid in accordance with hours worked are examples of instrumental activities. *Expressive* activities affect interpersonal relations within the organization and the establishment of and adherence to norms by organizational participants. Social parties, ceremonies, and pep talks are all expressive. Studies of experimental groups (Bales, 1953) have shown that the two sets of activities tend to be found in different persons, partly because they require incompatible role orientations and psychological characteristics. A study of business organizations by Rossel (1970) confirmed the utility of the distinction among managers. One manager described his role as follows: "My biggest and most important job is to see that the production schedule is met," whereas another manager stated, "I don't enjoy putting that kind of pressure [issuing orders] on people and I shouldn't have to," thus illustrating the contrast between instrumental and expressive orientations to leadership. Top management was found to be most strongly instrumentally oriented.[8]

Of organizations that tend to use coercion extensively, and whose lower ranks tend to be extremely alienated, the traditional prison is a typical example. Control of work for the organization and behavior within it tends to be divided between officials and informal leaders. The guards are officials, since their power is derived mainly from their positions and is largely independent of their personal qualities. However, much of the power to control the inmates lies in the hands of influential inmate leaders, who hold no organizational positions and rely largely on their personal influence, and hence are informal leaders. Although wardens, and to some degree guards, have some personal influence over inmates, as a rule it is minor. In this sense, there is no significant formal leadership in typical prisons. The ability of the prison to control the inmates depends largely on the amount of coercive power its officials command (e.g., how many guards there are) and on the relations between prison officials and informal inmate leaders. McCleery (1957) studied a prison in which the informal inmate leaders supported "law and order" until a change in personnel brought in prison officials who undermined the informal leaders by trying to build up their own personal power and leadership. This reduced the cooperation between the informal leaders and the officials and eventually triggered a riot—that is, the prison officials lost control of the organization. There is considerable doubt whether the higher in rank can serve as leaders for the lower ranks in coercive organizations. Officials, it seems, must either reduce the coerciveness of the organization or give up hope of effective formal leadership.

Expressive activities in the prison are controlled almost exclusively by inmate leaders, who set and reinforce the norms concerning right and wrong. The inmate leaders, for instance, determine if and when it is proper to speak to a guard and which crimes are more or less prestigious (murderers rank higher than rapists). Similarly, social relations are almost solely determined by the inmates and their leaders: "Stool pigeons" are ostracized, guards and other prison personnel are excluded. Prisoners make use of a colorful language to characterize social types: Approved are "right guy," "politician," "gorilla"; disapproved types include "square John" (who conforms to formal prison rules), "rat," "punk," and "ding" (shunned by everyone) (Sykes, 1958; Garabedian, 1964). Female prisoners use different terms (e.g., rats are called "snitchers" and peddlers "boosters") and they also make greater use of terms for homosexual partners (Giallombardo, 1966; Ward & Kassebaum, 1966). Prison officials have little control over these norms and relations. This is one of the reasons why rehabilitation efforts and psychiatric work tend to be unsuccessful in traditional prisons so long as the basic coercive structure is not changed.

Instrumental activities in the prison, especially the distribution of food and work, are more amenable to control by the organization and its officials, but even in this realm informal inmate leaders have a great deal of power. Food and other scarce items such as cigarettes, which are distributed by the prison, tend to be redistributed by the inmates to bring the division of worldly goods into line with their norms, to reward those high on the inmate normative scale and status structure, and to penalize those who are low on both. Similarly, the allocation of work in the prison is affected by pressures the inmates' leaders exert on the officials. Responding to such pressures is often the only way an official can maintain the inmate leader's cooperation, which is often required to maintain efficient organizational control. Furthermore, the inmates' control of instrumental activities extends to the production and acquisition of illicit goods and to the planning and execution of escape attempts. The officials' main instrumental control is ecological: It involves keeping the inmates in the prison and assigning them to various sections and cells.

Other organizations that rely heavily on coercive control have leadership structures similar to those found in a prison. However, the less coercion the organization uses, the more influence over the inmates' behavior it achieves, and the greater the probability that some formal leadership (e.g., leadership by higher ranks) will develop.[9] In the Japanese relocation camps in the United States during World War II, for instance, there was relatively less coercion than in the average prison. Although most of the camp personnel were treated as "officials" whose directives were followed because of their impersonal coercive—and sometimes remunerative—power, two staff members (especially the "people-minded" director) had a personal power that could be called leadership, though it was largely limited to the instrumental-administrative sphere (Leighton, 1945, pp. 226–241).

Correctional institutions in which juvenile delinquents are held tend on average to be less coercive than prisons (Street, Vinter, & Perrow, 1966). The same holds for mental hospitals—even the older type, which are often almost as coercive as prisons, but not quite. Moreover, because of the spread of the humanist viewpoint in society, there is a trend to increase the professional staff and to reduce the degree and frequency of coercion used in all these organizations. While initially much of the professional work done in these organizations may yield little because the inmates are too alienated to enter into a productive relationship with the treatment staff, as the professional staff increases in number and reduces the coercive nature of these organizations by substituting social rewards for physical punishments, the therapists' influence over the inmate population gradually grows, though it never approaches that of leaders in highly normative organizations.

In organizations that rely predominantly on normative controls, there tend to be few "officials" and few informal leaders; formal leaders effectively control most of the organizational participants. To the degree that informal leaders arise—within a parish, for instance—the tendency is to recruit them and gain their loyalty and cooperation by giving them part-time organizational positions—say as members of a church board. Or the informal leaders might break away to form their own religious organization. In any case, the tendency is for the informal leaders to lose this status within the given organization and for control to remain largely in the hands of the formal leaders. Fichter (1954, pp. 3–49) discusses the development in the Catholic Church parishes of positions that are filled by active lay leaders. They encompass athletic, welfare, and social activities, but are directly or indirectly controlled by the pastor. More recently, in large Protestant churches, there has been an increasing professionalization of leadership, with some of the activities formerly run by laity being taken over by paid workers. They are hired for religious education, counseling, recreational leadership, social work, and music, under the supervision of the ministers (Harrison, 1960; Thompson, 1975).

Control in normative organizations is much more dependent on personal qualities than it is in coercive organizations. Hence, through various selection and socialization processes, normative organizations endeavor to staff the organizational positions from which control is exercised with individuals who command personal influence, and thus combine positional normative power (e.g., the status of priest) with personal power (e.g., persuasive personality)—that is, are formal leaders. Individuals who lack personal power are often transferred to organizational positions in which no control over others is exercised, such as clerical or intellectual work. Such systematic efforts of normative organizations to provide leadership in formal positions, and the fairly high success of these efforts, make the evolution of informal leaders in these organizations unlikely.

Formal leaders in normative organizations are successful in exercising both instrumental and expressive control,[10] although they are more concerned with controlling expressive activities. Some religious organizations provide offices for both kinds of leadership. Expressive matters tend to be the main functions of the major line of priests and bishops, instrumental activities the main functions of secondary positions such as deacons. In other religious organizations, control of instrumental activities is left largely to the laity, while the organizations endeavor to maintain a monopoly of control over expressive matters—such as which prayers are to be said—in demanding adherence to the norms advocated by the church. Complete separation of the control of the two kinds of activities is impossible since instrumental matters (e.g., financing) affect expressive ones (e.g., the quality of Sunday or parochial schools), and vice versa. To ensure the superiority of expressive matters—which are more directly related to the religious goals—over instrumental ones, and to counter the drift toward goal displacement, religious organizations tend to insist on the superiority of the expressive leader over the instrumental one, whether the latter is an informal or a formal leader.

Just as prisons are typical coercive organizations, so religious organizations are typical normative organizations. The leadership structure of other highly normative organizations (such as the Communist party in Western societies) is quite similar to that of religious organizations (Selznick, 1952). Leadership is highly concentrated in organizational positions, such as the party secretary, and informal leaders are either given the position or expelled.

Hospitals are normative organizations too, in that the doctor has to convince the patient to follow his advice. When it comes to assessing medical competence, the layman has little basis for rational judgement. It is for this reason that the ability of the physician to make personal contact with the patient is an important one. Hence the emphasis on personal qualities of leadership frequently starts with selection for and socialization in medical school. Although competence is emphasized in the selection of medical students, they are also screened to see whether they have the potential for a "doctor's personality," often described as the ability to "impose one's will on the patient."[11] The relative weight this factor receives in the selection process is difficult to establish, but it seems researchers are more likely to underestimate it than to overestimate it. Though it is widely accepted that "personality" is more important for lawyers than doctors, future doctors do not think so. Among the medical students studied by Thielens (1958, p.

148), 40 percent considered "pleasing personality" to be the second most important factor making for a good doctor; "high intelligence" was listed as the first factor by 73 percent. Law students asked a parallel question about factors making for a good lawyer gave the attributes virtually identical weight: 73 percent listed intelligence first, and 44 percent put "pleasing personality" second.

Control in utilitarian organizations is more evenly divided among organizational officials, formal leaders, and informal leaders of the employees. Moreover, the main concern of these organizations is with instrumental control of such matters as production and efficiency, and not with control of relations and norms established by the workers, so long as these do not adversely affect the instrumental activities. The particular leadership pattern that evolves depends largely on the relative degree of alienation or commitment of the employees. In industries where the workers are extremely alienated, their informal leaders, whether "old hands" or union stewards, tend to control most of the expressive activities and a number of instrumental ones as well. In such factories, the foreman and higher-ranking supervisors, even if they wish to participate, are excluded from worker social relations, and the workers set the norms that determine a proper day's work, if and when foremen are spoken to, and so on. However, the factory usually determines at least what work is to be done and some of the specifications on how it is to be carried out. A case where the workers' group developed both an instrumental and an expressive leader is described in the classic study by Roethlisberger and Dickson (1939—discussed earlier in Chap. 4). The group is reported to have revealed

> general dissatisfaction or unrest. In some, this was expressed by demands for advancement or transfers; in others, by a complaint about their lot in being kept on the job. . . . I [the observer] then noticed that two of the workers in particular held rather privileged positions in the group and were looked up to by the rest of the members. On these two the group seemed to place considerable responsibility. Of A they said: "He can handle the engineers, inspectors and the supervisors. . . ." In speaking of B they expressed admiration for his work habits and capacities.

Although the instrumental capacities of B were respected, his expressive functions were not emphasized:

> "So-and-so talked too much a while ago, and B shut him up." All expressed appreciation of his willingness to help them. A, in his interviews, told of fights with supervisors and arguments with engineers and inspectors. "I made several machines work after an expert from the East said an adjustment was impossible." B told of helping other adjusters. He said that he threatened to punch one operator in the nose because he had let the supervisor know that he had finished early.

The observer summarized the situation:

The supervisory control which is set up by management to regulate and govern the workers exercises little authority except to see that they are supplied with work. It is apparent that the group is protected from without by A . . . and protected from within by one [B] capable of administering punishment for any violation of the group standards.*

The workers informally provided the expressive leaders and some of the instrumental ones, but the factory exerted some formal leadership in instrumental matters. Notice, however, that when alienation becomes quite high, workers may gain control of much of the work process itself.

In factories where the workers are less alienated, and in white-collar organizations, the formal leadership exerts considerably more control, especially over instrumental activities. The work carried out and its allocation among the various workers are largely determined by the organizational staff. Moreover, some of the expressive control, though rarely much of it, is acquired by those in organizational power positions. The norms followed by lower participants are much closer to those of the higher ranks, and social relations are not so sharply segregated. The Christmas party, after all, is typical not of the alienated factory, but of the less alienated business office. It is in factories where alienation is not high to begin with, and in other utilitarian organizations, that the organization can be successful in its efforts to increase commitment and to control the employees' expressive activities through such mechanisms as personnel departments, social workers, and the participation of lower ranks in decision making. The same techniques are often less effective in structures in which the participants are more alienated.

But even when alienation may be expected to be high, it may be possible to create, in lieu of commitment, what Burawoy (1979) calls "consent." In a study of a machine shop in which workers on a dull job were paid on a piece-rate basis, he shows that the opportunity to "make out" (earn a bonus) on the job converted work into a game through which workers were "sucked in," so that the challenges of the game themselves provided strong motivations and thus "manufactured" consent. To earn a bonus, workers had to develop complex skills, as well as develop harmonious relationships with auxiliary workers (inspectors, tool crib personnel, truckers, and others). In the process of becoming someone who plays the game well, workers developed prestige, self-confidence, and an identity in which they take pride. All this then acts to bind the worker to the factory as well as present him with a situation in which he has genuine choices, has some autonomy, and is therefore not the automaton that classic observers of factory workers sometimes claimed he was.

Many studies of leadership in utilitarian organizations have compared

*Quotations reprinted by permission of Harvard University Press, from Roethlisberger and Dickson, 1939, pp. 383–384.

leaders who use a style called "initiating structure" (putting pressure on workers to increase production) with those using a style called "consideration" (seeking rapport and good interpersonal communication), dimensions that are close to what we have called "instrumental" and "expressive." Although there was much hope that one style might prove "superior" (in productivity results) to the other, the data have not been supportive (Stogdill, 1974). This conclusion was predictable from compliance theory, since it holds that control is divided between formal and informal leaders, and that the commitment of workers must also be considered. Although some researchers are discouraged by the finding that, according to Mott (1972), at most from 10 to 20 percent of variance in output can be attributed to supervision, that is not a negligible percentage and hardly grounds for giving up. We would predict not that any one kind of leadership will be found to be more strongly associated with productivity than any other, but rather that a central variable will be whether the leadership (instrumental and expressive) is congruent with worker commitment and appropriate to the type of organization. In other words, we would urge a greater fine-tuning of research to take account of such interorganizational differences.

It should not be concluded that if an organization is low on formal leadership, it will not be able to achieve its goals effectively. Coercive organizations are built on the assumption that the officials cannot attain any leadership over the inmates, and hence they are equipped to deal with them by other means. Utilitarian organizations can function quite effectively with formal leadership of instrumental and some expressive activities. Normative organizations seem to be the only type that require considerable formal leadership for operation, and even these might do well with formal control of expressive activities and only some of the instrumental ones. Finally, as the study of the prison showed, even when leadership is highly concentrated in the hands of the lower participants, so long as the cooperation of these informal leaders can be gained and maintained by the prison staff, the inmates can be controlled effectively without any formal leadership.

## CONCLUSION

Further discussion of this subject would require detailed description and analysis of the nature of each kind of organization and the forms the distribution of leadership takes within it. This cannot be done in the limits of space available, nor is it necessary. Once the basic principles have been understood, they can be readily applied to whatever organization one is studying or wishes to examine.

First, the nature of power typically employed by the organization has to be determined: Is it coercive, normative, or utilitarian; and to what degree? Next, the typical orientation of the group of participants one observes has to be established. How alienated or committed are they? This might then be related to the place of leadership within the organizational power structure. Is its focus to be found in organizational positions (formal) or among lower participants who have no organizational power positions (informal)? Is the organizational leadership only instrumental, only expressive, or both? Through exploring answers to these questions, the compliance structure can be revealed.

## NOTES

1. Discussion in this and the following chapter draws on Etzioni, 1961 and 1975. It will be obvious that the authors prefer this theory over others, but the reader can make his or her own judgment after examining the evidence presented below.

2. Forms of control and their relationship to performance were discussed in Chapter 4. There is controversy over whether organizations in developing countries employ forms of control that allow only loose relationships between performance and reward, and whether such control is related to organizational effectiveness. Cf. Abegglen, 1958 and 1973; Cole, 1979. We shall discuss this question in Chapter 10.

3. A third kind of normative power—the power that peers exercise over one another—can also be distinguished, but since it does not derive from the organization as such, we do not consider it here.

4. Our comparison of the various forms of power and their combinations has implications for a controversy which has grown up about Olson's (1965) discussion of the "free rider" problem. He points to the problem created, especially in voluntary associations such as labor unions, in motivating participation when, with or without participation, the members will enjoy whatever benefits the union provides. The argument also applies to public or collective goods, such as the labelling of consumer goods or state policy on tariffs. Why, asks Olson, should anyone vote for such matters or take any trouble or pay something to support them when he or she will enjoy them anyhow, cost-free? But, as various critics have pointed out (Barry, 1978, Chap. II; Fireman and Gamson, 1979; Hirschman, 1982, Chap. 5), motives other than economic ones, such as ideological conviction or other normative powers, may play a role in such cases. Otherwise, few would ever bother to vote or participate, when we know that many do. Still, the free-rider problem remains a serious one in some situations, as, for example, in some social movements. In a study of the Three Mile Island accident, which damaged a nuclear power plant, Walsh and Warland (1983) find that 87% of the opponents (of restarting and/or water dumping at the plant) and 98% of supporters were what they define as free riders. Although one can quarrel with their definition, the percentages are far higher than most critics of this phenomenon would expect.

5. The typology classifies organizations according to who is the "prime beneficiary." The prime beneficiaries singled out are: the membership (called "mutual benefit," such as labor unions, farm federations, political parties), the clients (called "service," such as universities, schools, hospitals), the owners (called "business"), and the public at large (called "commonwealth," such as post offices, and state penal institutions).

6. Franklin's finding that controls in the newspapers and the hospital were predominantly utilitarian enables us to make an important point that some writers have missed. First of all, as already stated, names can be misleading: We need to *discover*, not assume, the compliance form. Although Etzioni (1975) classified newspapers as predominantly normative, he was thinking there of the professional reporters. Franklin included *all* nonsupervisory personnel, most whom *did* experience utilitarian control. As for hospitals, Franklin excluded patients, who in the original Etzioni discussion provided the main reason for classifying hospitals as normative. If attention is paid only to nonsupervisory employees, as in Franklin's study, then the focus of attention is on the utilitarian component of hospitals. The point is that one

must do research to discover what kind of compliance is actually present. Were this to be done, the conclusions of some analysts (e.g., Perrow, 1979, p. 161) might be modified.

7. Other studies showing varied degrees of support were made in the Finnish armed forces (Randell, 1968), basic training units (Smith, 1973), a basic science laboratory and an aerospace group in a large aircraft manufacturer (Miller, 1967), a public welfare agency (Hudson, 1973), and the financial and R&D divisions of four large industrial organizations (Greene & Organ, 1973). There are, as well, many other studies that make briefer use of the theory (listed in Etzioni, 1975, pp. 90–91).

8. Another finding was that the more the job called for worker commitment, the greater the likelihood that the immediate supervisor's leadership would be expressive—one more confirmation of the congruence hypothesis discussed earlier.

9. Reducing coercion often requires reducing some security measures, but there are limits to the degree this can be done.

10. In a study of a national sample of 3,039 teachers, Hodgkins and Herriott (1970) found that normative compliance was more characteristic of the primary grades (which stress building character and transmitting values). Data from higher grades showed a shift to more utilitarian compliance structures. Gamson (1966, 1967) found fascinating differences between utilitarian and normative orientations in comparing the natural and social sciences faculties in a small general-education college.

11. Whether such a focus on "personality" is desirable is severely questioned by research carried out by Freidson (1974), who finds that this kind of "professional dominance" is often used to keep from patients information that might be beneficial to them.

# CHAPTER EIGHT
# ORGANIZATIONAL CONTROL AND OTHER CORRELATES

The aim of organizational control is to ensure that rules are obeyed and orders followed. If an organization could recruit individuals who would conform on their own, or could educate its members so that they would conform without supervision, then there would be no need for control. Although this is never the case, there are very broad differences in the amount of control needed in organizations because of differences in recruitment and socialization of personnel.

## CONTROL, SELECTION, AND SOCIALIZATION

The role of recruitment, or selection, should be especially emphasized; the liberal-humanist tradition that prevails in the social sciences tends to underplay its importance and to stress that of socialization.[1] Actually, various studies indicate that a small increase in the selectivity of an organization often results in a disproportionately large decrease in the investments required for control (cf. Scudder, 1954). One reason is that a high percentage of the deviant acts are committed by a small percentage of the participants; hence, if these participants are screened out, the need for control declines sharply. Such selection is also "internal," as recruits drop out or, in the jargon of one executive, are "exit interviewed." The picture, then, that we should keep before us is one of a continually shifting makeup of participants, the particular mix at any given moment having important effects on the ease or difficulty of socialization.[2]

The amount of turnover is often underestimated: Census studies (from all sources) over the years have shown turnover averages to range from a low of 21 percent a year for service organizations to a high of 54 percent a year for manufacturing organizations (Price, 1977, Chap. 4).[3] The new manager, eager to institute changes in procedures or goals, may find it wise to be patient and allow for normal turnover to create opportunities to hire replacements who match his values or at least are not opposed to them. Such a strategy, though Machiavellian in concept, would seem to be no more than prudent; it would also absorb fewer resources than a program of extensive socialization. Of course, this strategy supposes the manager is free to choose replacements, which may not be true in many kinds of organizations.

It follows, then, that the degree to which an organization selects (or is allowed to select) its participants affects its control needs in terms of the amount of resources and effort it must invest to maintain the level of control necessary to achieve its goals. This degree of selection varies among the three types of organizations we have been considering. Coercive organizations are the least selective, accepting virtually everyone sent by such external agencies as the courts and the police. Notice, however, that when efforts are made to reduce coercion and to increase the use of other means of control—as when a rehabilitation program is tried in a prison, or a therapy program is launched in a custodial mental hospital—attempts are made to screen out the "toughest" inmates, to increase and improve the selection of new ones, and to reselect continuously the participants in a particular "open" ward. This has an interesting side effect: It maintains the appearance of an organization that relies highly on normative control while actually depending indirectly on coercive control. For instance, youthful prisoners in some states are allowed to work on a farm without bars or fences, but they know that if they run away, they are likely to be caught and sentenced to longer periods in a "closed" prison. Mental patients in "open" wards are often aware of the fact that if they "cause trouble," they will be locked in the "closed" ward.

Unlike typical coercive organizations, typical utilitarian organizations are highly selective. They often employ formal mechanisms—e.g., examinations, psychological tests, probation periods—to improve the selection of participants. All other things being equal, the higher the rank of the participant, the more carefully he is recruited and the less he is controlled once selected. However, the effectiveness of preselection depends heavily on the ability to identify the most promising candidates, and the evidence, from carefully controlled studies, is that the correlation of aptitude test scores with later organizational success is very low (averaging about .30 correlation according to Ghiselli, 1966). Further, increasing emphasis on credentials (Collins, 1979) has tended to overinflate admission requirements, leading to even lower correlations with later success because many of these credentials are actually irrelevant to work performance (Berg, 1970).[4]

Normative organizations vary primarily in their degree of selectivity. Some are extremely selective—most religious sects, for instance. Other religious organizations (e.g., the Roman Catholic Church) are highly unselective. The Soviet Communist party is highly selective; most democratic political parties in the West are highly unselective. Private schools are far more selective than public schools. In general, the more selective organizations are more effective and induce a deeper commitment from their participants than do organizations of lower selectivity. It should be pointed out, however, that these differences in effectiveness and commitment are only partial consequences of higher selectivity; in part, they are due to other factors that tend to be associated with selectivity, but are not results of it (cf. Reskin, 1979). Highly selective organizations are generally richer, and hence have more facilities available for achieving their goals. Highly selective schools, colleges, and hospitals often set social and professional norms that are used to evaluate the effectiveness of the whole category of organizations to which they belong, though these norms—for instance, the integrity required by the honor system—fit them much better than they do other organizations of the same category. Still, it seems that even if all these other factors were controlled, highly selective normative organizations would be more effective and generate stronger commitment than less selective ones. Such a claim is supported by studies of prestigious law firms (Smigel, 1964) when contrasted with smaller, struggling firms, as well as law schools that act as "feeders" for those firms (Lortie, 1959; Carlin, 1962).

Selection is based on the qualities participants possess when they enter the organization. Organizational socialization subsequently adapts these qualities to make them similar to those required for satisfactory performance of organizational roles (Cf. Long, 1978; Long and McGinnis, 1981). As Simon (1976) points out, the more effective the socialization, the less the need for control.

On the other hand, socialization is itself affected by the means of control used, since some kinds of control more than others create a relationship between higher and lower ranks that is conducive to effective socialization. That the socialization efforts of coercive organizations are usually frustrated is reflected in the limited success of their therapeutic or rehabilitation programs. Organizations that rely heavily on normative power are the most successful in terms of their socialization achievements. Modern schools are a prime example. Utilitarian organizations tend to delegate socialization to other organizations, such as vocational schools and universities, and prefer careful selection of socialized persons to doing their own socialization. This raises the important point that socialization and selection can partially substitute for each other. The *substitutability hy-*

*pothesis* suggests that the same level of control can be maintained by high selectivity and a low level of organizational socialization as by low selectivity and a high level of organizational socialization. (Of course, the amount of control needed is lower when selectivity and socialization are both high.)

For instance, although they are not necessarily aware of this, medical schools "fulfill" many of the premedical education requirements by selecting students who are relatives of professionals (especially doctors), which means that medical schools receive students who are already partially socialized—i.e., they have been introduced to many of the professional norms. Of one sample of 498 medical students, 50 percent had a relative who was a doctor, and 17 percent had a parent who was a doctor (Thielens, 1958). A study of medical students showed that there was little change in their basic normative orientation during their stay in medical school, when it could be expected that they would have undergone considerable socialization (Merton, Reader and Kendall, 1957). This is not to say that some socialization or value changes do not occur in training, as Becker et al. (1961) clearly demonstrate. Further, Haas and Shaffir (1977) report that medical students sustain a "cloak of competence" in the sense of adopting a style of presenting themselves as knowledgable by distancing themselves from others as well as by devaluing the role of psychosocial considerations in patient-relations (Haas and Shaffir, 1984). But, in spite of the research problems in studying these matters, a longitudinal study which compared male and female medical students (Leserman, 1981) reported that differences and shifts in orientation are more a function of selection processes than of socialization. In sum, the process of selection therefore leaves medical schools with a smaller job of socializing students to their professional norms than would be the case if they were not so selective.

The extent to which selection and socialization can substitute for one another is examined carefully in the following two studies. In a study of an experimental college, Gamson (1966, 1967) reports that valiant attempts to make up for low selectivity by extensive efforts at socialization were only marginally successful. There were high dropout rates in the natural science department, and the selection of a small number of "favored" students for special attention in a social science department. Ultimately, the college was forced to adapt its goals and high ambitions to the capabilities and motivations of its student body. Similarly, Taber (1969) argues from his research that at a small East Coast college that unless there is a certain minimum level of selectivity in recruitment, no educational organization can be very effective, no matter how extensive its attempts at socialization. Yet neither of these studies actually provides grounds for rejecting the substitutability hypothesis. They show, rather, that there are extremes at which no amount of socialization will make up for low selectivity. The result of lack of substitutability is shown to be low effectiveness, a finding that provides a refinement of the hypothesis.

A special form of the substitutability hypothesis has been addressed in criminological studies under the heading of "importation models" (does prisoners' behavior reflect the point of view they bring with them, i.e., selection) and "deprivation models" (is the prison socialization itself responsible for the behavior of its inmates?). Classical studies (Schrag, 1954, 1961; and Garabedian, 1964) supported the deprivation model, reporting prisoners' descriptions of admired types—"right guys" who violently opposed the guards and prison administration—and hated types—"square Johns" who supported the official social system. But later studies by Wheeler (1969) in Scandinavian prisons supported the importation model, since those prisons, while just as "deprivational" as American prisons, showed different patterns and much less violent behavior. Studies of women's prisons (Ward & Kassebaum, 1965; Giallombardo, 1966; Heffernan, 1972) tended also to support the importation model, since women's behavior was shown to be quite different from that of male prisoners in many respects. For example, as we mentioned in Chapter 7, women prisoners exhibit a more complex variety of social roles such as "butches" (aggressive masculine-appearing women), "femmes" (who play a more passive role), and "jailhouse turnouts" (who engage in lesbian behavior only in prison, reverting to heterosexual behavior on release). However, Thomas and Foster (1973), in a quantitative study, argue for the inclusion of both models, since each makes differential contributions to explaining prison behavior.[5]

## PERVASIVENESS

Means of control are used in all organizations to enforce the norms that set the standards of performance, but organizations differ markedly in the *pervasiveness* of the norms they attempt to enforce. Some organizations— prisons, for instance—have a limited pervasiveness; they attempt to control only some of the activities carried out on their premises. Actually, the prison is more pervaded than pervasive; that is, many of the norms affecting inmate behavior have been set and are enforced by outside social units, such as the communities from which the inmates come. Other organizations (e.g., hospitals) are highly pervasive; they attempt to control most of the activities that take place within them, but few of those carried on outside. Still other organizations (e.g., churches) attempt to set and enforce norms for activities that are carried on both when the participants are on the premises of the organization and when they are not. The latter types of organization pervades other social units.

In general, the more pervasive an organization is, the greater the efforts required to maintain effective control. Highly pervasive organizations, especially those that set norms for activities carried on outside the organization, almost inevitably have to stress normative control over participants' extraorganizational behavior. Low pervasiveness, on the other hand, can be enforced by any of the three types of means or combinations thereof, especially if the norms enforced require mainly visible conformity (e.g., attendance) and little "invisible" conformity (e.g., sense of responsibility).

The role of pervasiveness is illustrated in organizational settings that demand of their members high conformity on values. Often such conformity follows from the high degree of interdependence required by the work, which makes it necessary to have trustworthy colleagues. In a study of police socialization, Van Maanen (1973) shows how the need for dependable work partners is especially important during "hot calls" (those with potential for danger), as when someone has a gun or may actually be trying to injure or kill the policeman himself. In another study, that of a police academy, Harris (1973) found that such dangers at work led to a socialization focus on norms of defensiveness, professionalization, and depersonalization. Recruits are taught that they should be suspicious of everyone—not only potential criminals but also the press, politicians, lawyers, and others—since policemen can never anticipate when they might have to do something in self-defense (or anger) that would be difficult to explain to outsiders. Professionalism was emphasized for a similar reason; namely, being able to defend behavior as "good police practice" as well as conveying an image of themselves as guardians of law and respectability who could be trusted to do their work without public "meddling." Finally, depersonalization meant putting people into abstract categories and shunning personal involvement, which might interfere with objectivity in dealing with the emotionally charged situations in which they often find themselves.[6]

Such values, once acquired on the job, can hardly be prevented from spilling over into other areas of life. The result is a general shift in worldview. Studies of nursing students (Simpson, 1967; Psathas, 1968; Alutto, Hrebniak, & Alonzo, 1971) report a shift from an early "idealistic" view to a more practical, technical view of the work, which is also more functional for the crises nurses face. A more general value shift occurs among organizational executives. Kanter (1977), for example, reports a striking homogeneity of values among top executives in a firm that she studied, leading even to appearance:

> Managers at Indsco had to look the part. They were not exactly cut out of the same mold like paper dolls, but the similarities in appearance were striking. . . . The norms were unmistakable, after a visitor saw enough managers, invariably white and male, with a certain shiny, clean-cut look.*

*Reprinted by permission from Basic Books from Rosabeth M. Kanter, *Men and Women of the Corporation,* © 1977 Basic Books, Inc., p. 47.

Kanter relates such conformity to the need for trust among those whose work requires a high degree of discretion. Other studies show that such persons identify themselves totally with the company, making its values their own, to the point of insisting on them in their family life, their choice of friends, the education of their children, and their general style of life (cf. Gross, 1978).

## SCOPE

A factor that is substantively related to but analytically distinct from pervasiveness is organizational *scope*, which is determined by the number of activities carried out jointly by the participants in a particular organization. In organizations whose scope is narrow, participants share only one or a few activities (e.g., social activities). Participants in organizations whose scope is broad share several kinds of activities, as in labor unions that carry on social and cultural activities as well as collective bargaining. Total organizations are those in which maximum scope is attained, as in convents (Baldwin, 1957).

According to Goffman (1961):

> The central feature of total institutions can be described as a breakdown of the barriers ordinarily separating these three spheres of life. First, all aspects of life are conducted in the same place and under the same single authority. Second, each phase of the member's daily activity is carried on in the immediate company of a large number of others, all of whom are treated alike and required to do the same thing together. Third, all phases of the day's activities are tightly scheduled, with one activity leading at a prearranged time into the next, and the whole sequence of activities being imposed from above through a system of explicit formal rulings and by a body of officials.[7]†

There is no one-to-one relationship between scope and pervasiveness: An organization might set norms for more kinds of activities than are carried out jointly by participants, as the Communist party often does, or it might set norms for fewer activities than the joint ones, as in an army.

High scope enhances normative control, is a necessary condition of coercive control, and seems to affect utilitarian control negatively. High scope enhances normative control because it separates the participants from social groups other than the organization and tends to increase their involvement in it. A comparison of commuter and residential colleges illustrates this point. In commuter colleges, some educational effects are not attained and some are countered, because the students' involvement in the college as a social unit is limited, and because they have significant and

---

†Excerpt from *Asylums* by Erving Goffman. Copyright © 1961 by Erving Goffman. Reprinted by permission of Doubleday & Company, Inc.

active social ties to external groups, which often support different norms. All other things being equal, residential colleges can have a considerably deeper educational impact with the same investment in normative control. (Education is here considered in its broadest sense, including character development, rather than just the communication of skills and information.) The value of high scope for educational purposes is fully recognized by this study of a military academy:

> [A] clean break with the past must be achieved in a relatively short period. For two months, therefore, the swab is not allowed to leave the base or to engage in social intercourse with non-cadets. This complete isolation helps to produce a unified group of swabs, rather than a heterogeneous collection of persons of high and low status. Uniforms are issued on the first day, and discussions of wealth and family background are taboo. Although the pay of the cadet is very low, he is not permitted to receive money from home. The role of cadet must supersede other roles the individual has been accustomed to play. There are few clues left which will reveal social status in the outside world. (Dornbusch, 1955, p. 317)**

Other studies (e.g., Lovell, 1964) have explored the impact of such sequestration, not only in military organizations, but also in the training of musicians, railroaders, and pilots. Ritzer (1977, p. 85) points out that such separation speeds up the assimilation of organizational values because there is little interference from the outside world, allows for the "mortification of the self" the recruit brings with him, and protects the organization from media exposure of socialization failures as well as other embarrassments.

In the past, utilitarian organizations often attempted to maintain a broad scope, as in the company town; later, corporations were advised to provide their workers with educational, recreational, and residential facilities. However, the tendency more recently has been for corporations to reduce their scope in these areas. For example, cafeteria service is more often provided by an outsider than by the organization; the workers are now less frequently encouraged to bowl as a factory team; and business organizations attempt less often to counsel their employees on personal problems, feeling that such behavior is overly paternalistic or invasive of privacy.

Apart from this direct reduction in scope, there may be a natural movement toward a separation of work from other activities, as Diamond (1958) shows in his striking historical study of the Virginia Company of the early 1600s. The original European settlers of Virginia did not come, like the Pilgrims, seeking religious freedom. They did not even intend to stay in America, for they came for one reason only: to make money. Those who embarked for Virginia as employees or stockholders of the company hoped

---

**Reprinted by permission of SOCIAL FORCES.

to uncover another Mexico or Peru with stores of hidden wealth they might seize and hold by whatever means necessary. When this did not prove to be the case, they grew increasingly disenchanted and desired to return to England. To induce them to stay on, the company had to offer rewards, such as land ownership, exemptions from company duty, and most importantly, the importation of wives. As the men began to view themselves as settlers rather than employees or agents of the company, their behavior changed. Instead of living in company-provided barracks, they built private homes for their families. Instead of company rules, they banded together to create community laws they insisted were superior. An authentic political system began to supplant the company's chain of command, and even land ceased to be owned by the company. Private fortunes began to develop as the planter sought his own customers for his tobacco instead of selling it at a fixed price to the company. Social class differences emerged, upsetting formal relationships and, in the process, formal officials. Diamond (1958) writes:

> Secretary of State, John Pory, wrote Sir Dudley Carleton that "our cowe-keeper here of James citty on Sundays goes accowtered all in freshe flaminge silke; and a wife of one that in England had professed the black arte, not of a scholler, but of a collier of Croydon, wears her rought bever hatt with a faire perle hat band." (p. 473)*

In this manner, from 1607 to 1624, when the Crown revoked the company charter, Virginia passed from "organization to society."

The citizens of modern societies are socialized to shift constantly among various social units as the family, the community, and the work unit. The relatively high separation and low scope of all these units allows the typically modern mode of managing tension to operate. Tensions generated in one unit are released in another by changing partners, thus "localizing" rather than "totalizing" conflicts; and by shifting back and forth between social units in which rational, efficient behavior is demanded (a form of behavior that is particularly taxing) and those in which the norm is nonrational behavior (which is comparatively relaxing). Those utilitarian organizations that have a high scope, that fuse work and nonwork units, prevent both the localization of conflict and the shift of participants to units relatively free of rational considerations. This might explain the reduction in tensions resulting from the recent tendency to separate more fully work and nonwork units.[8]

Coercive organizations must maintain total scope, for unless the participants carry out all their activities within the one organization, they would have too many opportunities to escape. Moreover, the deprivational character of total scope, or separating the inmates from all nonorganiza-

*Reprinted by permission of the author and University of Chicago Press.

tional units, is used as a major means of punishment and hence of control. (For instance, a prisoner who has violated the prison's rules may find his sentence extended.) In a study of Finnish draftees, Randell (1968) offers evidence that broad scope may be related to greater uniformity of behavior. Insofar as this is the case, coercive organizations are able to control their members by reason of broad scope itself, quite apart from the effects of deprivation. Attempts to reduce the use of coercion and to rely more on normative power, as when rehabilitation or therapeutic programs are introduced, are frequently associated with efforts to reduce scope by allowing more visits by outsiders, initiating work programs outside the prison, permitting mental patients to spend weekends or the night at home, conjugal visits, and the like. Thus it can be seen that scope and coerciveness are related.

The usefulness of the compliance model in suggesting research hypotheses is borne out in a series of studies (employing causal modeling) that we call the Iowa State Compliance Studies since they were carried out by researchers at Iowa State University. The subjects included U.S. civil defense directors and college fraternities (for normative organizations), and managers of local farm supply and grain cooperatives (for utilitarian organizations). Causal analysis with path diagrams provides a "tough" test of compliance theory because the theory was originally shaped in terms of "correlates" and thus is more appropriately conceived of in system terms. Still, the results are worth examining.

Mulford, Klonglan, Beal, and Bohlen (1968) find support for what we called the substitutability hypothesis: When both socialization and selectivity were low among civil defense directors, effectiveness of the organization was also low. When both were high, so was organizational effectiveness. Increasing one to compensate for low levels of the other also increased effectiveness, though the relationship was not a linear one. Other studies introduce other variables (communication, salience, role tension) in complex causal models. In studies of the farm coops, Mulford, Klonglan, Warren, and Schmitz (1972) report that socialization and selectivity did not directly influence effectiveness, but scope did, and was found to have a dominant role. The results are suggested in the following diagram (see Etzioni, 1975, p. 410):

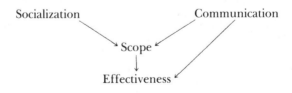

This diagram is a greatly simplified scheme of the original studies, for the evidence is that some variables have direct effects—for example, scope—

whereas others may operate *through* other variables—for instance, selection can affect the ease of socialization, which, in turn, affects scope, which then has positive effects on effectiveness.

## CONCLUSION

We would not argue that all the compliance theory propositions should be recast in causal terms. But studies such as these suggest that we can gain insight into how the propositions operate from causal studies, even though the causal direction may well turn out to be other than that hypothesized by some theorists, or may be interactive. The answer can only come from research.

### NOTES

1. The literature on adult socialization has grown to huge proportions; with emphasis on the special features that distinguish it from child socialization, such as content—biological drives versus overt norms; context—family versus work settings; and differences in degree of voluntariness. The main point stressed is that socialization is a lifelong process. See Mortimer and Simmons, 1978, and Van Maanen, 1976, for critical summaries.

2. Sociological studies of career achievement have tended to follow the Blau and Duncan (1967) model, often spoken of as "status attainment," in which attempts are made to predict a subject's occupational status by reference to the subject's father's occupation and education, the subject's own education, first occupation, and other variables. For a critical review, see Campbell, 1983. Our attention is on the individual's organizational experience, a subject that has not received as much attention. Some exceptions are provided by Gaertner, 1980, and Grandjean, 1981.

3. There is much variation both within industries and over time.

4. Studies of selection making use of education may be inadvertently taking a view of education more as a certifying variable than as one which provides a measure of job skills. See Faia, 1981.

5. A similar conclusion is reached by Irwin and Cressey, 1962; and Akers, Hayner, and Gruninger, 1974.

6. See also Westley (1970), who offers similar value justifications given by the police for the need to resort to violence.

7. See also Zurcher, 1967.

8. It is believed by some writers that the much-praised Japanese work organization is an exception to these claims because it continues to exhibit wide scope. However, that organization has certain unique features. The key elements are lifetime employment (actually up to age 55); the dependence of large organizations on closely bound satellite organizations that absorb much of the uncertainty of environmental change; a form of "bonus pay" that has employees subsidizing entrepreneurial risks; and the use of large numbers of "temporaries" (usually women) who can be discharged at will. All these elements are backed up by a form of paternalism, including such company-supplied benefits as vacations in company-owned resorts, sports facilities, dormitories, and even Shinto priests for those who wish to marry (cf. Cole, 1973, 1979, 1981; Clark, 1979; Vogel, 1975; Dore, 1973; and Marsh & Mannari, 1976). Such features make the "exportability" of the large Japanese organization dubious. In any case, these features add up to a picture of the Japanese organization as strongly normative, rather than utilitarian, or a mixture of the two.

# CHAPTER NINE
# ADMINISTRATIVE AND PROFESSIONAL AUTHORITY

The ultimate source of the organizational dilemmas reviewed up to this point is the incomplete matching of the personalities of the participants with their organizational roles. If personalities could be shaped to fit specific organizational roles, or organizational roles to fit specific personalities, many of the pressures to displace goals, much of the need to control performance, and a good part of the alienation would disappear. Such matching is, of course, as likely as an economy without scarcity and hence without prices. But even if all the dilemmas that result from the incomplete articulation of personality and organization were resolved, there would still remain those that are the consequences of conflicting tendencies built into the organizational structure.

Probably the most important structural dilemma is the inevitable strain imposed on the organization by the use of knowledge. All social units use knowledge, but organizations use more knowledge more systematically than do other social units. Moreover, most knowledge is created in organizations and passed from generation to generation—i.e., preserved—by organizations.

Yet, typically, the possessors of knowledge, especially scientific knowledge acquired through special education or research, are not found in the top command posts, but in the middle ranks, and often not in the regular line or command positions, but around them. These people are often referred as "experts," "professionals," "specialists," or by the names of their professions. How, then, can the top officers of the organization give "orders" to those who know more than they do about specialized matters? A structural dilemma is presented by the fact that administrative authority and professional authority based on knowledge are not only different but are often incompatible.

## ADMINISTRATIVE VERSUS PROFESSIONAL AUTHORITY

Administration assumes a power hierarchy. Without a clear ordering of higher and lower in rank, in which the higher in rank have more power and hence can control and coordinate the lower in rank's activities, the basic principle of administration is violated; the organization ceases to be a coordinated tool. However, knowledge is largely an individual property; unlike other organization means, it cannot be transferred from one person to another by decree. Creativity is basically individual and can only to a very limited degree be ordered and coordinated by the superior in rank. Even the application of knowledge is basically an individual act, at least in the sense that individual professionals have the ultimate responsibility for their professional decisions (But cf. Walters, 1982, on company doctors).

Students of the professions have pointed out that the autonomy granted to professionals who are basically responsible to their consciences (though they may be censured by their peers and, in extreme cases, by the courts) is necessary for effective professional work. Only if they are immune from ordinary social pressures and free to innovate, to experiment, to take risks without the usual social repercussions of failure, can professionals carry out their work effectively. It is this highly individualized principle that is diametrically opposed to the organizational principle of control and coordination by superiors—i.e., the principle of administrative authority. In other words, the ultimate justification for a professional act is that it is, to the best of the professional's knowledge, the right act. Professionals may consult their colleagues before they act, but the decision is the individual's alone. If in error, professionals will still be defended by their peers as long as they acted responsibly. The ultimate justification of an administrative act, however, is that it is in line with the organization's rules and regulations, and that it has been approved—directly or by implication—by a superior rank.

## THE ORGANIZATION OF KNOWLEDGE

The question is how to create and use knowledge without undermining the organization. Some knowledge is formulated and applied in private situations. In many kinds of medicine and law, much work is carried out in nonorganizational contexts—in face-to-face interaction with clients. But as the need for costly resources and auxiliary staff has grown, doctors face mounting pressures to transfer their work to organizational structures such as hospitals and other health-care facilities, and lawyers to law firms, legal divisions of corporations, or government agencies such as the public defender's office. Similarly, although artistic work is often thought of as the product of the isolated creative individual, Becker (1982) has shown how the artist is caught up in a network of teachers, resource facilitators, taste arbiters, and representatives of local and state governments. Much cognitive creativity, particularly in scientific research, has also become embedded in organizational structures, especially universities, for reasons similar to those that pertain to medicine and law.[1]

If this is true for the traditional professions, it is even more so for others. Accountants, engineers, nurses, social workers, chemists—as well as those who pursue the honorific title (and the privileges) of "profession," such as landscape planners, morticians, photographers, and industrial and public relations men and women—gravitate to organizations where the richness of resources and collaborative opportunities make their work most rewarding and effective. Some occupations, such as computer programming, pathology, and teaching, have hardly any existence apart from organizations.

How well these various professionals or would-be professionals adapt to life in the organization varies. We approach this question in the following way: Rather than classifying some occupations as "professions" and others as not, it is useful to think of a continuum from one pole, where the occupation has earned the right to call itself a profession, to the opposite pole, where the occupation is still struggling for recognition. Those at or near the professional pole may enjoy legal privileges and the right to control membership selection, training, and even prices for their services. Those at the opposite pole will have the legal right to practice their occupation, but in a setting with few protections and often serious competition from other occupations offering related services.

The closer an occupation approaches the profession pole, the more independence or autonomy its practitioners claim for themselves (Freidson, 1984), especially in organizations that bring them into conflict with administrators. When faced with attempts to control them, they will usually assert the claim that they cannot be dictated to because of their superior knowledge. However, even if there is a clear knowledge base, the claimed possessors of such knowledge are still not safe from attempts to control them. In a study of French medical practice, Jamous and Peloille (1970) conclude that even medicine's claim to professional status is based on what they call the "margin of indetermination" (the degree to which practice and knowledge have not been routinized). The more the professional knowledge is stripped of uncertainty and codified, the lower the power of the profession and the easier it becomes to train and control its members. Ritzer (1977, p. 58) argues that where there may not actually be a clear area of "indetermination," an occupation can deliberately try to create one by mystification—which, he believes, has been successfully done by lawyers around divorce actions and accountants in dealing with income tax questions.[2]

Where professional knowledge is either relatively low or else admits of systematization, as in many branches of engineering and nursing, for example, the degree of autonomy, and hence the ease of integration into the organizational structure, may involve less conflict with administrators who have superior rank though no more (or perhaps less) professional competence.

To some degree, organizations circumvent the problem of controlling knowledge by "buying" it from the outside, as when a corporation contracts for a market study from a research organization; i.e., it specifies the type of knowledge it needs, agrees with the research group on price, and then largely withdraws from control over the professional work. There are, however, sharp limitations on the extent to which knowledge can be recruited in this way, particularly since organizations consume such large amounts of knowledge and tend to need reliable control over its nature and flow.

There are two basic ways in which knowledge is handled within organizations:

1. Knowledge is produced, applied, preserved, or communicated in organizations especially established for these purposes. These are *professional organizations,* which are characterized not only by the goals they pursue but also by the high proportion of professionals on their staff (at least 50 percent), as well as by the authority relations between professionals and nonprofessionals, which are so structured that professionals have superior authority over the major goal activities of the organization (a point that is explored below). Professional organizations include universities, colleges, most schools, research organizations, therapeutic mental hospitals, the larger general hospitals, and social-work agencies. For certain purposes it is useful to distinguish between those organizations employing professionals whose professional training is long (5 years or more) and those employing professionals whose training is shorter (less than 5 years). The former we call *full-fledged professional* organizations; the latter, *semiprofessional* organizations.

Generally associated with these differences in training are differences in goals, privileges, and concern with matters of life and death. Full-fledged professional organizations are primarily devoted to the creation and application of knowledge; their professionals are usually protected in their work by the guarantee of privileged communication, and they are often concerned with matters of life and death. Semiprofessional organizations are more concerned with the communication and, to a lesser extent, the application of knowledge; their professionals are less likely to be guaranteed the right of privileged communications; and they are rarely directly concerned with matters of life and death.[3]

2. Professionals may be employed by organizations whose goals are *nonprofessional,* such as industrial and military establishments. Here they are often assigned to special divisions or positions, which to one degree or another take into account their special needs.[4]

We shall discuss the relationship between the two authority principles—that of knowledge and that of administration—first in nonprofessional organizations, then in full-fledged professional organizations, and finally in semiprofessional organizations.

## PROFESSIONAL AUTHORITY IN NONPROFESSIONAL ORGANIZATIONS

### Superiority of Administrative Authority

By far the largest and most common nonprofessional organizations are the production organizations that are privately owned and managed. The organizational goal of private business is to make a profit. The major means are production and exchange. While the professional deals with various aspects of the production and exchange process—that is, with means such as engineering, quality control, and labor relations—the manager (the corporation's equivalent of the administrator) is expected to coordinate the various activities in such a way that the major organizational goal—profit making—will be maximized.

In general, this has meant that chief executives are expected to have broad administrative interests rather than the specialized concerns of the knowledge professional. For example, a study conducted in 1950 (Newcomer, 1955, p. 92) reported the occupational backgrounds of business chief executives in the United States as:

| | |
|---|---|
| Administration: | 43.1% |
| Entrepreneurs: | 11.8% |
| Finance: | 12.4% |
| Engineering: | 12.6% |

Yet, some 30 years later, a study of the backgrounds of the chief executives of the top corporations (Kurtz & Boone, 1981, p. 30) showed the following percentages:

| | |
|---|---|
| Finance: | 17.7% |
| Administration: | 15.4% |
| Marketing, sales, retailing: | 12.6% |

| | |
|---|---|
| Legal: | 11.7% |
| Banking: | 11.6% |
| Production and operations: | 11.1% |
| Technical: | 9.7% |
| Founder: | 5.5% |

While the two studies did not use identical categories and hence are not directly comparable, the differences seem to show that organizations are tending toward drawing on people with some kind of knowledge base (not necessarily professional), as in the case of marketing, or, more clearly, law, and perhaps even "production" and "technical." Further, it was estimated in the early 1970s that approximately half of all top executives possessed master's degrees and 25 percent had doctorates (Steele & Ward, 1974). However, much of the shift toward higher degrees appears to be more a reflection of the general increase in education in society, as well as the fact that the MBA has become almost a union card for business executives. Still, in spite of the expansion in *use* of knowledge professionals in industry, an authority on business organization comments: "Yet, at the very top major strategic decisions are still made by generalists without great reliance on mathematics or computers, and middle managers are not disappearing" (Webber, 1975, p. 453). In sum, the specialists are not displacing the generalists, though some specialist backgrounds (e.g., legal) may be more relevant to an environment in which the government plays an increasing role, as well as to other environmental changes (we discuss some of these in Chapter 10).

In general, the goals of private business are consistent with general orientations. The economic orientation of the organization and the bureaucratic orientation of the administrative role share an inclination toward rational combination of means and development of rational procedures to maximize goals, which are considered as given. The social and cultural conditions that support modern economic activities also support modern general administration. Professional and technical orientations are less compatible.

When people with strong professional orientations take over managerial roles, a conflict between the organizational goals and the professional orientation usually occurs. Homans (1950, pp. 369–414) reports an interesting case in which the influence of professionally oriented participants was greater than in most corporations. He discusses an electrical equipment company that was owned, managed, and staffed by engineers. Management, which was in the hands of administration-oriented engineers, suffered from pressure to pursue uneconomic goals by the professionally oriented design engineers. The design engineers were charged with being indifferent to profit-making. This caused considerable tension between the managerial and professionally oriented groups, tension to which this company was especially sensitive because of its high dependence on professional work and its special ownership structure. A power struggle resulted, which ended with a clearer subordination of the design engineers (staff) to the managerial engineers (line). This was mandatory "if the company was to survive and increase its sales," as Homans put it. The treasurer (a nonprofessional in this context) became the most influential member of the new management. In short, in a corporation where the professionals exerted a strong influence, the existence of the organization was threatened, considerable internal tension was generated, and finally the organizational power structure was changed toward a more usual structure, with the professionally-minded more clearly subordinated. In other words, the organizational authority structure was made more compatible with the goals of the organization. The orientations of managers and the goals of private business seem to match. When a professional orientation dominates, it tends to "displace" the profit goal of privately owned economic organizations.

On the other hand, when technology is changing rapidly, as it is in the "high-tech" industries such as semiconductors and computer manufacturing, telecommunications, robotics, aerospace, and biotechnology, scientist-innovators may occupy a more prominent place in management. But even here we would expect their prominence to last only so long as the firm remained small and in the hands of its founder-entrepreneurs (who would also display generalist managerial skills). With growth and bureaucratization, we would expect such specialists to take on a narrower, advisory role.

### Professional-Administrative Conflict

As organizations come to require increasing amounts of expertise, administrators find they must develop ways of integrating the professionals who provide such expertise into the organization. Here a genuine dilemma arises: The very expertise and independence of judgment that administrators desire from professionals is contradictory to the simple model of obedience usually employed by administrators. Professionals have a strong sense of identification with their occupation, derived from a lengthy period of socialization in university or graduate schools, and they operate under strong controls by colleagues and professional association norms or rules. Gouldner (1957–58) drew a distinction between "cosmopolitans" and "locals" (using colleges as the basis for his research), as follows:

| | COSMOPOLITANS | LOCALS |
|---|---|---|
| *Loyalty to the organization* | Low | High |
| *Commitment to specialized or professional skills* | High | Low |
| *Reference group orientation* | Outer | Inner |

For example, a professor of chemistry might see himself or herself as *primarily a chemist* committed to special research or laboratory skills, accepting only the standards adhered to by other chemists all over the world, and willing to shift employment to a different college if he or she could thereby become a better chemist. Or, instead, the professor might see himself or herself as *primarily an employee* of the college who teaches chemistry there and has little or no commitment to research, but rather a primary orientation to the needs of the teaching department, a strong loyalty to the college, and an unwillingness to consider outside offers. Clearly, the more the professional expert in any organization sees himself or herself as a "cosmopolitan," the more conflict we can expect between that person and the administration.[5]

In a classic discussion, Dalton (1950), noting that professionals are often put off to one side of the organization chart, where they may, following military practice, be called "staff" in contrast to those in the direct line of command, who are called "line," claimed that there was continuing "staff-line conflict." The staff in the industrial organizations he studied were usually younger and much more likely to be college-educated than the line, although the latter had greater organizational experience and hence resented advice and suggestions from the relatively inexperienced staff. Furthermore, the two groups were divided by differences in patterns of speech and dress, recreational preferences, and the like. In these areas, the higher-ranking line was often closer to the lower-ranking line than to the staff. Thus the tensions between staff and line derived not only from their varying structural position in the organization but also from their different social backgrounds.

Since Dalton did his research, the educational and many of the background differences he reported have been greatly reduced, if not altogether eliminated. But the orientations to the organization (the local-cosmopolitan differences) remain. Major points of conflict are: The professionals resist what they see as "bureaucratic rules," not out of any sense of superiority but simply because they see themselves as bound by professional rules that are research-tested or practice-tested means for carrying on their work. For similar reasons, they resist bureaucratic standards of quality or acceptability as simply irrelevant to those the profession demands. It follows, then, that professionals find it difficult to accept supervision from those less knowledgeable than themselves, except over purely bureaucratic matters such as time of work—but even here they may prefer to set their own hours, which may be *more* demanding than those of the organization (Kornhauser, 1963; Scott, 1966; Gross, 1967).

Attempts to mitigate such conflict take a variety of forms, one of the more popular being that of offering to professionals a "dual ladder": that is, the option of either competing for promotions with line or other staff, or of staying in their own unit and accepting the rewards of higher salary and movement up a "step system" of honorific rewards and "perks." They may be offered greater amounts of laboratory space, authority to purchase equipment without the approval of higher line officers (with maximum dollar amounts specified), the opportunity to attend professional meetings, and so forth. Yet such devices do not do away with conflict (and may even increase it as professionals become encapsulated in their own "world"), but as may be recalled from our critique of the Human Relations theory in Chapter 4, some conflict is structural and cannot and should not be done away with. We may hope that such "horizontal power conflict" (Landsberger, 1961; Strauss, 1962; Gross, 1964) will produce more rational decisions as each party to the conflict is forced to take the other into account. This is not to make a case for compromise as such, but rather for meeting objections and criticism that are often well worth considering (Hall, 1982, pp. 151ff.).

Despite the possible advantages to the organization of such conflict, it must be remembered that we are here dealing with organizations whose goal is nonprofessional (e.g., profit making). Therefore it is usually desirable for administrators to have the major (line) authority and thus the final say, since they direct the major goal activity and are responsible for the overall success of the organization. Professionals are hired for their advice and assistance, which must be integrated into the organization. Thus it is functional for professionals to occupy a *secondary* place in the organization, and therefore be ultimately subject to administrative authority. This is generally the case in corporations and armies. The situation is very different in professional organizations, as we now will see.

## PROFESSIONALS IN PROFESSIONAL ORGANIZATIONS

In full-fledged professional organizations, the staff-professional line-administrator correlation, insofar as such distinctions apply at all, is reversed. Although administrative authority is suitable for the major goal activities in private business, in professional organizations administrators are in charge of secondary activities; they administer *means* to the major activity, which is carried on by professionals. In other words, to the extent that there is a staff-line relationship at all, professionals should hold the major authority and administrators the secondary staff authority. Administrators should offer advice about the economic and organizational implications of various activities planned by the professionals. But the final decision is, functionally speaking, in the hands of the various professionals and their decision-making bodies, such as committees and boards. Professors decide what research they are going to undertake and to a large degree what they are going to teach; physicians determine the treatment to be given to the patient.

Administrators may raise objections. They may point out that a certain drug is too expensive or that a certain teaching policy will decrease the number of students and endanger the financial health of a university. But functionally the professional is the one to decide to what degree these administrative considerations should be taken into account. For example, in a study of a large medical center, Goss (1961) found that physicians were quite willing to accept the assignment of students, patients, or examining rooms. However, the supervisor (himself a physician) was careful to confine himself to advising physicians whenever he noted something of interest on a patient's chart. In other words, when it came to patient care, any notion of "obeying" the supervisor was regarded as the height of irresponsibility. In this area, the physician had to make decisions on his own authority.

It is interesting to note that some of the same complaints made against professionals in nonprofessional organizations are made against administrators in professional organizations: They are said to lose sight of the major goal of the organization in pursuit of their specific limited responsibilities. Professionals in private business are sometimes criticized as being too committed to science, craftsmanship, and abstract ideas; administrators in professional organizations are deprecated because they are too committed to their specialties—"efficiency" and economy.

Many of the sociological differences between professionals and managers in private business are reversed in professional organizations. Professionals enter professional organizations younger and in lower positions (i.e., as students, research assistants, or interns) than managers do. But the range of mobility of administrators is usually relatively limited, and a professional is more likely to reach the top position of institutional head.

In private business, overinfluence by professionals threatens the realization of organizational goals and sometimes even the organization's existence. In professional organizations, overinfluence by the administration, which takes the form of ritualization of means, undermines the goals for which the organization was established and endangers the conditions under which knowledge can be created and institutionalized (as, for instance, academic freedom).[6]

## Who Is Superior?

Heading a professional organization constitutes a special dilemma. It is a typical case of institutionalized role conflict. On the one hand, the office should be held by a professional in order to ensure that the commitments of the head will match organizational goals. Having a professional at the head of the authority structure means that professional activity will be recognized as the major goal activity, and that the needs of professionals will likely receive understanding attention. On the other hand, organizations have needs that are unrelated to their specific goal activity. They have to obtain funds to finance their activities, recruit personnel to staff the various functions, and allocate the funds and personnel that have been recruited. Organizational heads must know how to keep the system integrated by giving the right amount of attention and funds to the various organizational needs, including secondary ones. A professional may endanger the integration of the professional organization by overemphasizing the major goal activity to the neglect of secondary functions. He may lack skill in human relations. In short, the role of head of professional organizations requires two incompatible sets of orientations, personal characteristics, and aptitudes. Whether the role is performed by a lay administrator or a typical professional, one set of considerations is likely to be emphasized to the detriment of the other.

The severity of the dilemma is increased because of the motivational pattern of typical professionals. Most successful professionals are not motivated to become administrators. Because of their commitment to professional values and their ties to professional groups, they are likely to refuse to accept low-level administrative positions, which often are the required training grounds for those who would be higher administrators.[7] To a considerable extent, university academic administrators reinforce those views in their own public statements. Lunsford (1970), in a study of 526 university administrators, describes them as a notoriously self-effacing group who deny any trace of ambitiousness, and who regard themselves as temporarily doing a job before returning to academic teaching or research. How much such claims are self-justifying myths is difficult to say.[8]

A similar situation prevails in hospital administration. For instance, in one mental hospital, Stanton and Schwartz (1954) report that the role of administrative psychiatrist was filled by those at the beginning of their training period. It was considered an undesirable chore that must be endured before one could turn to the real job. Psychiatrists who completed their training tended to withdraw to private practice. The case of general hospitals is more complex; partly because of the increasing role of government and third-party payment sources such as Blue Cross, as well as different forms of health-maintenance organizations, and partly because of the growth of clinics involving outpatient treatment. While physicians continue to play a dominant role (and to avoid direct administration), administrative complexities have enlarged the role of lay administrators, as we shall see in the following discussion.

The general unwillingness of professionals to assume directive responsibilities is a continuing problem faced by hospitals and other professional organizations.

### The Professionally Oriented Administrator

There are various solutions to this dilemma. The most widespread by far is the professionally oriented administrator. Such administrators combine a professional education with a managerial personality and practice. Goal as well as means activities seem to be handled best when such persons are the institutional heads. Because of their training, they are more likely to understand the special needs of a professional organization and its staff than lay administrators, and because of their personal characteristics, they are more likely to be skilled in handling the needs and requests of professional colleagues as well as those of the administrative staff.

There are various sources of professionally oriented administrators. One is the professionals themselves. In universities, the career often begins with committee chair assignments, the discovery by the person that he or she has administrative talents, and the revelation that the activity is challenging and has its own rewards. If the person has talent and if the committee work attracts favorable attention, the academic may then be nominated for an administrative post. At first the person (if chosen) will keep one foot in his or her academic specialty. As the administrative work becomes more time-consuming (and/or the person is promoted to higher administrative posts), the administrator must give less time to his or her specialty, which often results in anguish and problems of dissonance. Some may decide to return to their academic positions (perhaps because of sudden shifts in higher administration leading to their removal, or for other reasons). Problems of "reentry" are often serious, though some may be fortunate enough to receive a year's leave of absence for retooling (Gross & McCann, 1981).[9]

It is not clear whether people who elect an administrative career (partial or full) are less productive or less eminent than their colleagues, but the time required for administration does make continued productivity difficult. Sometimes administrators (especially higher administrators) are chosen precisely *because* of their eminence in a scientific or scholarly field (Birnbaum, 1971), which confuses the picture. For these reasons, any assessment of the "quality" of administrators is questionable. Still, it is true that university higher administrators, especially presidents, are overwhelmingly drawn from academic positions (Wilson, 1942, p. 85; Ferrari, 1970, p. 81). Whatever their eminence as academicians, they do understand and accept academic values.

For mental hospitals and often for clinics, a second source of professionally oriented administrators is special training. In recent years, there has been a movement toward developing training programs for specialized administration. A considerable number of teachers, for example, return to universities to take courses in administrative education before they become school principals. Similarly, physicians and lawyers may attend workshops and special programs dealing with health-service administration or the management of law offices. While these people may have the same professional or specialized skill base as the professionally oriented administrator, their commitment to administration is stronger, they have fewer ties with professionals, and hence are less strongly supportive of the professional goals of the organization.

Besides the administrator who was, originally, trained as a professional (the professor who became a dean, the physician who became a clinic administrator), some professional organizations are directed by *lay administrators*. These are persons who have no special training in the activities associated with the goals of the professional organization, but who have degrees in business administration or, commonly, in hospital administration.

Why this development has occurred in voluntary hospitals (and, by implication, in other professional organizations) is examined in research carried out by Perrow (1961). He first points out that all organizations must accomplish the following tasks: (1) secure necessary capital and basic legitimization of activity; (2) marshall the necessary skills; and (3) coordinate the activities of its members as well as the relations of the organization with other organizations and clients and consumers. Perrow takes the view that the power holders making policy at the top of the organization will vary according to which of these tasks is most problematic for the organization—a process he illustrates with hospitals. He finds they tend to go through stages. First they are dominated by trustees, then by medical staff, and ultimately (in today's larger hospitals) by administrators, often lay administrators.

In the earliest period Perrow studied (the early part of the 20th century), the crucial problem was acquiring capital and operating funds. Since hospitals lacked precise indicators of efficiency, yet used donated funds, they had to involve community representatives—trustees—in the authority structure. Such persons legitimated the status of the hospital, assured that funds were used properly, and tried to see that community needs—as they perceived them—were met. The trustees usually favored conservative financial policies, tended not to delegate decision making, and often saw their position as a vehicle for personal prestige. Since this form of domination was found in the early history of hospitals, usually before the development of extensive medical knowledge, there was little resistance from medical staff, and the superintendent (as he was often called) had little power. Such hospitals often served a particular ethnic or religious group (there were Methodist hospitals, Jewish hospitals, and the like).

The second stage of organization resulted from the enormous advances made in medical knowledge in recent years. Power passed from the trustees to the medical staff, though the trustees usually continued to play a crucial role in securing needed funds. As doctors took control, they emphasized extensive facilities, low hospital charges, high-quality services, and often elaborate time- and energy-conserving conveniences and other devices that helped them advance their own careers, as well as keep in the forefront of medical advances. They tended (and still tend) to minimize administrative skills, regarding the nonphysician administrator as simply a "housekeeper." Policy matters were decided by medical chiefs of sections. Physician domination usually goes hand in hand with a preference for private patients, and often affiliation with a university-based research center to provide a mix of treatment, training, and research functions.

In the third and present stage, as expenses mount, and as each hospital demands access to costly equipment and diagnostic facilities, hospitals are being forced to share facilities and thus to work out modes of joint control. It also is necessary to contract with other agencies, to engage in complex relationships with government agencies and insurance or other payment organizations. These trends enhance the value of the lay administrator, often someone with an MA in Hospital or Health Service Administration.[10] The lay administrator frequently enlists physician support for his role by acting as an intermediary with the trustees or other fund sources that assist doctors in the pursuit of their professional interests. At the same time, the lay administrator will apply the brakes to the eagerness of doctors for complex, overly expensive equipment. He may also minimize research, preventive medicine, and training, which sets the stage for conflict, as well as the development of conflict-resolution strategies. It is also possible in this stage that administrators may begin to share power, leading to multiple leadership with different functional roles assigned to medical staff, trustees, and the administrator himself.

The developments charted by Perrow apply not only to voluntary hospitals but also to other voluntary organizations such as social service agencies and privately sponsored correctional institutions for juveniles.[11] However, *non*voluntary service organizations—for instance, county and military hospitals, county welfare agencies, and adult correctional agencies—have seldom exhibited trustee control at any stage; control is usually by a government committee. Also, they are rarely so dominated by professionals as voluntary hospitals are by medical staff. Instead, they may experience administrative dominance from the start, often with a low level of professionalism. However, this situation is beginning to change in the more modern federal facilities and even in a few prisons and custodial institutions.

Where lay administrators dominate, there may not only be conflict with professional staff but also goal displacement. For example, although mental hospitals are dedicated, in principle, to therapy, custodial functions may be overemphasized, so that tranquilizers are used to control patients rather than to treat them. Or patients may be released with the claim that they will be "better and more humanely treated" in the local community, when actually the motive is to reduce costs (Scull, 1977). Similarly, Scott (1967) shows how workshops for the blind that were intended to train visually impaired persons in basic industrial skills so they could become self-sufficient were pressured into becoming efficient by contractual obligations for their products. The result was that the workshops began to hire and prefer "normals," who would help them meet their production goals, and the original training goals were displaced. Even universities may face such pressures, particularly when research goals compete with the training needs of the local community. These pressures may be particularly strong in the case of public universities, which must justify their activities to state legislatures.

When there are dangers such as these, a lay administrator may fail to appreciate the special needs of the professional staff. The problem may become more pronounced as organizations grow large and administrators lose contact with professional staff altogether.

## Center of Authority

It will be recalled from Chapter 5 that Weber's bureaucratic theory assumed that there is one major structure of authority (the line). It may be very complicated and have many branches, but it always has one center of authority where final decisions are made and conflicts can be resolved. The main authority line is directly related to the primary goal activity of the organization, and only indirectly to secondary (means) activities.

In professional organizations, there seems to be no line in this sense. The hospital, for instance, has been cited as an organization with two lines of authority, one professional and one administrative (Smith, 1955; Henry, 1954). However, in hospitals and other professional organizations, only the administrative (that is, the nonprofessional) line is structured in a bureaucratic way, with a clear line and a center of authority. Various department heads (of maintenance, security, admissions, and the like) are subordinated to the administrative director, and through him to the head of the organization.

Gross and McCann (1981) report striking differences in education and job experience between the topmost nonacademic figure in universities (often with vice presidential rank) and the academic vice president. Only 16.7 percent of nonacademic vice presidents have PhDs in contrast to 79.6 percent of academic vice presidents. Over 73 percent of academic vice presidents have had previous academic jobs in contrast to 34.2 percent of nonacademic vice presidents. Thus the nonacademic administrators have remarkably different career lines, which makes it unlikely that they play key or influential roles in organizational policy. Instead they form the head of a line that is responsible mainly for secondary or support activities. But it is that line (which includes lower-level administrators, registrars, purchasing agents, grounds staff) that has a clear authority structure. The professors, who conduct the major goal activity, do not form an authority structure in the regular sense of the term. As far as university research is concerned, for example, faculty members are considerably free from direct control by superiors. (This holds to a large degree for the substance of their teaching as well.) As McHenry and associates (1977) show, even the department chairperson is a colleague who coordinates schedules and performs other administrative activities, but only encourages or facilitates the professional staff in their conduct of their specialized activities. He does not "direct" them—or at least attempting to do so would likely be dysfunctional for the teaching or research process.

Of course, there are many sources of control other than line orders and direct supervision of performance, especially the rewards and sanctions exerted by informal pressures of peers. But since most of these mechanisms also function in nonprofessional organizations, in addition to supervision, one can safely state that there is less control in professional organizations than in other organizations. Moreover, as far as the major goal activity is concerned, such control does not take the form of a hierarchy with superiors who issue orders and require performance reports. The typical professional is not under such control. This does not hold true for students, research assistants, and interns, who are not part of the collegiate, peerlike organizational structure.

There are three areas of activity in professional organizations: (1) major goal activities, carried out by professionals and almost completely under the authority of the professional who performs the activity or directs the semiprofessionals and nonprofessionals who perform it; (2) secondary activities, performed by administrators and nonprofessional personnel under their control; and (3) secondary activities performed by the professionals. The last area includes preparing statistics, participating in public-relations activities, and allocating facilities. In the first area, there is no established hierarchy; in the second, the hierarchy does not involve professionals. In the third area, there is often a clear hierarchy and administrative predominance, and here it is easy to misunderstand the nature of the professional organization and to see the professionals as part of an administrative line structure. But so far as any hierarchy exists in this realm, it is limited to secondary activities; where the main goal activities are concerned, there is much professional autonomy.

In sum, the dilemma of combining professional and administrative authority is handled in professional organizations (ideally) by dividing the responsibilities so that the goal activities are controlled by the professionals, the means activities by the administrators, with the whole structure supervised by a middleman who has greater administrative skills and authority than the average professional, and more professional authority and competence than the average administrator because of his professionally oriented administrative training and experience. Still, there is no complete solution to this dilemma; studies of professional organizations report strains on this score, especially in those areas where professional considerations clash with means considerations.

## THE SEMIPROFESSIONAL ORGANIZATIONS

The basis of professional authority is knowledge, and the relationship between administrative and professional authority is largely affected by the amount and kind of knowledge the professional has. The relationship described in the preceding section holds largely for organizations in which professional authority is based on long training (5 years or more), when questions of life and death and/or privileged communication are involved, and when knowledge is created or applied rather than communicated. When professional authority is based on shorter training, involves values other than life or privacy, and covers the communication of knowledge, we find that it is related to administrative authority in a different way.

First of all, professional work here has less autonomy; that is, it is more controlled by those higher in rank and less subject to the discretion of the professional than in full-fledged professional organizations, though it is still characterized by greater autonomy than blue- or white-collar work. Second, the semiprofessionals often have skills and personality traits more compatible with administration, especially since the qualities required for communication of knowledge are more like those needed for administration than those required for the creation and, to a degree, application of knowledge. Hence these organizations are run much more frequently by the semiprofessionals themselves than by others.

The most typical semiprofessional organization is the primary school. The social-work agency is the other major semiprofessional organization. A semiprofessional sector, rather than a full-fledged organization, is found in the nursing service of hospitals.[12]

The goal of the primary school is largely to communicate rather than to create or apply knowledge. The training of its professionals, on average, falls below 5 years of professional education. The social-work agency is less typical since it applies knowledge, but it is semiprofessional in the fairly short training period involved (though social workers in private practice, especially in family therapy, may receive more training than many others), in the fact that questions of life and death are usually not involved (though threats of suicide and other psychiatric problems may be important in selected cases), and in that privileged communication may not be strictly maintained (e.g., social workers may be required to divulge information in the courts). A unique feature in social work is the use of what Scott (1969, pp. 102–110) calls "therapeutic supervision," that is, psychiatric concepts are employed to deal with worker-supervisor conflict. For example, a social worker's disagreement with her supervisor's suggestion may be interpreted as due to unconscious forces in the worker's personality. The consequences can be a hiding of feelings and a failure to deal with conflict. Though therapeutic supervision may be a form of normative power, the result can be manipulation of a subordinate by a superior, however much each may deny or even be unaware of the process.

Nurses apply knowledge, but their training is much shorter than that of doctors, and the question of what treatment to administer is concentrated (at least officially) in the hands of physicians. This statement is less true of nurse-practitioners and new nursing specialties associated with midwifery and complex technologies such as intensive care, inhalation therapy, and some forms of rehabilitation, but still, the nurse's subordination to the doctors is profound. One of her key roles is to assist the doctor, even to the degree (Katz, 1969) of preventing knowledge of physician errors, uncertainty, and ambiguity from reaching the patient. She is usually given more autonomy—sometimes even total discretion—where therapeutic medical knowledge stops, as in case of incurable or senile patients, where comfort, nurturance, and ease of pain may be the only aids left.

The work of these groups is less autonomous than that of the professions discussed earlier. Their workday is tightly regulated by the organization; their duties at work are comparatively highly specified. In cases where performance is not visible—e.g., social work, because it is done in the field; or teaching, because it is conducted in the classroom[13]—detailed reporting on performance is required, and supervisors are allowed to make surprise visits to check on work being done. Nurses are directly observed and corrected by doctors and by superior nurses. Such supervision is not characteristic of the mechanisms of control found in the full-fledged professional organizations. Inspectors are not widely used to drop in on a professor's classroom to check on his teaching, especially not in the better universities. No doctor will be asked to report to an administrative superior on why he carried out his medical duties in the way he did or stand corrected by him.[14] The external examinations used in schools to evaluate teachers are rare in universities.[15]

Furthermore, much of the supervision in semiprofessional organizations is done by people who are themselves semiprofessionals or professionals. Almost all school principals have been teachers. Few have been recruited directly from training courses for school administration, and almost none are lay administrators. Virtually all social-work supervisors have been social workers. Few have assumed supervisory positions early in their careers, and again, almost none are lay administrators. The same is true of nursing. Thus while the semiprofessionals are more supervised than the professionals, the supervision is more often conducted by their own kind.

There is some deprofessionalization in these organizations, as there is in full professional ones. Those teachers who are less committed to children—that is, the least "client-oriented"—are more likely to be administration-conscious and to become principals. Few principals, unless the school is particularly small, continue to teach other than in an occasional, ritualistic way. Similarly, social-work supervisors tend to be people who were more organization-oriented and less client-oriented in their field-work days, and they see few if any clients once they move up in the hierarchy.

Not all the differences between professional and semiprofessional organizations can be traced to the differences in the nature of the professional authority. Part of the problem is that the majority of semiprofessionals are of lower-middle-class or working-class origin (Simpson & Simpson, 1969, pp. 200–201), and many have chosen semiprofessional occupations as a relatively easy way up, rather than from intrinsic interest in the work. Another factor of major significance is the high concentration of women in these fields. This fact has led in the past to interrupted careers, as women married or were forced to take time out to raise children, the net result being lower wages and other problems. Although these factors are changing as women elect full-time, lifetime careers to an increasing extent, their position is still a difficult one in view of opposition from powerful male elites and the fact that their occupations are typically practiced in large-scale organizations where bureaucratic controls are strongest. The irony, as Ritzer (1977, p. 180) points out, is that the semiprofessional occupations actually are characterized by indeterminancy and uncertainty, the very bases of professional mandate. The intimate relationship of nurse to patient, of social worker to client, and of teacher to student cannot really be routinized. Nor can one dub such fields "marginal." In sum, they contain the raw materials for professionalization, but are hampered by the factors we have mentioned—social class origins and organizational location. There are some signs of change, but the battle for professional status has still to be fought.

In semiprofessional organizations, professional and administrative authority are related in a way different from that found in professional organizations. As already noted, control through organization regulations and superiors is much more extensive, though not as extensive as that of blue- or white-collar workers, and it is done mainly by semiprofessionals themselves. As in professional organizations, the articulation of the two modes of authority is not without strain. The semiprofessional subordinates tend to adopt the full-fledged professions as their reference group in the sense that they view themselves as professionals and feel that they should be given more discretion and be less controlled. Teachers resent the "interference" of principals, and many principals try to minimize it. Social workers rebel against their supervisors. Nurses often feel that they are more experienced than the young intern or more knowledgeable than the older supervisor, and hence should not be expected to submit themselves to the command of either.

Before leaving the subject of semiprofessional organizations, a word should be said about "lower participants" in those organizations (and, for that matter, in all organizations, including professional ones). Here we refer to people at the very bottom, such as attendants in mental hospitals and prison guards, as well as stenographers and secretaries, laboratory assistants, and maintenance men. Scheff (1961) has shown how the attendants in a mental hospital can make or break a psychiatrist's career by the difficulties or ease they create in arranging patients for group sessions, and by assisting in or resisting forms of therapy that require active attention during the many hours when the psychiatrist is absent. Crozier (1964) in a classic study showed how maintenance men in a French tobacco monopoly were able to accumulate power by virtue of the fact that they were the only ones who knew how to repair essential machinery. Mechanic (1962) refers to secretaries whose knowledge of office secrets or where resources may be secured use the power that gives them to exact privileges or deference from even the highest-status persons in the organization. However, it is a mistake to make too much of the "power" of such participants because it is largely negative or veto power. They can hold things up, but they do not make policy or initiate action. That kind of power remains with the professionals or the higher supervisors.

## Contextual Factors

Every comparative statement made throughout this discussion should be read as though prefaced by the clause "all other conditions being equal." But since they never are equal, some of these conditions and the effects of their variation should be spelled out.

## EXTERNALIZATION VERSUS INTERNALIZATION

All organizations rely to some degree on other organizations and collectivities for the fulfillment and regulation of some of their functions. The point of interest here is which functions are handled by the professional organization and which are externalized. The more that professional functions are internalized and administrative functions externalized, the closer the organization comes to the ideal type of professional or semiprofessional organization.

The school is particularly close to the ideal type. It has few administrative problems to begin with because its scope is narrow. It relies considerably on families, the community, social workers, the police, and others to minister to most of the nonprofessional needs of its clients. Hospitals, on the other hand, have a broad scope: They take care of most of the nonprofessional needs of their patients. Hence hospitals have a greater percentage of nonprofessional staff and many more administrative problems than schools. Universities are from this viewpoint similar to schools. Boarding schools, on the other hand, are very different in their personnel structure and administrative problems because they are so broad in scope (cf. Lefton & Rosengren, 1966).

Research organizations differ considerably among themselves in degrees of externalization and internalization of nonprofessional functions. Some research organizations are incorporated into university structures to a high degree, and many of their administrative functions are externalized. Other research organizations are comparatively independent and have to finance their activities themselves. This type usually has a stronger administrative control structure.

At the other end of the continuum are research organizations that are incorporated into nonprofessional and even authoritarian organizations, such as the armed forces. As several studies show, there seems to be considerable confusion in the structure of these research organizations. Military principles of organization and behavior are mixed with professional ones. Strict observation of the protocol of the military hierarchy is demanded in some situations and professional, collegial relations are encouraged in others. The heads of many research organizations in the United States armed forces are professionally oriented administrators. This can be explained in part by the fact that although these research units are broad in scope, they rely to a large degree on other military units for supply and for regulation of many of their nonprofessional needs. Thus administrative problems are minimized.

Of special interest from this viewpoint is a study that examines the effect of nationalization on the organizational structure of hospitals in England. It shows that when administrative responsibilities were taken over by a higher-level administrative unit, the heads of subordinated hospitals became more professionally oriented (Sofer, 1955). This finding can be compared to the relationship between the superintendent's office and the school principal: As more administrative tasks are assumed by the superintendent, the principal can devote more time and energy to his professional function—improving the quality of teaching.

## SINGLE VERSUS MULTIPLE PROFESSIONS

Another factor that impinges on the balance between professionals and administrators, and on the relationship between this balance and the process of goal implementation, is the number of professions cooperating in one organization and their mutual attitudes. The greater the number and the higher the tensions among them, the greater the need for a neutral administrator as final authority. The grammar school is from this point of view on one end of the continuum; it has but one professional group, the teachers. The university is on the other end; it has a large number of professional groups (departments). When there is strong rivalry between faculty groups—as, for instance, between the humanities and the natural sciences—a layman is often more functional as a university president than a professional would be. In general, the university administrator often functions as an arbitrator among different professional groups.

When organizations contain competing professionals, as is the case in hospitals or clinics where resources are scarce and the established professions face competition from newer, emerging fields, then conflict may become bitter, especially since each profession is likely to feel that it is acting in the best interests of its own patients or clients. Research-oriented persons may be considered "impractical" by treatment-oriented personnel, and the former may view the treatment staff as out-of-date or worse. De Santis (1980) describes a continuous battle among the various medical specialties, where allergists have boundary disputes with dermatologists and otolaryngologists, cardiologists battle specialists in internal medicine, and pathologists conflict with radiologists. Nor is there any easy solution to such conflicts, although she reports that these specialists prefer to settle their disputes informally rather than face the prospect of a "settlement" by formal means or through a ruling of a higher medical body.

## PRIVATE VERSUS PUBLIC ORGANIZATIONS

One of the most important dimensions for the study of professional organizations is the way they are owned and financed. Many professional organizations are partly financed through contributions or from tax money. Clients' fees play very different roles in various organizations; in some cases, they have no role at all, and in others, they are the most influential criterion for action. Another aspect of the same problem is the way the professionals are compensated. Sometimes they are paid salaries, at times they receive fees from the organization or from clients. These factors impinge on the relationships between the administrators and the professionals, especially in organizations with a profit goal, because they determine to a considerable degree who represents that goal—the professionals or the administrators.

From the viewpoint of professional goals, the distorting potential of a lay administrator seems to be highest in those "private" professional organizations where professionals are salaried. In those public organizations where the professionals are not salaried and the administrators represent public interests, the distorting potential may be minimized. Between these two poles exists a whole gamut of alternatives. Their study will shed further light on the relations between professional and bureaucratic authority.

## NOTES

1. For example, of the total of $3.9 billion that the U.S. government obligated to the 100 universities and colleges receiving the largest amounts for research and development in Fiscal 1982, about one-half went to only 20 universities; the top 10 universities alone accounted for about 30% of all the money, a figure which has changed little in recent years (*Federal Support to Universities, Colleges, and Selected Nonprofit Institutions, Fiscal Year 1982*, 1984, pp. 51–52). Similar concentrations (in some cases, even more striking) are found in other countries where the government is the only or the major source of research funds.

2. If this is the case, it may be related to the fact that law (or, to take another example, the ministry) does not make its case for professional status on any claim of scientific knowledge to begin with, just as accountancy (or social work, for example) does not involve knowledge claims (alone). Both are more accurately characterized as involving a systematization of established practice.

3. It should be emphasized that these are quite arbitrary distinctions that make no attempt to take account of the many differences in detail among various training programs, some of which may go beyond or fall short of these training periods. Indeed, some groups try to gain the mantle of "professional" by artificially increasing the training program. Similarly, the issue of "life and death" is always relative: Engineers erecting a bridge or constructing a building are concerned with "life and death" (if they are negligent), and there are many medical and legal specialties (plastic surgery, perhaps, and property and contract law) that are rather remote from life-and-death issues. Nor, finally, do we mean anything pejorative by the term *semiprofessional*. We wish merely to emphasize the fluidity of the concept, as well as the likelihood of historical changes in professional status. Surgery was of low prestige in the Middle Ages, and obstetrics was once the province of midwives. On the other side, the clergy have lost status over the last century.

4. A third form of organization, which is less common, is omitted from our discussion. This is the "service organization"—for instance, the Stanford Research Institute, ABT Associates, or some independent survey organizations—in which professionals are provided with the instruments, facilities, and auxiliary staff required for their work. However, the professionals are not employed by the organization or subordinated to its administrators. They may be on the staff at nearby universities, or in private practice.

5. The local-cosmopolitan distinction has been subjected to criticism and further research over the years. By and large, it has stood up rather well, though actual situations are more complex than suggested by the dichotomy (see Berger & Grimes, 1973).

6. It should be stated that the picture presented is to some extent an "ideal type," which will be found to vary in particular settings (cf. Perkins, 1973; Richman & Farmer, 1974). For example, in times of financial strain, especially in state universities and colleges that depend on legislative funding, the administration may play a critical role in decision making about the termination of programs or may even suspend tenure for short periods. Even here, however, most administrative officers will consult with faculty, though they may not be bound by the consultation. Indeed, state law may (and usually does) place the actual legal responsibility for university programs in the administrators' hands.

7. Partly this rejection of such lower-level administrative positions in universities as assistant dean and dean flows from lack of familiarity with the complexities of administration, as well as the low valuation placed on these activities. Riesman (1970, p. 76) sees a resemblance between faculty views of administrators and the general "cult of amateurism" in American culture: "what is wanted [for a university administrator] is a Ph.D. who temporarily gives up his profession to become a part-time amateur manager, and either actually hates such work or appears to despise it."

8. Cohen and March (1974), starting from a perception of universities as "organized anarchies," see the president as having little power to offer very much direction in any case.

9. Tracing administrative careers is a difficult process. The picture presented in the text is based on data from the Gross-McCann (1981) study, as well as anecdotal reports by the senior author in interviews with administrators.

10. A survey carried out in 1979 (Gifford, 1979) reported that just over one-half of chief executive officers of hospitals held the degree of Master of Hospital Administration, 12.6 percent held other master's degrees, 22.7 percent held bachelor's degrees, and only 4.9 percent held MDs or other doctorates.

11. Universities continue to insist that their top officer be a bona fide academic with appropriate degrees, even though it may be years since that person taught courses in his or her specialty area or did any research. However, on the larger campuses, and particularly in statewide systems of public universities, the administrative problems have become so overwhelming that academics have found they must share decision-making power with statewide coordinating councils, the public, and legislatures and governors' offices.

12. Others who may be found in semiprofessional settings are pharmacists (Kronus, 1975) and personnel directors (Ritzer & Trice, 1969). These occupations also exhibit various degrees of strain because of their close association with business, which means that often they are practiced in nonprofessional organizations such as factories or chain stores.

13. Lortie (1969) finds that schoolteachers exhibit what he calls a "dedicatory ethic," which elevates service and the other intrinsic satisfactions of teaching. Therefore they value contact with their students over the orientation to colleagues that is one of the hallmarks of the more professionalized occupations.

14. However, there are controls of an informal sort, such as Grand Rounds in which surgeons must justify, before colleagues, a questionable surgical practice, or explain why healthy tissue (as reported by the hospital pathology department) was removed. Bosk (1979) points out that such controls are gentle and more in the character of "don't do it again" than severe sanctions or criticisms. See also Abbott (1983) on the values associated with codes of ethics.

15. However, in some countries, such external examinations (e.g., those set by the University of London in some Commonwealth countries) may be quite common, enabling persons to obtain prestigious degrees by special arrangement in their home countries.

# CHAPTER TEN
# ENVIRONMENTS
# OF ORGANIZATIONS

A critic of the classic Hawthorne studies once stated to one of the writers:

> The basic trouble with those studies is that they ignored the fact that the Great Depression was coming on and people were being laid off. Is it surprising that workers "restricted output"? They didn't want to work themselves out of a job. The researchers should have looked out the windows of the shop to what was going on outside. The environment—that was the missing thing.

It took some time for researchers to learn the lesson, but learn it they did, as they would have had to, even without Hawthorne. For the environment was literally demanding their attention. Legal and political changes forced organizations to give attention to constraints such as controls on pricing and affirmative action, as well as to become "more responsible" in the public interest. Powerful unions could tie up whole sectors of the economy, and new competitors from foreign countries threatened entire industries such as steel and automobiles. The environment was not only becoming complex, it was changing rapidly. Strategies that organizational leaders would take years to develop might prove out-of-date as soon as they were put into operation.

As leaders struggled to deal with the environment, researchers began to ask what soon became the basic question, the one to which we devote this chapter: *Do organizations react to their environments,* coping as best they can? *Or,* instead, *do organizations control their environments,* imposing structure on disorder, achieving dominance and predictability? As we shall see, there is no simple answer, but the evidence comes down in greater support of the second position: Control *is* achieved, but once achieved, is easily lost, as the environment shifts again to offer new challenges. In sum, we need to keep a dynamic perspective before us, being ever ready to throw out old, accepted generalizations as new shifts in the world, as well as in research, reveal new problems and new knowledge. We can rarely predict what will happen, but we are getting better at it.

In order to understand how organizations deal with their environment, we will have to examine that environment more carefully. We proceed by following these steps: (1) First we survey the *organizational revolution,* which has given us a world of organizations, especially large ones. (2) Next we examine the great historical changes that led to the invention and dispersal of the key organizational form, namely, the *corporation.* With the picture of the emergence of the environment now more clearly before us, we examine our basic question on whether organizations react to or control their environment. We look at (3) *Contingency* theory, which sees organizations as reacting to or coping with environmental forces, and (4) *Strategic Choice* theory, which sees organizations occupying a more dominant role. A major way in which organizations exert such control is next examined, namely, (5) the establishment of *interorganizational linkages,* such as organizational "sets" and "networks," by which organizations unite their efforts or, in some cases, seek to establish power over other organizations. We end by asking what all these changes mean for the individual—the customer, the member of the public, or the employee. Are they well served by such organizational dominance?

## THE ORGANIZATIONAL REVOLUTION

Industrialization presages major changes in all societal sectors. The rise in educational standards and achievements, the spread of political consciousness, secularization, the rapid growth of science, the decline of the family, the increase in social mobility—all are associated with industrialization. We refer to all these related changes as *modernization.*

A central element of modernization is the development of many large organizations. After all, factories were not simply structures to house new machines, they were also places where work relations assumed a new form. The rise in education presupposed the emergence of schools and led to the development of universities. In politics, the party—a mass organization— took over what had been the exclusive domain of cliques and cabals. The bureaucratic state emerged from the ruins of feudal society. In all these areas, some organizations existed before the Industrial Revolution. The Italian city-states had developed some fairly large and complex commercial organizations. There were universities in medieval Europe. State bureaucracies operated in ancient Egypt, in Imperial China, and in Byzantium.

But these organizations were few in number, encompassing only a small fraction of the members of the society, and many of the principles of effective organization—as specified by the Classical theory of administration or the Weberian Structuralist approach—were not observed. Recruitment to the Chinese bureaucracy was not based on specialized knowledge or other bureaucratic merits as much as it was on general philosophical knowledge, with stress on the ability to recite and write poetry. Organizational positions were not separated from social status; recruitment was limited largely to the gentry. The allocation of rewards for organizational performance was not monopolized by the organization. In late medieval France, for instance, judges were compensated by the litigants rather than by the court. It was only with modernization that there emerged a great number of organizations, characterized by similarity of structure, encompassing a large part of the population, and penetrating into a wide spectrum of social spheres.

This change is reflected in the fact that despite the growth in size of the employed population, the proportion of the self-employed in the United States has dropped from 25 percent in the year 1900 to around 8 percent in 1980. Of a total labor force of 106 million in 1981, nearly one-half (46 percent) work for organizations with 100 or more employees, a figure that is a modest definition of a "large" organization. A corresponding concentration of persons can be seen in institutions of higher education (about half of students attend institutions with 10,000 or more students), voluntary associations (over 80 percent belong to associations with 50,000 or more members), prisons (about 45 percent of prisoners are housed in prisons with 700 or more prisoners), churches (seven churches account for almost two-thirds of all church membership), hospitals (46.7 percent of admissions are to hospitals with at least 300 beds), and labor unions (93 percent of members belong to unions with at least 50,000 members).[1] This is not to say that small organizations have vanished, or are about to vanish. Construction continues to be carried out by small crews; many retail stores, especially boutiques or others that pride themselves on "personal service," remain small; and, of course, there are organizations such as juries, examination boards, orchestras, and councils of war, which must be small to enable intensive interaction to go on. Further, large organizations themselves spawn smaller ones, which act as service facilities for them (e.g., restaurants that spring up around a large factory) or as subcontractors for smaller components that the factory requires. Indeed, large aircraft or defense contractors discover that in order to qualify for large government contracts, they may be required to subcontract to many smaller organizations in several states (even to foreign countries, if the company plans to sell its products to those countries). Still, in spite of the survival of small organizations, the organizational landscape has become increasingly dense with large organizations.[2]

## CHANGES IN THE HISTORICAL ENVIRONMENT:
## THE COMING OF THE CORPORATION

Modernization helped create the setting in which complex organizations, small or large, could arise and develop. It allowed for differentiation so that functions formerly carried out within the family—production and allocation of products and services, social integration (e.g., tribal rituals to keep families together), and normative integration (e.g., the handing down of folklore)—can be separated. Organizations have taken over production and allocative functions, while the family has retained social and normative integration. Weber (1958) described how this process, aided by rationalization and secularization, was particularly stimulated by the Protestant Reformation, as well as by other changes associated with the coming of modern science and bureaucratization.

As these vast structural changes were occurring, a new form of complex organization was invented, the limited liability corporation, which was to prove so successful that it has been imitated by schools, small church congregations, PTAs, and even universities, many of which might be better off with a more collegial form. The dominance of the corporation is so vast that it is important to understand how it came into existence.

We referred in Chapter 1 to "corporate actors"—organizations that are like persons in that they can take action on their own behalf. The concept was known to the ancients, but beginning in about the 12th century, it began to develop new functions. Coleman (1974) describes the situation for the case of the church. In Germany in the Middle Ages, a landowner might build a church on his land and arrange for a priest to conduct services there, at first mainly for his own household. Later, others might be allowed to participate. As the generations went by, the priests in the church began to argue that the landowner no longer had full feudal rights over the church and the land on which it stood. By then, there would have grown up generations of serfs whose only task was to serve the church, and who could not be treated in quite the same way as the serfs who toiled on the land. As the rights of the landowner dwindled, he began to see himself not as the owner or lord over the church, but simply as its patron.

But if the landowner no longer had rights over the church, then who did, and who was responsible for it? Not the priest, surely, for he might become ill or die, or move on to another church. The question became more pressing as the church's rights grew and it collected an independent income from lands and resources that were willed to it by others. Who, then, owned the land itself, the building, and the rights to the income? The law had some difficulty with this question at first, but gradually it hit on the fiction of declaring that the saint for whom the church was named was the "owner." The result was that, many years after their death, Coleman notes with tongue in cheek, St. Peter, St. Paul, and St. James became extensive landowners. The priest was then regarded as the "guardian" of the saint's property. Soon the fiction was further extended, so that the church was considered a sort of infant under the guardianship of the priest. But lawyers were careful to separate the priest—and, indeed, any other person—from ownership or any rights in the church. In this manner, a total separation was made between any living persons and the corporate actor that the church had now become.

Similar developments, which we shall not discuss, took place with boroughs and other corporate units, which also began to be separated from the persons who happened to be employed in them. Such corporate units now had the ability to levy taxes or fines, to collect tolls, and even to purchase, in the names of the church or borough, other real property. Still later, a new change was made by the invention of the "trust." Under primogeniture, a person could pass on his personal possessions to whomever he pleased, but on the death of the owner, land had to go to the eldest son, which allowed the feudal lord to exact a tax at the time of succession. To evade this tax, the concept of the trust was invented. A landowner would, *in his own lifetime,* pass on his land to a set of trustees, whom he would instruct on what he wanted done with his land now and after his death. So on his death, the land would remain in the hands of the trust. Whenever a particular trustee died, he would be replaced, so, in theory, the trust could go on forever.

Through these devices the concept of the corporate actor took on ever more flexible uses and power. It could act on its own, entirely apart from whoever happened to be the manager or trustee at any given time, could buy and sell property on its own behalf, and run landed estates indefinitely. The law treated these corporate actors as if they were persons, applying the whole corpus of law (developed for persons) to them.

From these beginnings, then, came the modern private corporation. The early factories in England and on the Continent were run by families or single individuals known as entrepreneurs, who would use their own money to buy supplies, contract with workers to manufacture a product, and then sell the output. But such persons and families were highly limited in the amount of money they controlled, and therefore the scale of their enterprises was also limited. When an entrepreneur went broke or died, the company he had formed died with him. But this arrangement was adequate for the putting-out system, which dominated English manufacture between the 15th and the 18th centuries.

The putting-out system took two forms. In the *domestic system,* the entrepreneur traveled around the countryside with supplies and distributed them to families in their homes, or in small workshops where groups of craftsmen gathered together, such as spinners, weavers, glaziers, potters, blacksmiths, tinsmiths, locksmiths, joiners, millers, and bakers.

This system was adequate for textiles, clothing, metal goods (such as nails and cutlery), watchmaking, and for the hat, wood, and leather industries.

Where work could not be taken home, as in coal, tin, and copper mining, a *subcontracting system* was used, which is vividly described by Dobb (1963):

> In blast-furnaces there were the bridge-stockers and the stock-takers, paid by the capitalist according to the tonnage output of the furnace and employing gangs of men, women, boys and horses to charge the furnace or control the casting. In coal-mines there were the butties who contracted with the management for the working of a stall, and employed their own assistants; some butties having as many as 150 men under them and requiring a special overseer called a "doggie" to superintend the work. In rolling mills there was the master-roller, in brass-foundries and chain-factories the overhand, who at times employed as many as twenty or thirty; even women workers in button factories employed girl assistants. When factories first came to the Birmingham small metal trades "the idea that the employer should find, as a matter of course, the work places, plant and materials, and should exercise supervision over the details of the manufacturing processes, did not spring into existence"; and even in quite large establishments survivals of older situations persisted for some time, such as the deduction from wages of sums representing the rent of shop-room and payment for power and light. (p. 267)*

The subcontracting system persisted in the early factories. Foremen sometimes added to their own supervisory function the practice of taking a few machines on their own account and hiring labor to operate them. It was common in carpet and lace mills, ironworks, potteries, building and civil engineering projects, in transport and quarrying. In the United States, such subcontracting in iron and steel continued almost to the end of the 19th century.

But both the domestic and subcontracting systems had certain major defects. For one thing, they were highly inefficient. Domestic production was difficult to supervise effectively, so productive quality varied from cottage to cottage. Any division of labor would have wreaked havoc in the system because one unit would have had to wait on another before it could do its work. Another problem was the difficulty of moving material around, not to speak of the losses from theft in transit. There was no real control over embezzlement, and there was a basic lack of dependability and frequent turnover. The entrepreneur might discover that a whole family or group of artisans had moved on to another county, or that a subcontractor had taken his crew away when he found he could get a better price from another owner.

But all of these problems were secondary to a much more serious one; namely, the system proved completely unequal to handling the demands

*Reprinted with permission of International Publishers Co., Inc.

presented by the growing state, by the coming of international trade, and by the emergence of wealthy middle classes. These changes created huge new markets for products. The state wanted gunpower, uniforms for its armies, coins, and ships. The middle classes wanted luxuries such as porcelain, glass, soap, furs, silk, velvet, and spices. Producing such goods in sufficient quantities to satisfy demand required a scale of operations totally beyond the old entrepreneurs. As two examples, in England, there was a demand for masts for military vessels and felt for men's hats. Both the beaver skins for the hats and the timber for the masts could be found only on the West Coast of North America or in Hudson's Bay, places far away from England or the Continent, and even from the new settlements on the East Coast of North America. To get such goods required ships and expensive machinery, warehouses and wharves, as well as the investment of a lot of money. A ship might be gone for a year or more, and therefore investors had to be willing to wait and not depend on the quick turnover that had characterized the putting-out system. Further, there was great risk from storms and pirates, as well as competition from the ships of Spain, France, Holland, and Russia. If a single person risked his own money and his ships were lost, he would be ruined. So a new way had to be developed for gathering together large sums of money, yet by an arrangement that would minimize the risk to any one investor.

The answer was found in the limited liability or joint-stock company. It appears to have been invented either by Italian bankers or by German merchants of the Hanseatic League. Two of the largest such companies were the Dutch East India Company and the British East India Company, the latter of which became practically a full-blown government. The state granted a charter to a group of persons to form such a corporation; this corporation then became an actor in its own right. It could sue or be sued in its own name, irrespective of the individuals who ran it, and it had perpetual succession. People came and went, the corporation remained. This organization gathered little bits of money from many persons, and therefore could amass huge sums. Yet each person only stood to lose what he had contributed. Nor was he responsible for the debts of the organization, such as what it owed for large capital investments in ships, land, or buildings. Those were the responsibility of the corporation itself, not of *any* persons in it.

Once this corporation came into existence, investors were mainly concerned with making money and had little interest in its management. Some of these corporations grew to huge size, until today they have millions of shares and hundreds of thousands of investors.[3] Furthermore, many of these stockholders are not persons but are themselves corporate actors, such as pension funds, insurance companies, mutual funds, money market funds, or large investment banks. In this way, we get a separation of the ownership from the management (which we discussed earlier).

Exactly how independent the managers are is the subject of debate (Herman, 1981), but it is indisputable that they have a great deal of freedom and are often subject only to general monitoring by major stockholders. The corporate form has been adopted by social-work agencies, universities, and other organizations where trustees or regents act like boards of directors, but where presidents and other administrative staff enjoy much discretion and are power holders by virtue of the organizations they head.

## THE BASIC QUESTION: DO ORGANIZATIONS CONTROL THEIR ENVIRONMENTS?

We come now to the dilemma faced by the managers of organizations. In one sense, they have a great deal of autonomy to chart the course of the organization, to make decisions on goals and products, to take risks in moving into uncharted areas of endeavor, to spend large sums of other people's money on expensive equipment, to hire and fire. Yet that "autonomy" is constrained, not only by laws and other political and moral restraints, but also by the autonomy possessed by the managers of *other* organizations. In a world of organizations, the significant environment is made up of other organizations. For example, in the United States, there are around 2 million corporations and about 12 million partnerships and sole proprietorships. The question is: When so many organizations (of so many kinds) jostle one another in societal space, to what extent must their managers be content to react, as best they can, to the environment, and to what extent can they employ strategies to impose order on that environment?

The two questions have each become the subject of what are called "theories" (though they might better be called "claims"): the first is often called *Contingency theory,* and the second may be called *Strategic Choice theory.*[4] Although put in this way, the two positions would seem to be directly opposed, we shall see that often their defenders are paying attention to different parts of the society.

## CONTINGENCY THEORY

### Cross-Cultural Studies: An Early Expression of the Contingency Theory Position

Perhaps the earliest expression of what later came to be called Contingency theory was in cross-cultural research on organizations. When confronted with the clear fact that generalizations developed for organizations in Western or industrialized countries did not apply to less developed or

Third World countries, analysts took one of two positions. One position argued for a basic "logic of industrialism" that was the same the world over: There were certain inescapable features of organization structure that would be found everywhere. Organizations would become increasingly specialized and complex as they grew in size. Those developments, in turn, would create a structural need for coordination of the organizations, which, because of their large size, could not be directed from the top. The result would be increasing decentralization of decision making. To make sure that decentralization did not result in different parts of the organization working at cross-purposes, increased formalization would be required. As organizations became more formalized, managers would have to pay increasing attention to ability and performance as opposed to ascriptive considerations such as family or ethnic origins.

When confronted with the fact that Japanese organizations (which really started this whole discussion) offered what was (loosely) called "lifetime employment" (in clear contradiction of the formal organization principle of hiring and firing for ability and performance), and when it was further pointed out that these organizations also took into account ascriptive factors (family, special personal needs), the "logic of industrialism" proponents either saw these as "temporary" aberrations, or else as masking what went on behind the scenes (people were not actually fired, true, but they were "asked to resign"; people who were kept on when their performance faltered were simply being retrained). Their point was the organizations everywhere *had* to be alike structurally because of the requirements of industrialization.

The opposite claim was made by what was called the "culture-specific" position. These scholars maintained that there were many roads to industrialism, that all countries did not need to follow the model of England after the Industrial Revolution, but could move in different ways. The state, for example, might play a much larger role by directly importing trained specialists who might enable a country to move to industrialized status in only two or three generations. The economy might be stimulated by forced savings or in other ways to provide incentives for shifts of younger persons into new occupations. The discovery of valued national resources (such as oil or metals) might enable Third World countries to piggyback their modernization programs on their newfound wealth or strategic geopolitical position. Ascriptive or "traditional" features might be used so that loyalty to a family or to a regime could be enlisted in the service of organizational work—in other words, loyalty to the Emperor might be translated into loyalty to Honda Motors.

The dispute between the two positions, though it generated much research, was not settled by this research, for predictably, the evidence came down mostly on a middle ground. For example, Child and Kieser (1979), comparing 82 British companies and 51 West German companies, found that in both countries size was correlated with degree of specialization and with hierarchical levels, as logic of industrialism predicted. But, as the culture-specific position predicted, there was *more* centralization in Germany than in England (in decisions on operational matters such as marketing, production, and purchasing), in keeping with the greater respect for authority found generally in Germany—a cultural difference.

A study by Jonsson and Neuhauser (1979) of Swedish and U.S. hospitals came to a similar conclusion. It was found that the average patient stay is longer in Sweden, but costs are lower—a neat trick that surely the United States would do well to follow. However, when disease, type of surgery, and comparable diagnostic tests are held constant, the average length of stay is about the same in both countries. The longer average stay in Sweden is simply due to the fact that Swedish hospitals accept more patients with chronic diseases, who "inflate" the average figures. So medicine, surgery, and hospital practice are much the same, structurally, in both countries. The cost difference comes from the fact that most patients in Sweden are treated by doctors who are on hospital staff, whereas most U.S. patients are treated by private doctors—a cultural difference that leads to more doctors per patient in the United States, who create more work for hospital personnel in terms of diagnostic tests and special procedures, with consequent higher costs. Further, U.S. hospitals must hire larger clerical and administrative staffs to process third-party payments (Blue Cross, Medicare, Medicaid, etc.) to pay the doctors, resulting in further costs. In sum, doctors practice much the same medicine in both countries, and hospitals perform the same tests and procedures, but private medicine and third-party payments increase costs in the United States.

Studies of more "exotic" societies have shown rather stronger cultural differences. For example, Hofstede (1979, 1980), in a study of "power distance" between subordinates and superiors in 39 different countries, finds such differences to be much higher in the Philippines, Mexico, and Venezuela, for example, than in Austria, Israel, Denmark, or New Zealand.[5]

No matter. The critical point for us is that studies in general claim that *both* "logic of industrialism" *and* cultural features will "explain" the structure of organizations. What the scholars in either tradition end up demonstrating is a *deterministic* position. In one case, managers *must* follow a "logic of industrialism." They have no choice whether to centralize or decentralize, specialize or not: The "logic" forces them to behave in a predictable way. The culture-specific position offers no greater opportunity for individual variation. Instead of following the "logic" imperative, managers are seen as having no choice but to do whatever the culture requires of them. Managers will be more domineering in Venezuela than in Denmark, no matter how decentralized the organizational structure may be. In sum, neither perspective offers much scope for initiative or autonomy on the part of managers. Managers can only "react" to the logic or to the culture.

### Contingency Theory Proper

Other writers, while staying away from the logic-culture controversy, were showing, in a different way, that managers were relatively powerless to control their environments. These researchers (who self-consciously called themselves "Contingency theorists"—a label they wore with pride) sought to demonstrate that the environment of modern organizations was so complex and so rapidly changing that the best *any* organizational manager could hope to do was simply to react, and he might not even be successful at that. Too slow or inadequate a reaction would lead to disaster.

These writers began with a serious attempt to "describe" the environment in structural terms, seeking to identify "dimensions." Once they identified them, they then sought to show that such variables were correlated with organizational performance, leaving the strong suggestion that if correlations were high, this showed managers were reacting to the environment.[6] Since the environment was so complex and changing so rapidly, it could hardly be argued that managers were *making* it complex or making it change (though, collectively, such a result might occur; see Weick, 1977). The best, then, that managers could hope for was to quickly identify what was going on in the environment and then seek to cope with it as rapidly as possible.

Most researchers took their lead from the early work of Emery and Trist (1965), who claimed that environments varied from what they called "placid-randomized," with little change or relationships among organizations, all the way to "turbulent" environments, which were highly interconnected as well as undergoing rapid change in rate of connection. Although they offered only a conceptual argument (with an example drawn from the experience of a British company), the concept *turbulent* caught on and has become a catchword in many managerial circles. Terreberry (1968) went on to argue that there was a trend toward such turbulence, with environments becoming ever more complex and changing ever more rapidly. Other writers (e.g., Jurkovich, 1974; Dess and Beard, 1974) have offered different pictures of the dimensions of organizational environments, but most revolve about various measures of the complexity of the environment (how many other organizations there are, how clustered they are, how different they are) and the amount of change (whether it is rapid or slow, predictable or random). An example is shown in Figure 10-1.

We have already met one of the earliest tests of Contingency theory in our discussion (Chapter 2) of the study by Lawrence and Lorsch (1967) of firms in the container, food processing, and plastics industries, which showed that there was no "one best way" to organize, and that the "best way" depended on whether the environment was complex and rapidly

*Environmental Capacity:* The relative level of resources available to an organization within its environment, varying from lean or low-capacity to rich or high-capacity environments.

*Environmental Homogeneity-Heterogeneity:* The degree of similarity between the elements of the domain population, including individuals and organizations. Varies from undifferentiated or homogeneous to highly differentiated or heterogeneous environments.

*Environmental Stability-Instability:* The degree of turnover in environmental elements. (Note that high turnover may still be patterned and is thus predictable.)

*Environmental Concentration-Dispersion:* The degree to which resources, including the domain population and other elements, are evenly distributed over the range of the environment. Varies from random dispersion to high concentration in specific locations.

*Domain Consensus-Dissensus:* The degree to which an organization's claim to a specific domain is disputed or recognized by other organizations.

*Turbulence:* The extent to which environments are characterized by an increasing interconnection between elements and trends, and by an increasing *rate* of interconnection.

---

Source: Howard E. Aldrich, *Organizations and Environments,* Englewood Cliffs, NJ: Prentice-Hall, Inc., 1979, Table 3.2, p. 64. Reprinted with permission.

**FIGURE 10-1.   Dimensions of organizational environments.**

changing or was simple and placid. In plastics, products were continually changing, with intensive focus on research on how to beat competitors to the market. At the same time, knowledge of customer preferences was highly uncertain. However, production was much less uncertain; once a product was developed, it could easily be routinized in a production process. Important differences among departments were found in such matters as interpersonal attitudes, time perspective, and personal goals—all of which added up to what the authors called "differentiation." The container firms, on the other hand, were far less differentiated, and they were also operating in more placid, less competitive environments. This led the authors to generalize that the degree of internal differentiation in an organization is directly related to the degree of differentiation in the environment.[7]

The study was very popular and widely cited, but later research, using more sophisticated methods, has not been strongly supportive. Many of the problems revolve about the difficulty of measuring the environmental "dimensions," which turn out to be highly complex in themselves. Another issue has revolved about the widespread use of *perceptual* measures (e.g., managers' perceptions that their environment is changing predictably versus managerial perceptions that it is not; cf. Duncan, 1972). Such perceptions have been found (e.g., by Tosi, Aldag, & Storey, 1973) to correlate poorly with objective measures. Defenders argue that it is perceptions that predict behavior, but it can be argued in return that objective change will produce effects whether perceived or not.

Still, research goes on. For example, a study by DuBick (1978) of 73 news organizations (in 67 metropolitan centers) supports the theory, at least in part, in that he is able to show that internal differentiation among newspapers (specialization of departments, for example) is correlated with the complexity of the environment in the city (e.g., as measured by diversity of ethnic groups and occupational differentiation). However, he also reports that such relationships tend to be strongest where competition is also strongest. At newspapers in cities without competition, organizational decision makers have much more discretion as to how they will organize their news-gathering or writing teams. In sum, only when the environment imposes strong constraints on organizations (as when newspapers must compete with other newspapers) can one say that it is "determining" or strongly influencing the internal organization of the newspaper.

Other researchers have been less aggressive in showing *direct* relationships between organizations and their environments, preferring instead to say that the environment offers challenges or limits. Some writers have emphasized the influence of the "density" of the organizational environment on the formation of new organizations. The implication is that the presence of many organizations of a similar type creates an atmosphere, as well as examples that other organizations will be influenced to follow (cf. McCarthy & Zald, 1977). For example, Fennell (1980) carried on a study of hospitals in which she was able to demonstrate that expansion of hospital services was more closely related to "keeping up" with what other prestigious hospitals offered than with patient needs. Although the argument is that the hospital administrators had "no choice" but to follow the lead of other hospitals, one could imagine that *some* administrators might refuse to do so, hoping that satisfying patient needs would generate sufficient support for continued operation. Still, such a course of action would be risky.[8]

A balanced position is the widely reported work by Stinchcombe (1965) in which he points up the importance of basic environmental resources as preconditions for the emergence of organizations. He calls attention to the importance of literacy and basic education, a money economy, a population aware of the potential benefits of organization, but free from dependence on traditional elites who may resist new organizations as destructive of established status relationships (Pennings, 1980, offers a similar list). Some economists (Williamson, 1975) argue that organizations are likely to *arise* to manage economic transactions when such transactions become too costly or too complex to be managed directly. Such is likely to be the case when transactions become unspecifiable in detail (as in employment contracts), and when there are small numbers of people involved and "opportunism" (cheating) becomes easy. These are cited as "market failures" showing the need for organizations. Such an argument is more reasonable and less deterministic than the assumption that there is any direct relationship between environment and what happens in organizations, but it still stops short of telling us that organizational leaders and elites can actually manipulate the environment or even create one more suited to their needs. Therefore we can classify such work as extensions of the Contingency theory, though with less commitment to an extreme position.

A recent variant—actually a radical form—of the Contingency approach has been labeled "population-ecology" theory. The theory is basically Darwinian, even making use of the terms employed in Darwinian evolutionary theory. Organizations are found to *vary* (e.g., bureaucratic versus professional, variations by industry), and over time some will adapt better, and hence survive, while others will fail. The most obvious example is the high mortality rate of small as compared to large organizations. Eventually, the form of the survivor organizations will be imitated by other organizations that seek to survive, or whatever form the survivors assume will become the dominant form. An example might be bureaucratic structure (in contrast to traditional or kinship-based structures). Aldrich and Reiss (1971) applied this theory in a study of the extent to which white shopkeepers were succeeded by blacks or Puerto Ricans in 648 businesses in three inner-city neighborhoods between 1966 and 1972. Such inner-city areas were found to be less hospitable than other areas to businesses because of the slow increase in median family income, as well as population loss and lower business profits. A fairly stable rate of white owners leaving was accompanied by an increasing rate of replacement by blacks or Puerto Ricans. Most of the business sites were not reoccupied as businesses, however, but were converted to nonprofit use. Only when most white owners had left were minority businessmen able to compete. This fact, the authors suggest, meant that the white owners had been more efficient exploiters of available resources, especially in consumer goods and retail food sales.

A defense of population-ecology models in theoretical terms is offered by Hannan and Freeman (1977), who point to the inertial features of organizations that make it difficult for them to change in the face of environmental demands. Such features include investment in training as well as in capital equipment, the established political arrangements within the organization, frictional barriers to entry or exit, and the difficulties organizations face in getting outside support for proposed changes. The theory is only just beginning to be used, but one of the problems with it is immediately evident: Testing requires a large number of organizations, substantial proportions of which must "die" over a measurable period of time. The case is clearest for small organizations, and those who use this approach will find it essential to pay attention to them.[9] Much of the research on complex organizations, as we have seen all through this book, is on *large* organizations, and these fail much less frequently. So those using such an approach will have difficulty finding cases among the most important organizations.[10]

## THE STRATEGIC CHOICE THEORY

In general, then, the Contingency theory sees organizations as *reacting* to their environments. They "cope" as best they can. The Strategic Choice theory offers a much larger role to *discretion*.

In his classic work, Thompson (1967) described organizations in this way, although his book is rarely cited in discussions of Strategic Choice theory. Thompson pointed out that rationality norms themselves dictate a more active role than Contingency theory suggests. Organizations are seen as *buffering* themselves from environmental influences by protecting their technical core through such devices as stockpiling of materials and supplies in anticipation of difficulties or shifts in the environment, as well as by storing outputs in inventories. In the face of environmental fluctuations in demand and supply, organizations will seek to *smooth out* ups and downs by offering premiums (as utility firms do to those who will use the service during rough periods rather than in peak periods), or special promotions or sales during slow periods. If buffering and smoothing prove insufficient, organizations will seek to *anticipate,* by planning, market surveys, and other devices. For example, knowing that its mailboxes fill up between 4:30 and 5:00 in the afternoon (when secretaries drop off company mail on their way home), the post office may offer a special incentive for early mailing, such as assurance of local delivery on the following day. When all three techniques fail, organizations can *ration* their facilities, as mental hospitals do by establishing front and back wards, thus restricting their limited psychiatric services to patients who show a good chance of profiting from them. Similarly, the post office will give priority to first-class mail, leaving junk mail for mass deliveries when time is available.

Some (e.g., Perrow, 1979, pp. 189 ff.) have offered similar general defenses of Strategic Choice theory (especially Child, 1972, who used the term *strategic choice*) but the only conclusive defense must come from research. We turn now to a brief survey of major findings so far uncovered.

In a study of 40 widely dispersed branch offices of a large U.S. brokerage organization, Pennings (1975) examined the claims of Contingency theorists that there should be a close fit between environmental and organizational structural characteristics. What he found was that, with some exceptions,[11] such environmental variables as perceived competition, uncertainty, instability, number of competitors, feedback specificity, and demand volatility were not related (or were negatively related) to such organizational variables as vertical communication, participativeness, meetings, power distribution, specialization, and social interdependence. In other words, a branch manager apparently was free to use his own discretion about employee participativeness, number of meetings, and how specialized the branch would be, irrespective of the kind of environment in which the branch found itself operating. Nor was the fit between organization and environment related to effectiveness (as measured by losses due to errors, morale, and anxiety or by various production measures). Although the study can be faulted on certain methodological grounds (see Aldrich, 1979, pp. 139–140), one cannot argue away empirical findings unless the design is fatally flawed, and Pennings' was not. His study, employing the best of available methods, simply did not support Contingency theory, but argued instead for a good deal of autonomy on the part of branch managers and staff.

Another approach is suggested by Hirsch (1972), whose original research argues strongly for the importance of examining the *industry,* an aspect of the environment that most researchers neglect. He examines "cultural products"—books, records, and movies; that is, those things serving esthetic or expressive rather than more clearly utilitarian functions. The organizations that manufacture these products act as intermediaries in a vast industry system: In the manner of construction foremen, they bring together small groups of creative people (artists, writers, etc.) for one particular performance, book, or movie. They pay them for that one performance or book, and then the creative artists (or craftspersons) disperse, only to be reassembled (though not necessarily the same individuals) for new performances or products. At the same time, the producers face an environment characterized by demand uncertainty and cheap technology (it costs relatively little to manufacture records or to print books). Demand uncertainty means that the producers, however arrogant they sometimes sound, really do not know what makes a best-seller book or a hit record. They are constantly confronted with a book that had none of the ingredients for success but became a top seller, or a record by an unknown artist that immediately became a favorite.

The producers also face uncertainty at the output boundary: To market the books or records, they need to establish relationships with sales organizations or with disk jockeys and radio station producers (without violating any laws on bribery or other forms of what is called "payola"). At the same time, they seek to influence the media by trying to get new products mentioned or discussed as "news stories" rather than nakedly through advertisements (though they use advertisements too, of course).

In the face of such uncertainties in the cultural product environment, Contingency theory might predict that producers could do little more than try to react fast to whatever changes the environment presented them with. However, Hirsch finds that the producers move instead to fashion an environment that enables them to maintain control. This they do through three strategies.

1. They generate a proliferation of contact men. Producers make use of many talent scouts and others who provide a constant flow of information secured from agents, authors, writers, and other publishers. These

talent scouts must be allowed a good deal of discretion if they are to be able to forecast new trends and to scour the countryside in search of talent.

2. Since they cannot predict which record or book is going to be successful, producers engage in overproduction and differential promotion. That is, instead of selecting a few books, for example, and spending a lot promoting them, they produce *many* books, including some that compete with each other, and let the chips fall where they may. This means that the authors of the competing books are sacrificed as early consumer preference decides which book the producer will promote. Once a book begins to take off, advertising and support will be withdrawn from other books and focused on the one likely success to make it an even greater success.

3. The producers coopt reviewers and opinion leaders, not directly, but through advertising, publishers' parties, special "meet the stars" cocktail parties, and other devices—all intended to get a book, movie, or record talked about. After such treatment, some radio disc jockeys, for example, may begin to *believe* that a record is going to be a hit and play it over and over again (whether they like it or not), thus helping ensure that it *will* be a hit because the public has come to expect to hear it. Since radio stations depend on "Top 40" and similar program formats to attract advertising revenue, other disc jockeys must play the record, which makes it an even bigger hit.

In sum, Hirsch presents a picture of organizational executives reaching out to control their world, though not always successfully.[12]

## SETTING UP INTERORGANIZATIONAL LINKAGES: A MAJOR APPROACH IN THE SEARCH FOR STRATEGIC CHOICE

One of the ways in which organizations seek to control their environments is by setting up linkages with other organizations, often in complex networks, and then employing such connections to regularize the inflow of information and reduce uncertainties in resource supply and other contingencies.[13] Although much of this work is reminiscent of the traditional interest of students of organizations in such matters as interlocking directorates of corporations and banks, it is new in that it is much more strongly based in theory and less concerned with the general question of seeking to "prove" that a power elite dominates or with other questions pursued by neo-Marxists and others interested in macrosociological matters. Instead, the interest is in trying to discover how such interorganizational networks actually operate, as well in demonstrating that they show support for a strategic control approach (as opposed to contingency approaches).

Generally, attention focuses on the following variables: (1) how closely connected or coupled the various organizations are (loose coupling may allow for flexibility so that organizations can respond to local conditions without affecting the entire network, as when supermarkets are allowed to stock locally produced or favored merchandise items); (2) whether ties are single (e.g., research universities may be part of a single accrediting system) or multiple (as when universities in the same athletic conference also agree on a no-raiding policy for their academic faculty); (3) whether a single organization in the network begins to assume control over others through its unique access to valued resources (as when a teaching-research hospital is taken as a prestige model by other hospitals, which may then seek to purchase complex diagnostic equipment that seriously strains their financial resources); and (4) whether there develops an administrative structure that effectively knits the network together through authoritative control (as illustrated in Stern's 1979 study of the evolution of the National Collegiate Athletic Association from a loose voluntary confederation of universities to one that determines access to the Olympics for college athletes, sets the terms for football bowl games participation, imposes fines, and in effect controls intercollegiate athletics).

The primary social *process* through which interorganizational linkages form is believed to be some form of *social exchange*. Most analyses (e.g., classic studies by Blau, 1964; Homans, 1974) build on a fundamental study by Emerson (1962), who analyzed exchange in terms of the twin variables of power and dependence. The basic ideas can be laid out as follows.

Organizations establish links by exchanging information, personnel, funds, equipment, and other needed inputs, all of which we call, for short, "resources" (Levine & White, 1961). The process is illustrated in Figure 10-2.

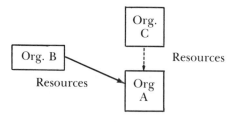

**FIGURE 10-2.  Power-dependence relationships.**

If we regard Organization A as the "focal organization" (meaning simply the organization we are paying attention to), then we ask where it obtains its needed resources. If it obtains them from B, then Emerson concludes that Organization A is *dependent* on Organization B, or, obversely, Organization B has *power* over Organization A to the extent that it can withhold those resources or demand special privileges or deference in exchange for them. However, Organization A is less dependent on B to the extent that it can draw on *alternatives* (such as Organization C, connected by a dotted line in Figure 10-2). The more it can do so, the less is Organization B's power over A. In turn, A's dependence on C increases, as does C's power over A. If A can draw on both B and C or play off one against the other, then more complicated power plays become possible. The model assumes a freedom to negotiate among organizations, and therefore holds constant legal or other controls that may affect such freedom. For example, Organization B might wish to take advantage of its power over A to force it to merge with it, but it might be constrained by legal regulations against such mergers (e.g., antimonopoly laws).

Although simple in concept, the model rapidly becomes complex as we investigate ways in which one organization seeks power over another by increasing dependence or by seeking to restrict the other organization's freedom to seek alternatives. In turn, organizations seek to reduce their dependence by trying to *do without* the needed resource or by keeping their options open by *seeking alternatives*.

Let us look briefly at each of these possibilities. We will make use of examples from interpersonal relationships (as well as interorganizational relationships), since they often illustrate the point we are making and can be applied directly to organizations.

### Interorganization Strategy 1: Doing Without

The strategy of doing without is illustrated by consumer boycotts, as when labor unions in the California agricultural market sought to get people to stop buying California grapes or lettuce. This strategy has an august history and much sanction in philosophy, witness the appeals of Thoreau and others who advocated simple living by reducing one's dependence on the products of complex organizations. It is part of the appeal of communes, which not only make their members do without things because of the usual inefficiency of their production methods, but turn such inefficiency into a positive virtue. The leaders claim that *consumption* is evil, that the automobile, for example, is simply not worth what it costs in lives and pollution as well as in the worker degradation that goes into producing it. The result is a denigration of production itself.

Doing without has been a major approach of some of the world's great religions, as in the case of monasticism, and of revolutionary ideologies that seek to wean people from an existing government by reducing their dependence on its goods and services. It is not surprising that revolutionary movements are often ascetic, as in preindependence India, where Gandhi sought to weaken British power by encouraging Indians to become less dependent on it as well as less awed by the pomp and glory that England represented.

In the face of such attempts to get people to do without organizational products and services, organizations take countermoves. For example, commercial firms seek to bind customers to them by service policies on goods they sell and by encouraging the use of credit cards. In turn, once people get accustomed to carrying less money, they become more and more dependent on their credit cards. The use of nonstandard parts and fittings in military hardware may be important in binding client organizations to military suppliers. In a related maneuver, a giant manufacturer of computers and word-processors may seek to dominate a market by offering a basic unit which is not compatible with those of potential competitors, forcing purchasers to make use of the giant's peripheral equipment. In turn, competitors may retaliate by making sure their peripheral equipment *is* compatible with that of the giant.

Firms seek to encourage materialistic values in their employees by such devices as offering them discounts on company products or incentive systems that pay off in trips to Bermuda or Acapulco. So, too, celebration of patriotic ideals in annual ceremonies helps to fortify the power of established governments, and the belief in the value of a church's blessings helps to strengthen the power of church officials.

Doing without as a strategy is less common in interorganizational relations than in organization-person relationships, since organizations simply cannot function without funds, information, and other resources. One form organizational doing without does take is the decision to phase out products or portions of the organization that represent potential threats (as when one company decided to cease manufacturing napalm because of public protests, concluding that the loss of revenue was more than offset by the gains in public acceptability). Doing without is also seen in decisions of firms to eliminate union dependencies by moving operations to a nonunion region (such as some parts of the U.S. South) or even to foreign countries, where the firm often gets to do without legal or other governmental controls.

The special conditions under which health agencies can do without coordinating agencies is examined in a study by Litwak and Hylton (1966). Community Chests emerged because all local agencies found they had to raise funds and believed it would be to their mutual benefit to prevent repetitive calls by clients on the same fund sources. However, they were not equally dependent on the Community Chest. Some, such as Catholic social-work agencies, cooperated with other agencies but refused to join Community Chests unless they eliminated Planned Parenthood groups. Others, such as some national cancer associations, already had a dependable national market (because of the general public's fear of cancer) and thus had no need to participate in local Community Chests. A partial situation existed for many Jewish agencies, which participated in the local Community Chest for family and recreational programs, but conducted their own campaigns on issues addressed to the national Jewish constituency, such as research on anti-Semitism or aid to Israel.

In all these cases, the local Community Chest persisted because it served some important interdependency needs. However, the Social Service Exchange suffered a different fate. This organization was common at a time when social-work agencies gave out money, clothing, housing, food, and other material goods to needy clients. It was clearly necessary to have a coordinating agency to prevent clients from receiving duplicate allotments from different agencies—hence the Social Service Exchange. But in the 1930s, when the federal government took over most material assistance programs, the private social-work agencies turned their attention to psychiatric casework. The latter required little if any communication among agencies, since clients were unlikely to seek duplication of such services, and whatever information that was necessary could be secured directly from the client. For these reasons, then, agencies found they could do without the Social Service Exchanges, with the result that the number of such exchanges declined precipitously.

### Interorganizational Strategy 2: Seeking Alternatives

The other strategy available to organizations that desire to reduce their dependence on other organizations, and hence the power of such organizations over them, is to seek to shift their patronage elsewhere—that is, to seek alternatives. Whether an organization can do so depends on three major factors: (1) whether an alternative in fact exists; (2) how much, if any, information the organization has about alternatives and how reliable that information is; and (3) the costs of making a shift.

1. In the case of public utilities that supply power to cities, it may be possible to respond to threatened coal miners' strikes by shifting from coal to oil or gas. Many utilities did shift to oil when oil was cheap, and it is noteworthy that there followed a long period of relative labor peace in coal mining, with few of the strikes that seemed almost endemic to the industry when John L. Lewis headed the mineworkers' union. When oil prices rose to the point where the digging of coal in marginal fields became feasible, utilities considered shifting back, and interestingly, there was an upsurge in militancy on the part of coal miners.

Another example of alternatives is the relationship of the United Automobile Workers to the three major automakers. Here a single union confronted three automakers, which were forbidden, by antimonopoly laws, to cooperate in dealing with the union. The union would deal with one company at a time, often choosing the one in the weakest position, say when it was tooling up for production of new-model cars. When such a company gave in to union demands to prevent an interruption in production, the settlement would become the pattern that other companies were told they must follow. In this instance, the manufacturers had no alternative so long as unionization of autoworkers was nearly universal. But the picture changed when German and Japanese imports offered serious competition to American auto manufacturers. The auto companies still had no alternatives, but the buyer did, and this weakened both the companies *and* the unions' control of the market. One result has been the nearly unprecedented acceptance of wage and benefit reductions ("givebacks") in union settlements in order to help the companies compete. It should also be pointed out that (as of this writing) the companies are seeking other alternatives by establishing joint operations with foreign car manufacturers— resulting, in some cases, in "job exporting," much to the chagrin of the autoworkers.

2. Alternatives may exist, but organizations may not have reliable information about them. In the case of relations between organizations and their individual clients, a striking illustration is provided by students and universities. The universities obtain information about prospective students by requiring them to take nationally standardized tests, such as the Scholastic Aptitude Test, the Graduate Record Examination, and other special exams required for admission to law or medical school. This information is reliable, having gone through careful methodological screening by scientific survey organizations. But students, on their side, have only such sources as university catalogues, which, not surprisingly, are full of attractive pictures and broad statements of little practical value. Some volumes of references, such as *Barron's Profiles of American Colleges* and the *International Handbook of Universities,* offer better information, but even they depend largely on what information the universities are willing to supply, and they tell little about informal relations, student culture, and other factors that affect the student's experience and success.

Another example that has been much talked about in recent years is the proposal to increase the freedom of choice of parents by not requiring that they register their children in the local public school, but instead offering them vouchers ("good for 1 year's education") that they can present to the school of their choice (Cohen & Farrar, 1977). Although the matter is controversial for many reasons—not least among them the danger that schools will develop public relations staffs to "peddle" themselves in the manner of toothpaste and deodorants—one problem has been the unavailability (to parents) of reliable information on schools. The scheme, though given much publicity and some testing, has not met with general public acceptance.

Organizations will, as indicated in the case of university student testing, usually have much better information sources. Divisions of research and marketing will be assigned to secure data on other organizations. Often organizations will establish exclusive relationships with sources of supply, or insist on exclusive treatment of their merchandise in department stores. In addition, corporate inspectors or other field staff will generate continuous information on whether such exclusive contracts are being honored.

3. An organization (or person) cannot take advantage of an alternative if the cost of shifting is too high. The invention of the corporation made the ability of stockholders to shift to other corporations practically cost-free (little more than brokers' fees). Further, information on shares traded on the major stock exchanges is so widely available, carefully monitored, and standardized that the cost of gathering it has been greatly reduced. One result is that when the representative of one company serves on the board of directors of another, and that director discovers that the company is in difficulty, he is likely to quickly urge his own company to sell its shares rather than to try to modify the behavior of the directed company. Such behavior helps ensure the independence of managers of firms from the outside members of their boards of directors, further contributing to their autonomy.

In this connection, Coleman (1974) makes an interesting observation. He sees a business as operating in four markets: a capital market, a raw materials market, a labor market, and a product market for customers, as illustrated in Figure 10-3.

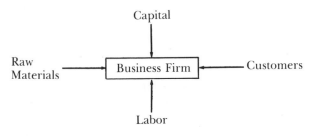

**FIGURE 10-3.  Business markets.**

A power-dependence analysis suggests the following: The owners (the stockholders), who make up the capital market, have power because they can shift their ownership quickly by selling their stock. The result is that the business firm is beholden to them and dependent on pleasing them. The suppliers of raw materials can often shift their business to other companies (in the absence of exclusive contracts), and therefore the business firm has an incentive to pay them good prices to keep them from shifting. In the case of unionized industries, the workers will be unified and kept productive through high wages. The only unit without power, then, is likely to be the customers, who are attracted by advertising and salesmanship. The arrangement will benefit owners, suppliers, stockholders, and sometimes workers, with the firm having the least incentive to please the customer, especially in large oligopolistic industries, where customers (including other firms) have little choice. The result, writes Coleman (1974), is:

> the curious paradox of increasing incomes and increasing wealth, on the one hand, and an increasingly shoddy set of things on which to spend that wealth. (pp. 61–62)*

Where the customer is another organization, however, as when a manufacturer sells its output (such as automobile batteries) to another manufacturer (an automobile manufacturer), then information is likely to be much more reliable, owing to inspection and testing of completed products, as well as the existence of a regularized relationship that the supplier is motivated to continue. Such a relationship, in turn, may provide an incentive for the two firms to merge in order to assure the regularity of the supply.

The role of alternatives as a factor determining interorganizational power is examined by Randall (1973) in a study of the response of the Wisconsin State Employment Service to a shift from its usual general job placement mandate to a focus on human resource development. This policy change was a deliberate charge to reach the disadvantaged, improve their employability, help develop suitable jobs for them (employers were even urged to redesign jobs for this purpose), and follow up the experience of clients in job situations. Two major factors affected experience: the size of firms in the district, and the presence or absence of community action agencies. The Employment Service met with a much better response in districts with small firms than it did in those with large firms. Large firms were much less dependent on the Employment Service for personnel. They had their own personnel divisions, which performed all the activities that the Employment Service did (such as recruiting, testing, and screening), and since they usually paid higher wages, they could afford to be choosy about whom they hired. When badgered by the Employment Service, their reaction was, if anything, to increase their independent activities, particularly since they firmly believed that such criteria as the disadvantaged lack (education, maturity, etc.) were essential for employment success. On the other hand, small employers could not afford their own employment services, and thus were inclined to cooperate with the Employment Service, particularly since they paid lower wages to begin with and had always hired the disadvantaged anyhow.

The other factor affecting success was the presence of a community action agency that competed for the same clients as did the Employment Service. In fact, since the community action agency's major activity was often job finding, it saw the Employment Service as a stodgy, overly bureaucratized, agency that could not handle its new human resource devel-

---

*Reprinted with permission of publisher, W. W. Norton and Co., Inc.

opment role. In turn, the Employment Service offices in districts that contained such agencies increased their activity levels substantially. Thus the presence of a competing agency gave the *client* (the disadvantaged person) alternative agencies to choose between, which led both agencies to "court" him or her. Whether such competition is, on balance, desirable (perhaps a cooperative attitude and a division of labor might have served the disadvantaged even better), the reality is that interorganizational power largely determines the distribution of resources to both organizations and their clients.

Other analysts have sought to trace more complex interorganizational relationships.[14] For example, Turk (1977) focuses on the city as a location in which interorganizational relationships can be examined. The physical proximity of organizations will have some influence on their willingness to establish linkages with one another. However, Turk takes the view that whether organizations will work together or conflict depends on the kind of municipal government that exists and the extent of citywide consensual voluntary associations. For example, he finds that the correlation between the need for funds for the poor (or for hospitals) and the likelihood that a Model Cities network (or a hospital council) will be established is greater in cities where city governments are larger and more diversified and the voluntary associations are consensual than in cities where city government is not diversified and voluntary associations are absent. In some sense, then, organizations "use" the kind of government or voluntary associations available to establish coalitions or coordinate efforts.

One of the most widely cited examples of interorganizational linkage has attracted attention from a policy standpoint because of concern for control of corporate behavior and the public interest. We refer to corporate interlocks (Pennings, 1980; Mariolis & Jones, 1982), meaning when managers or directors serve on one another's boards of directors (a direct interlock) or when two representatives of different corporations both serve on the board of a third corporation (indirect interlocks). Such ties were objects of suspicion at least since their condemnation by (later) Supreme Court Justice Brandeis (1933, p. 35). Although the subject is highly controversial and a favorite of radical critics, the evidence is far from clear, perhaps because it is not easy to collect data. Among the largest corporations, either financial or nonfinancial, around 80 percent or more of the directors are directors of a single corporation only, and only from 10 to 13 percent are on the boards of as many as two corporations. Further, there is evidence that among the largest companies, the number of interlocks has steadily declined, at least since the passage of the Clayton Act (1914), which restricted such interlocks (Bunting & Barbour, 1971). Nevertheless, in some industries, the proportion of such interlocks is very high, and they are found in the largest corporations. Dooley (1969), who examined the top 250, and Mariolis (1975), who examined the top 797 (compiled from various FORTUNE magazine lists), report average numbers of interlocks from eight to ten. When Herman (1981) collected data on oil companies and compared them to a "control group" (a random sample of 20 of the 200 largest nonoil companies), he found many more interlocks as well as other kinds of linkages among oil companies (Table 10-1).

Besides direct and indirect interlocks, there are joint ventures, a major form of organization in the oil and gas industries (as well as the iron and steel, mining, and chemical industries). In a joint venture, two or more companies pool expenses for exploration, research, or common bidding to a government, and share the subsequent revenues. These are certainly cosy relationships (Herman calls them "quasi-mergers"). Although they are of questionable legality, governments may actively encourage them, as the U.S. government did in the mid-1920s, when it helped Exxon and Mobil gain access to the Iran Petroleum Company for strategic reasons and because of the fear of oil shortages, even though the joint venture was incompatible with antitrust law principles. In the 1960s and later, Exxon and Royal Dutch/Shell were joint participants in over 150 ventures outside the United States, and most other oil companies were involved in many other kinds of joint ventures that had the obvious effects of monopolizing or controlling some sector of an economy or critical supply lines. Table 10-1 lists other kinds of linkages, such as a common investment bank, major club memberships, and common legal counsel.

It is impossible to "prove" that such ties add up to a conspiracy or other nefarious plan, but the number of these linkages among the oil companies is very much larger than found in the "control group." Considering the Classical interest in interlocks, it is interesting that the dominant form of tie is the joint venture and common membership on federal advisory bodies. Researchers would seem to be advised to pay greater attention to such ties. On the other hand, those who wish to make a case that intercorporate ties are *not* important might take some comfort from the fact that Herman found *comparatively* few such ties in the 20 large corporations that made up his "control group." Perhaps the problem of intercorporate ties is largely confined to the oil industry though we are inclined to doubt it (see Whitt, 1981).

## PREDICTING INTERCORPORATE LINKAGES: THE ROLE OF CONCENTRATION

Such figures as we have been quoting are, unfortunately, patchy, and we would wish for more systematic and inclusive analyses. Pfeffer and Salancik (1978) offer a highly suggestive hypothesis about the process that motivates organizations to establish ties with one another, and then test the hypothesis with data on mergers, interlocks, and joint ventures. They hypothesize

**TABLE 10-1  Interlocks and Other Ties Among 20 Oil Company Majors and Among a 20-Company Control Sample of Large Corporations, 1975**

| TYPE OF LINKAGE | OIL COMPANY PAIRS CONNECTED BY PARTICULAR LINKAGE (190 POSSIBLE TIES) | | CONTROL COMPANY PAIRS CONNECTED BY PARTICULAR LINKAGE (190 POSSIBLE TIES) | | TOTAL OIL COMPANY TIES | | TOTAL CONTROL COMPANY TIES | |
|---|---|---|---|---|---|---|---|---|
| | (1) NO. | (2) % OF 190 | (3) NO. | (4) % OF 190 | (5) NO. | (6) % OF TOTAL* | (7) NO. | (8) % OF TOTAL* |
| Direct interlock | 0 | 0 | 6 | 3.2 | 0 | 0 | 6 | .9 |
| Indirect interlock | 46 | 24.2 | 79 | 41.6 | 70 | 5.2 | 114 | 17.8 |
| Major joint venture | 106 | 55.8 | 0 | 0 | 254 | 18.8 | 0 | 0 |
| Minor joint venture | 176 | 92.6 | 1 | 0.5 | 2,501 | 0 | 1 | 0 |
| Common auditor | 27 | 14.2 | 21 | 11.1 | 27 | 2.0 | 21 | 3.3 |
| Common investment bank | 42 | 22.1 | 40 | 21.1 | 42 | 3.1 | 41 | 6.4 |
| Common representation on federal advisory board | 190 | 100.0 | 52 | 27.4 | 697 | 51.5 | 94 | 14.7 |
| Common major club membership | 135 | 71.1 | 172 | 90.5 | 354 | 0 | 447 | 0 |
| Common representation on nongovernment advisory or research body | 112 | 58.9 | 128 | 67.4 | 263 | 19.4 | 364 | 56.9 |
| Common legal counsel | 0 | 0 | 0 | 0 | 0 | 0 | | |
| Common major ownership of voting stock | 0 | 0 | 0 | 0 | 0 | 0 | | |
| Total no. of ties | | | | | 4,208 | 100.0 | 1,088 | 100.0 |
| Mean no. of ties | | | | | 210.4 | | 54.5 | |
| Total minus clubs | | | | | 3,854 | | 641 | |
| Mean (minus clubs) | | | | | 192.7 | | 32.1 | |
| Total minus clubs and minor joint ventures | | | | | 1,353 | | 640 | |
| Mean (minus clubs and minor joint ventures) | | | | | 67.7 | | 32.0 | |

*Total ties minus clubs and minor joint ventures.

From: Edward S. Herman, *Corporate Control, Corporate Power*, a Twentieth Century Fund Study. Copyright © 1981 by the Twentieth Century Fund, Inc. Table 6.7, p. 209.

that the amount of interorganizational linkage will exhibit an inverted U-shaped relationship, being low when there are either very many firms in an industry or very few, and high when the concentration is moderate, as shown in Figure 10-4. The argument is that when there are a great many organizations in a field or industry, no one or small group can much affect the industry and therefore there is little point in seeking linkages or ties. Also, when there are very few organizations, they are highly visible to one another and can tacitly take one another into account without having to establish direct ties (which, in any case, are often forbidden by law). In a familiar process known as "price leadership" or "parallel pricing," a large steel company, for example, will announce that it is raising the price of certain grades of steel. The announcement functions as a "market signal" (Spence, 1974) to other large steel companies, which then consider whether to raise their prices to the same level. If they follow suit, prices have been raised without any direct ties. If they do not, then the first company lowers its price back to what it was, thus again coordinating action without direct contact.

On the other hand, when there are just enough organizations to make linkage worth engaging in, we may expect them to be common. Pfeffer's (1972) data on mergers in manufacturing support the hypothesis, as does Pfeffer and Salancik's study (1978, p. 166) of officer and director interlocks in competing firms in the same industry. Finally, Pfeffer and Nowak (1976) report further confirming data for joint ventures among firms in the same industry.[15]

Since interlocks and similar ties are often illegal, we would expect that the U-shaped argument might also predict corporate crime, particularly antitrust violations. Indeed, a number of studies do support this argument. Burton (1966) found that firms in the intermediate range of size concentration had the greatest number of penalized antitrust violations. On the other hand, Hay and Kelley (1974), in a study of 62 price-fixing cases, found that the highest proportion of conspiracies occurred in *highly* concentrated industries (rather than in the moderate range), while Posner

**FIGURE 10-4. Industrial concentration and intercorporate linkages.**

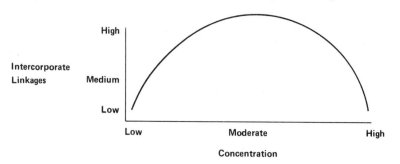

(1970) found no significant relationship between concentration and antitrust activity over a 79-year period. Such a mix of findings is not surprising because many factors other than firm concentration enter into figures on penalization for antitrust violations. An obvious one is the decision of government agencies to prosecute some firms and not others (often an agency is willing to settle for a plea of *nolo contendere* and a promise to cease future violations rather than face a criminal suit, which requires proof "beyond a reasonable doubt"). In addition, other features of the environment, such as scarce resources, may lead organizations to take chances that get them into trouble (e.g., Staw & Szwajkowski, 1975; Gross, 1979; Vaughan, 1980; Mars, 1982). Still, as suggested by Clinard and Yeager (1980), interorganizational ties provide a potentially fruitful area of research for students of corporate crime.

## STRATEGIC CHOICE THROUGH INTERORGANIZATIONAL NETWORKS

In recent years, another approach to strategic control has been explored—the invention of *networks* (Cook, 1977). That is, some organizations have sought to control their organizational environment by stimulating or forming networks of various kinds, and then seeking control of the network, or at least the establishment of norms and "rules of the game" for all the network's members. Research on such networks builds on earlier studies of networks among *persons,* where the interest was in whether some networks were more efficient as work groups than others. Classic studies by Bavelas (1951), for example, isolated experimental subjects in cubicles, wherein their ability to pass information to one another about solutions to simple problems was controlled by different networks. "Circle" and "all-channel" networks were relatively decentralized, since all persons shared in processing information; whereas a "wheel" required information from the other persons to pass through a central person, and thus was centralized. In general, it was found that centralized networks are more efficient (because they process information more rapidly and with less cost, and because they impose an obvious organization on the group). However, other researchers have reported that decentralized organizations do better with more complex tasks and those requiring innovation and creativity (see Blau & Scott, 1962).

The same kind of thinking led to work on relationships among organizations, but networks of the Bavelas kind were not found, which led to studies of more complex networks. For example, Tichy, Tushman, and Fombrun (1979)[16] suggest that relationships can be characterized by the following dimensions: size (number of organizations in the network), density (number of links as a proportion of possible links), clustering (number of dense regions), centrality (whether one or a group of organizations dominates), stability (degree to which the network keeps its shape or endures), presence of stars, bridges, gatekeepers, and isolates. Similarly, Aldrich (1979) calls attention to the special role of "linking pin organizations" (such as coordinating bodies), and of factors that act to stabilize networks, such as dependence, resource control, and what he calls "multiplexity" (redundancy of relationships—the more ties, the more stable the network). However, these works are speculative[17] and have not stimulated any substantial amount of field research. Although some studies are certainly suggestive (e.g., Clark's 1965 study of how a committee of science teachers came together to form a research innovation arm of the textbook industry, or Becker's 1970 study of the adoption of measles immunization and diabetes-screening programs by state health departments), it remains uncertain how network analysis in the formal sense, or at the theoretical level, might contribute to further research. One problem is that interorganizational networks are often unstable, consisting as they do of coalitions formed for limited purposes over short periods of time (as in a joint venture). When the venture is completed, either the network breaks up, or some of the organizations stay in it only for a brief period.

One kind of network that offers interesting possibilities has been called the "organization set." As first introduced by Evan (1966, 1976), the concept (drawing on Merton's work on role sets) referred to the other organizations with which a particular organization ("the focal organization") exchanged persons, information, or products or services. Those from whom the organization received those resources were called the "input set"; those to whom the organization delivered its outputs (products, information, etc.) were dubbed the "output set." Evan offered hypotheses, such as: "the higher the concentration of input organizational resources, the lower the degree of autonomy in decision-making of the focal organization"; and "the greater the size of the organization set, the lower the decision-making autonomy of the focal organization" (illustrated in coalitions, as, for example, when a large trade association of California druggists organized a boycott against a major toothpaste manufacturer which had withdrawn its support of "fair-trade" contracts with the druggists).

A quite different use of the term *organizational set* is offered by Caplow (1964, Chap. 6), to refer to organizations of a given type that are visible to one another. Examples include the psychology departments at major universities in a country (or in the world), the Methodist churches in a moderate-sized city in the United States, the football clubs in Melbourne, Australia, or in Rio de Janeiro, Brazil, the manufacturers of tires for automobiles or the symphony orchestras in urbanized countries. The striking fact about such sets is that they are *stratified,* often in regularized patterns. Certain psychology departments, for example, are freely conceded to be "better" than others in productivity or training of students, some football clubs are richer or more prestigious than others, eight firms account for over half the production of rubber tires in the United States, Canada, and the United Kingdom, and certain symphony orchestras are usually conceded to be the "top" orchestras by both players and listeners. Organizations at the top act as models for, or even control, those further down.

Moreover, the stratification is often clustered. Thus, in the United States, a tiny group of universities seem to be qualitatively different from those further down. They hire one another's graduates and form almost a caste. The next level down, while clearly major universities, attract less able students, and their faculties are often quite responsive to the "call" from the top layer. In turn, these universities may offer striking rewards (such as distinguished professorships) to attract major figures from the top universities. Still further down are universities whose goals seem to be different from those of the top two levels; they emphasize local service to the community and the importance of teaching and student contact. There may also be a fourth level of marginal institutions in continuing danger of losing their accreditation. Different clusters characterize small liberal arts colleges, denominational colleges, state colleges, and more specialized teaching institutions. Another kind of stratification occurs in sports leagues (Gross, 1979), where there may be major leagues, minor leagues, bush leagues, and what is sometimes called "Siberia." Often these leagues form themselves into cartels in order to control the available talent, bring order into contests, and make sure that games are worth seeing (that is, involve opponents of roughly equal ability, because otherwise a game is of little spectator interest).

During the late 1890s, a series of mergers consolidated more than 200 formerly independent iron and steel makers into 20 much larger rival entities. Most of the new firms were confined to only a few facets of steel making, but after their formation many mapped out programs of integrating vertically to cover the whole spectrum from ore mining through fabrication. Charles Schwab, then president of Carnegie Steel, foresaw that this would lead to excess capacity and sharp price competition. He communicated his views to J. P. Morgan, who organized a merger among 12 of the prior consolidations. (For his labor, he realized promotional profits estimated at $62.5 million.) The end product was U.S. Steel, which at the time of its creation controlled roughly 65 percent of all domestic blast furnaces and finished steel output.

The present situation is not so concentrated but there is still a clustering, with some firms in the big leagues. For example, in 1977 the four largest firms in the category "Blast Furnaces and Steel Mills" accounted for 45 percent of the value of shipments, and 8 firms accounted for the next 20 percent. Forty-two firms shared the next 30 percent, and 345 "Bush League" steel firms divided up the remaining 5 percent. Here are some other examples (the figures are from the Bureau of the Census, *1977*

*Census of Manufactures,* 1981): In "Photographic Equipment," the top four firms accounted for 72 percent of value, leaving 698 others to divide up the rest. In "Tires and Inner Tubes," the top four companies took care of 70 percent of value, leaving the remaining 30 percent to 117 other firms. In "Soaps and Detergents," the top four absorbed 59 percent, leaving 41 percent for 551 other firms. Other industries are not so concentrated (e.g., in "Radio and TV Communications Equipment," the top four firms account for only 20 percent of value, and "Pharmaceuticals" (surprisingly) comes out with a top-four concentration of 24 percent). Some industries are actually quite fragmented (in these terms): In "Commercial Printing: lithographic," seven machine products in the top four account for only 6 percent.[18]

The tendency is for the market to get broken up into segments, with strong product differentiation and varying degrees of vertical integration, or into clusters in which firms are in what might be called different leagues. A small steel firm does not try to compete with U.S. Steel or Bethlehem Steel. It must be content to produce a special type of steel for a special market in which it enjoys acceptance. So, too, Control Data treads carefully in the mainframe computer market, which is dominated by IBM; it finds the going easier in the highly sophisticated market represented by the universities and the government space programs. Firms, like teams, are careful not to take on opponents out of their league (although in business, unlike sports, the elite "teams" do not exhibit any reluctance to clobber the minor league "teams," unless constrained by antitrust laws.) So, too, in hiring and in recruiting students, universities will usually stay in their "league," seeking a different function or goal (e.g., a liberal arts college may send its outstanding graduates on to a distinguished research university), a different market (state universities depend on legislatures as opposed to student fees for funds), and often different sources for their faculties (community colleges are often reluctant to hire PhDs from universities, finding such persons too "stuck up" and inappropriately socialized for the jobs they will be expected to carry out in such colleges).[19] In this way, colleges monopolize and control access, determine standards, and, in effect, dominate their educational niche.

## CONCLUDING COMMENT

Whatever the future of network analysis, there seem to be very bright prospects for interorganizational studies and for the further exploration of the ways in which environments and organizations interpenetrate. What, then, of the question to which we addressed ourselves at the beginning of this chapter: Do organizations react to or do they control their environments? Occasional examples may, of course, be found at both extremes.

Small shops exhibit high mortality in the face of arduous economic circumstances, and giants sometimes do fall (as have most railroads, for example). Even a firm like Chrysler found itself requiring government assistance. On the other hand, a few organizations seem to totally dominate their environments; public utilities in some states, IBM in the mainframe computer market, and, of course, government-supported monopolies in many countries. Still, even where organizations are free to deal with one another, the evidence generally seems to support the claim that they do effectively control their environments. Their strategies do not always work, but they are getting better all the time. One contributor to their power is surely social science itself, which produces a continuing outpouring of findings on organizational behavior. Does this mean that the study of organizations is a "science"? That is certainly the goal of organizational researchers, and so far the results encourage continued effort.

Yet a final question remains: If organizations do dominate or control their environments, that may be good news for stockholders and managers, but does it mean that the consumer is well served? We earlier cited an analysis that suggested the opposite. The consumer is dispersed, has little market power, and often receives inadequate information. So the consumer—whether customer, client, student, hospital patient, or simply member of the "public"—may not be well served by the organization's domination of its environment.

And what of the member of the organization below the managerial level—the low-level supervisor, the workers, the laboratory assistants, the teachers, the employees generally? As we saw in earlier chapters, they are often powerless in large organizations. There are efforts to increase their participation, but the movement in that direction has been slow.

In the end, then, we are left with the question of how the individual can control the outputs of organizations, as well as his own career and fate within the organization. Perhaps the only way to control organizations is for people to form their own organization, such as consumer organizations. But that requires resources, education, energy, and, above all, organizational know-how. Still, it is far from impossible, and the increasing role of the large organization and of its interrelationships with other organizations strongly suggests that we must learn not only how organizations work—the concern of this book—but also how to form effective organizations of our own.

## NOTES

1. These figures are drawn from the following sources: U.S. Department of Commerce, 1980; U.S. Department of Commerce, 1972, Table 5; Department of Health, Education and Welfare, 1976, p. 105; Warner and others, 1967, p. 290; U.S. Department of Justice,

1975, pp. 26–27; Yearbook of American and Canadian Churches, 1977, pp. 233–240; Hospital Statistics, 1977 Edition, pp. 10–11, Table 3; Bureau of Labor Statistics, 1974.

2. It is important not to exaggerate the dominance of large corporations. For example, Herman (1981, Table 6.2, p. 191) draws together data on concentration from 1909 to 1975, showing that the 200 largest nonfinancial corporations in the U.S. accounted for between a low of 33 percent and a high of 57 percent of assets of all nonfinancial corporations (the 57 percent figure was for 1933—it was 34.9 percent in 1975). The figures for sales were considerably lower. But the extent of concentration remains controversial and a never-ending source of debate. For example, some recent discussions (with data) where conclusions are often very different, include: Mintz and Schwartz, 1981; McCaffrey, 1982; Allen and Panian, 1982; Kerbo and Fave, 1983; Freitag, 1983.

Further, such concentration is uneven. In 1975, large firms (defined as those with assets of $250 million or more) controlled less than one third of the assets in agriculture, construction, trade, and services. But such firms did control more than half the assets in mining, manufacturing, transport and utilities, and banking and finance. The latter four industries together accounted for 45.6 percent of the national income. Concentration seems especially large in manufacturing, but U.S. figures are actually lower than those for many other industrialized countries.

3. Some examples: Inland Steel has 18 million shares outstanding among 69,000 stockholders; Weyerhauser Lumber has 60 million shares and 29,000 stockholders, Ford Motor Company, 108 million shares and 382,000 stockholders. The largest privately held firm is American Telephone and Telegraph with over half a billion shares and 3 million stockholders. (These figures are for the mid-70's.) Further, such dispersal of ownership has increased over the last 45 years. The modal category was 5,000–19,999 shareholders in 1929. By 1974, the model was 50,000–99,999 shareholders (Herman, 1981, p. 21).

4. There is variation in choice of terms. For example, Schmidt and Kochan (1977) distinguish between *power-dependency* approaches (those that emphasize the domination of one organization over others) and *exchange* approaches (in which there is "mutual benefit"). Both, it seems to us, involve questions of strategic choice, though how equal or unequal the resulting relationship among organizations might be is an empirical question. Pfeffer (1982) uses the term *resource dependence* theory in much the same way as we use strategic choice.

5. Lammers and Hickson (1979, Chapter 22) claim support for a typology of organizational forms ("Latin," "Anglo-Saxon," and "Third World" or traditional) that they believe are revealed by cross-cultural studies.

6. Such correlations are often carried out with path analysis, which leads directly to conclusions on causation. For example, a study by Meyer and Brown (1977) of the formal structure of 229 city, county, and state finance agencies reports that time of origin, environment, and other structural features are related. But the conclusion, after the statistical evidence is presented, goes much further than simply claiming that a "relationship" exists: "A causal chain from origins (that is, time of origin) and the environment to formalization to hierarchy to decentralization is thus posited" (p. 384).

7. Galbraith (1973, 1977) gives an "information-processing" view of the theory. Under conditions of greater task uncertainty, more information must be processed internally, which affects the degree of specialization, decentralization, and other structural features.

8. A general argument to this effect is offered in a theoretical paper by Meyer and Rowan (1977). Basically they contend that organizations (especially those subject to direct legitimization by influential constituencies) will exhibit rules and structure that are institutionalized—that is, *considered* essential—whatever their actual operational effects might be. So a hospital will have an intensive care unit for newborn babies at least partly because a modern, effective hospital *should* have such a unit. So, too, a university of high quality must maintain "appropriate" departments, whatever the enrollments may be. Such activity, Meyer and Rowan say, has "ritual significance." As to how organizations actually perform, they believe that actual operations are "decoupled" from the rationalized myths used to justify the claimed operations. Goals are kept deliberately ambiguous or vacuous, and inspection and evaluation are "ceremonialized."

9. Scott (1981, p. 204) draws a similar conclusion, namely, that natural selection perspectives work better with small organizations, and resource dependency perspectives (discussed below) with larger and more powerful organizations.

10. Hannan and Freeman (1984) defend population-ecology theory against the charge that it applies mainly to small organizations by showing that it can also explain why large organizations survive better than small ones. They show the result to be partly a matter of *structural inertia* (the ability to reproduce structure) and partly a matter of age (large organizations often being older). On the other hand, Starbuck (1983) denies that large organizations do actually survive better, thus raising the question of what it is that is being explained. Clearly, we are not at the end of this discussion.

11. The exceptions were resourcefulness (richness of the environment as measured by average income, balance in bank accounts, and amount of donations to the local United Fund), and complexity (diversity of various kinds of stock brokerage transactions).

12. For example, in another study, Hirsch (1975) compares pharmaceutical manufacturing firms with phonograph record companies over a 15-year period (1950–1965). Both seek to control three aspects of their environment: pricing and distribution, patent and copyrights, and external leadership. But in this case, the record companies are found to be much less effective in such control, and therefore much less profitable. Similarly, Meyer (1982), in a study of how hospitals in the San Francisco Bay area coped with what he calls an environmental "jolt" (a surgeons' strike), found *some* were badly hurt (by a reduction in income), and others were able to weather the storm by drawing on financial reserves, reducing staffs, and centralizing power, or by offering diversified services less dependent on surgical admissions. So even in cases of "jolts," a reaction model tells us little about how organizations handle their environments.

13. The description of such networks had attracted the attention of some mathematically inclined students, e.g., Galaskiewicz and Marsen, 1978; Laumann and Pappi, 1976.

14. Such complex interorganizational models are described in theoretical works by Benson (1975), Hall, Clark, Giordano, Johnson, and Van Roekel (1977), and Burt (1980).

15. In a summary of data, Pfeffer (1982, pp. 201–202), good scientist that he is, reports other studies that offer inconsistent or nonsupporting data for the hypothesis. However, the studies cited suggest less that the hypothesis is wrong than that further specification as to detail is necessary.

16. Tichy, Tushman, and Fombrun (1979) actually offer illustrations from interpersonal interactions. We have adapted these to interorganizational relationships.

17. Which is not to deny that they will prove productive for future research. Some works of considerable mathematical complexity have strong empirical implications, e.g., where there may be theoretical reasons for expecting certain predicted orders of dominance in certain networks, as in Marsden's (1983) criticism of the experimental work on networks done by Cook and Emerson (1978), and Cook et al. (1983).

18. Concentration ratio figures must be handled with caution. They can be affected drastically by how the category is defined (the broader the category, the lower the concentration); by the nature of the product (e.g., ready-mixed concrete shows a low figure because it is too costly to ship it over long distances, but the industry *is* concentrated within local areas; the same is true of newspapers); and by concentrating on domestic production (e.g., auto figures are directly affected if limited to U.S. manufacturing). Still, such ratios are widely used because they are easily available and other, more precise estimates are not. See Scherer, 1980, Chap. 3.

19. But see Morrison and Freedman, 1978, who cast doubt on this claim.

# REFERENCES

ABBOTT, ANDREW, "Professional Ethics," *American Journal of Sociology*, 1983, 88: 855–885.

ABEGGLEN, JAMES C., *The Japanese Factory: Aspects of Its Social Organization.* Glencoe, Ill: 1958.

ABEGGLEN, JAMES C., *Management and Worker: The Japanese Solution,* Tokyo: Sophia University Press, 1973.

ACKER, JOAN, AND DONALD R. VAN HOUTEN, "Differential Recruitment and Control: The Sex Structuring of Organizations," *Administrative Science Quarterly,* 1974, 19: 152–163.

ADAIR, JOHN C., "The Hawthorne Effect: A Reconsideration of the Methodological Artifact," *Journal of Applied Psychology,* 1984, 69: 334–345.

AIKEN, MICHAEL, AND JERALD HAGE, "Organizational Alienation: A Comparative Analysis," *American Sociological Review,* 1966, 31: 497–507.

AIKEN, MICHAEL, AND JERALD HAGE, "Organizational Interdependence and Intraorganizational Structure," *American Sociological Review,* 1968, 33: 912–930.

AKERS, RONALD, NORMAN S. HAYNER, AND WERNER GRUNINGER, "Homosexual and Drug Behavior in Prison: A Test of the Functional and Importation Models of the Inmate System," *Social Problems,* 1974, 21: 410–422.

ALBROW, MARTIN, *Bureaucracy,* New York: Praeger, 1970.

ALDRICH, HOWARD E., "Technology and Organizational Structure: A Reexamination of the Findings of the Aston Group," *Administrative Science Quarterly,* 1972, 17: 26–43.

ALDRICH, HOWARD E., *Organizations and Environments,* Englewood Cliffs, NJ: Prentice-Hall, 1979.

ALDRICH, HOWARD E. AND A. J. REISS, JR., "Police Officers as Boundary Personnel," in H. Hahn (ed.), *The Police in Urban Society,* Beverly Hills, CA: Sage, 1971, pp. 193–208.

ALLEN, MICHAEL PATRICK, AND SHARON K. PANIAN, "Power, Performance, and Succession in the Large Organization," *Administrative Science Quarterly*, 1982, 27: 538–547.

ALLEN, MICHAEL PATRICK, SHARON K. PANIAN, AND ROY E. LOTZ, "Managerial Succession and Organizational Performance: A Recalcitrant Problem Revisited," *Administrative Science Quarterly*, 1979, 24: 167–180.

ALUTTO, JOSEPH A., LAWRENCE G. HREBNIAK, AND RAMON C. ALONZO, "A Study of Differential Socialization for Members of One Professional Occupation," *Journal of Health and Social Behavior*, 1971, 12: 140–147.

ALVESSON, MATS, "The Limits and Shortcomings of Humanistic Organization Theory," *Acta Sociologica*, 1982, 25: 117–141.

ARGYRIS, CHRIS, *Understanding Organizational Behavior*, Homewood, Ill: Dorsey, 1960.

ARGYRIS, CHRIS, "Personality and Organization Theory Revisited," *Administrative Science Quarterly*, 1973, 18: 141–167.

ATHANASIOU, R., "Job Attitudes and Occupational Performance: A Review of Some Important Literature," in J. P. Robinson, R. Athanasiou, and K. B. Head (eds.), *Measurement of Occupational Attitudes and Occupational Characteristics*, Ann Arbor: University of Michigan, Institute for Sociological Research, 1969, pp. 79–98.

ATKINSON, J. M., AND J. HERITAGE, *Order in Court: The Organization of Verbal Interaction in Judicial Settings*, London, Macmillan/SSRC, 1979.

BACHARACH, SAMUEL B., AND EDWARD J. LAWLER, *Power and Politics in Organizations*, San Francisco: Jossey-Bass, 1980.

BACHMAN, JERALD G., AND JOHN D. BLAIR, "'Citizen Force' or 'Career Force'? Implications for Ideology in the All-Volunteer Force," in Nancy L. Goldman and David R. Segal (eds.), *The Social Psychology of Military Service*, Beverly Hills, CA: Sage, 1976, pp. 237–253.

BALDRIDGE, J. VICTOR, AND ROBERT A. BURNHAM, "Organizational Innovation: Individual, Organizational, and Environmental Impacts," *Administrative Science Quarterly*, 1975, 20: 165–176.

BALDWIN, MONICA, *I Leap Over the Wall*, New York: Signet, 1957.

BALES, ROBERT F., "The Equilibrium Problem in Small Groups," in Talcott Parsons, Robert F. Bales, and Edward A. Shils (eds), *Working Papers in the Theory of Action*, Glencoe, Ill: Free Press, 1953.

BARON, JAMES N., AND WILLIAM T. BIELBY, "Bringing the Firm Back. In: Stratification, Segmentation, and the Organization of Work," *American Sociological Review*, 1980, 45: 737–765.

BARRY, BRIAN, *Sociologists, Economists, and Democracy*, Chicago: University of Chicago Press, 1978.

BAUGHER, DAN (ED.), *Measuring Effectiveness*, San Francisco: Jossey-Bass, 1981.

BAVELAS, ALEX, "Communication Patterns in Task-Oriented Groups," in Daniel Lerner and Harold D. Lasswell (eds.), *The Policy Sciences*, Stanford, CA: Stanford University Press, 1951, pp. 193–202.

BECKER, HOWARD S. ET AL., *Boys in White*, Chicago: The University of Chicago Press, 1961.

BECKER, HOWARD S., *Art Worlds*, Berkeley, CA: University of California Press, 1982.

BECKER, MARSHALL H., "Sociometric Location and Innovativeness: Reformation and Extension of the Diffusion Model," *American Sociological Review*, 1970, 35: 267–282.

BENDIX, REINHARD, *Max Weber: An Intellectual Portrait,* Garden City, NY: Doubleday, 1960.

BENDIX, REINHARD, AND LLOYD H. FISHER, "The Perspectives of Elton Mayor," in Amatai Etzioni (ed.), *Complex Organizations: A Sociological Reader,* New York: Holt, Reinhart, and Winston, 1961, pp. 113–126.

BENNETT, H. STITH, *On Becoming a Rock Musician,* Amherst: University of Massachusetts Press, 1980.

BENNETT, W. LANCE, AND MARTHA S. FELDMAN, *Reconstructing Reality in the Courtroom: Justice and Judgment in American Culture,* New Brunswick, NJ: Rutgers University Press, 1981.

BENSMAN, JOSEPH, AND ISRAEL GERVER, "Crime and Punishment in the Factory: The Function of Deviancy in Maintaining the Social System," *American Sociological Review,* 1963, 28: 587–598.

BENSON, J. KENNETH, "The Interorganizational Network as a Political Economy," *Administrative Science Quarterly,* 1975, 20: 229–249.

BENSON, J. KENNETH, "Organizations: A Dialectical View," *Administrative Science Quarterly,* 1977, 22: 1–21.

BERG, IVAR (with assistance of Sherry Gorelick), *Education and Jobs: The Great Training Robbery,* New York: Center for Urban Education by Praeger Pub., 1970.

BERG, IVAR, M. FREEDMAN, AND M. FREEMAN, *Managers and Work Reform: A Limited Engagement,* New York: Free Press, 1978.

BERGER, P. K., AND A. J. GRIMES, "Cosmopolitan-Local: A Factor Analysis of the Construct," *Administrative Science Quarterly,* 1973, 18: 223–235.

BERGER, PETER L., AND RICHARD JOHN NEUHAUS, *To Empower People: The Role of Mediating Structures in Public Policy,* Washington, D.C.: American Enterprise Institute, 1977.

BERLE, A. A., AND GARDINER C. MEANS, *The Modern Corporation and Private Property,* New York: Macmillan, 1932.

BERLINER, JOSEPH S., "A Problem in Soviet Business Administration," *Administrative Science Quarterly,* 1956, 1: 86–101.

BETTMAN, JAMES R., AND BARTON A. WEITZ, "Attributions in the Board Room: Causal Reasoning in Corporate Annual Accounts," *Administrative Science Quarterly,* 1983, 28: 165–183.

BIGELOW, D. A., AND R. H. DRISCOLL, "Effect of Minimizing Coercion on the Rehabilitation of Prisoners," *Journal of Applied Psychology,* 1973, 57: 10–14.

BIGUS, ODIS, E., "The Milkman and His Customer: A Cultivated Relationship," *Urban Life and Culture,* 1972, 1: 131–165.

BIRD, CAROLINE, *The Invisible Scar,* New York: D. McKay, 1966.

BIRNBAUM, ROBERT, "Presidential Succession: An Interinstitutional Analysis," *Educational Record,* 1971, 52: 133–145.

BLAKE, R. R., AND J. S. MOUTON, *Building a Dynamic Corporation Through Grid Organization Development,* Reading, MA: Addison-Wesley, 1969.

BLAU, PETER M. *The Dynamics of Bureaucracy,* Chicago: University of Chicago Press, 1963, 2nd ed.

BLAU, PETER M., *Exchange and Power in Social Life,* New York: Wiley, 1964.

BLAU, PETER M., "A Formal Theory of Differentiation in Organizations," *American Sociological Review,* 1970, 35: 201–218.

BLAU, PETER M., *Inequality and Heterogeneity,* New York: Free Press, 1977.

BLAU, PETER M., AND OTIS D. DUNCAN, *The American Occupational Structure,* New York: Wiley, 1967.

BLAU, PETER M., AND RICHARD A. SCHOENHERR, *The Structure of Organizations,* New York: Basic Books, 1971, Chap. 8.

BLAU, PETER M., AND W. RICHARD SCOTT,    *Formal Organizations,* San Francisco: Chandler, 1962.

BLAUNER, ROBERT,    "Work Satisfaction and Industrial Trends in Modern Society," in W. Galenson and Seymour M. Lipset (eds.), *Labor and Trade Unionism,* New York: Wiley, 1960, pp. 339–360.

BLAUNER, ROBERT,    *Alienation and Freedom: The Factory Worker and His Industry,* Chicago: University of Chicago Press, 1964.

BLOCH, MARC,    "The Advent and Triumph of the Watermill," in Marc Bloch, *Land and Work in Medieval Europe,* Berkeley: University of California Press, 1967.

BLUMBERG, PHILLIP I.,    *The Megacorporation in American Society,* Englewood Cliffs, NJ: Prentice-Hall, 1975.

BOSK, CHARLES L.,    *Forgive and Remember,* Chicago: The University of Chicago Press, 1979.

BRANDEIS, LOUIS D.,    *Other People's Money, and How the Bankers Use It,* Washington, D.C.: National Home Library Foundation, 1933.

BRAVERMAN, HARRY,    *Labor and Monopoly Capital,* New York: Monthly Review Press, 1974.

BRAYFIELD, ARTHUR H., AND WALTER H. CROCKETT,    "Employee Attitudes and Employee Performance," *Psychological Bulletin,* 1955, 52: 396–424.

BRUCE, STEVE, AND ROY WALLIS,    "Rescuing Motives," *British Journal of Sociology,* 1983, 34: 61–70.

BUNTING, DAVID,    "Corporate Interlocking, Part IV." Cited in Herman, 1981, p. 200.

BUNTING, DAVID, AND JEFFEREY BARBOUR,    "Interlocking Directorates in Large American Corporations, 1896–1964," *Business History Review,* 1971, 45: 317–335.

BURAWOY, MICHAEL,    *Manufacturing Consent,* Chicago: The University of Chicago Press, 1979.

BURAWOY, MICHAEL,    "Between the Labor Process and the State: The Changing Face of Factory Regimes Under Advanced Capitalism," *American Sociological Review,* 1983, 48: 587–605.

BUREAU OF LABOR STATISTICS,    *Directory of National Unions and Employee Associations,* 1973, 1974.

BUREAU OF NATIONAL AFFAIRS,    "Employee Performance: Evaluation and Control," *Personnel Policies Forum Survey,* No. 108, February 1975, pp. 2–4. Cited in French, 1982, p. 323.

BURT, RONALD S.,    "Autonomy in a Social Topology," *American Journal of Sociology,* 1980, 85: 892–925.

BURTON, J. F., JR.,    "An Economic Analysis of Sherman Act Criminal Cases," in J. M. Clabault and J. F. Burton, Jr. (eds.), *Sherman Act Indictments, 1955–1965: A Legal and Economic Analysis,* New York: Federal Legal Publications, 1966.

CAMPBELL, JOHN P., AND ROBERT D. PRITCHARD,    "Motivation Theory in Industrial and Organizational Psychology," in Marvin D. Dunnette (ed.), *Handbook of Industrial and Organizational Psychology,* Chicago: Rand McNally, 1976.

CAMPBELL, RICHARD T.,    "Status Attainment Research: The End of the Beginning or the Beginning of the End?" *Sociology of Education,* 1983, 56: 47–62.

CANTY, D.,    "Evaluation of an Open Office Landscape: Weyerhaeuser Co.," *American Institute of Architects Journal,* 1977, 66: 40–45.

CAPLOW, THEODORE,    *Principles of Organization,* New York: Harcourt Brace, 1964.

CAREY, ALEX, "The Hawthorne Studies: A Radical Criticism," *American Sociological Review*, 1967, 32: 403–416.

CARLIN, JEROME E., *Lawyers on Their Own*, New Brunswick, NJ: Rutgers University Press, 1962.

CARLSON, RICHARD O., "Succession and Performance Among School Superintendents," *Administrative Science Quarterly*, 1961, 6: 210–227.

CARROLL, GLENN R., "Dynamics of Publisher Succession in Newspaper Organizations," *Administrative Science Quarterly*, 1984, 29: 93–113.

CAUDILL, WILLIAM, *The Psychiatric Hospital as a Small Society*, Cambridge, MA.: Harvard University Press, 1958.

CHILD, JOHN, "Organizational Structure, Environment, and Performance: The Role of Strategic Choice," *Sociology*, 1972, 6: 1–22.

CHILD, JOHN, "Organizational Structure and Strategies of Control: A Replication of the Aston Study," *Administrative Science Quarterly*, 1972a, 17: 163–177.

CHILD, JOHN, "Parkinson's Progress: Accounting for the Number of Specialists in Organizations," *Administrative Science Quarterly*, 1973, 18: 328–348.

CHILD, JOHN, AND ALFRED KIESER, "Organizational and Managerial Roles in British and West German Companies: An Examination of the Culture-Free Thesis," in Cornelis J. Lammers and David J. Hickson (eds.), *Organizations Alike and Unlike: International and Interinstitutional Studies in the Sociology of Organizations*, London: Routledge and Kegan Paul, 1979.

CHINOY, ELY, *Automobile Workers and the American Dream*, Garden City, NY: Doubleday, 1955.

CLARK, BURTON R., *Adult Education in Transition*, Berkeley: University of California Press, 1956.

CLARK, BURTON R., "Interorganizational Patterns in Education," *Administrative Science Quarterly*, 1965, 10:224–237.

CLARK, RODNEY, *The Japanese Company*, New Haven, Conn.: Yale University Press, 1979.

CLARK, S. D., *The Church and Sect in Canada*, Toronto: University of Toronto Press, 1948.

CLEGG, STEWARD, AND DAVID DUNKERLEY, *Organization, Class, and Control*, London: Routledge and Kegan Paul, 1980.

CLINARD, MARSHALL B., AND PETER C. YEAGER, *Corporate Crime*, New York: Free Press, 1980.

COHEN, DAVID K., AND ELEANOR FARRAR, "Power to the Parents?—The Story of Education Vouchers," *The Public Interest*, 1977, No. 48, pp. 72–97.

COHEN, MICHAEL, AND JAMES G. MARCH, *Leadership and Ambiguity: The American College President*, New York: McGraw-Hill, 1974.

COHEN, MICHAEL D., JAMES G. MARCH, AND JOHAN P. OLSEN, "A Garbage Can Model of Organizational Choice," *Administrative Science Quarterly*, 1972, 17: 1–25.

COLE, ROBERT E., *Japanese Blue Collar*, Berkeley: University of California Press, 1973.

COLE, ROBERT E., *Work, Mobility, and Participation: A Comparative Study*, Berkeley: University of California Press, 1979.

COLE, ROBERT E. (ED.), *The Japanese Automotive Industry: Model and Challenge for the Future?* Ann Arbor: Center for Japanese Studies, University of Michigan, 1981.

COLEMAN, JAMES S., *The Asymmetric Society*, Syracuse, NY: Syracuse University Press, 1982.

COLEMAN, JAMES S., *Power and the Structure of Society*, New York: Norton, 1974.

COLLINS, RANDALL, *Conflict Sociology*, New York: Academic Press, 1975.

COLLINS, RANDALL,   *The Credential Society*, New York: Academic Press, 1979.

COOK, JOHN D., SUSAN T. HEPWORTH, TOBY D. WALL, AND PETER B. WARR,   *The Experience of Work: A Compendium and Review of 249 Measures and Their Use*, London: Academic Press, 1981.

COOK, KAREN S.,   "Exchange and Power in Networks of Interorganizational Relations," *Sociological Quarterly*, 1977, 18: 62–82.

COOK, KAREN S., AND RICHARD M. EMERSON,   "Power, Equity, and Commitment in Exchange Networks," *American Sociological Review*, 1978, 43: 721–739.

COOK, KAREN S., RICHARD M. EMERSON, MARY R. GILLMORE, AND TOSHIO YAMAGISHI,   "The Distribution of Power in Exchange Networks: Theory and Experimental Results," *American Journal of Sociology*, 1983, 89: 275–305.

CORWIN, RONALD,   *A Sociology of Education*, New York: Appleton, Century Crofts, 1965.

COSER, LEWIS,   *The Social Functions of Conflict*, Glencoe, Ill: Free Press, 1956.

CROZIER, MICHAEL,   *The Bureaucratic Phenomenon*, Chicago: The University of Chicago Press, 1964.

CUMMINGS, THOMAS G., AND EDMOND S. MOLLOY,   *Improving Productivity and the Quality of Work Life*, New York: Praeger, 1977.

CYERT, RICHARD M., AND JAMES G. MARCH,   *A Behavioral Theory of the Firm*, Englewood Cliffs, NJ: Prentice-Hall, 1963.

DALE, ERNEST,   *Planning and Developing the Company Organization Structure*, New York: American Management Association, 1952.

DALTON, MELVILLE,   "The Industrial 'Rate Buster': A Characterization," *Applied Anthropology*, 1948, 7: 5–18.

DALTON, MELVILLE,   "Conflicts Between Staff and Line Managerial Officers," *American Sociological Review*, 1950, 15: 342–351.

DALTON, MELVILLE,   *Men Who Manage*, New York: Wiley, 1959.

DAVIES, CELIA, SANDRA DAWSON, AND ARTHUR FRANCIS,   "Technology and Other Variables: Some Current Approaches in Organizational Theory," in Malcolm Warner (ed.), *The Sociology of the Workplace*, London: George Allen and Unwin, 1973, Chap. 5.

DAVIS, L. E., AND A. B. CHERNS (EDS.),   *Quality of Working Life*, New York: Free Press, 1975.

DEMERATH, NICHOLAS J., RICHARD J. STEPHENS, AND R. ROBB TAYLOR,   *Power, Presidents, and Professors*, New York: Basic Books, 1967.

DIAMOND, SIGMUND,   "From Organization to Society: Virginia in the Seventeenth Century," *American Journal of Sociology*, 1958, 63:457–475.

DENZIN, NORMAN K.,   "Crime and the American Liquor Industry," in *Studies in Symbolic Interaction*, Greenwich, Conn: JAI Press, Vol. 1, 1978, pp. 87–118.

DESANTIS, GRACE,   "Realms of Expertise: A View from Within the Medical Profession," in Julius Roth (ed.), *Research in the Sociology of Health Care*, Greenwich, Conn: JAI Press, 1980, pp. 179–236.

DESS, GREGORY G., AND DONALD W. BEARD,   "Dimensions of Organizational Task Environments," *Administrative Science Quarterly*, 1984, 29: 52–73.

DIAMOND, SIGMUND,   "From Organization to Society," *American Journal of Sociology*, 1958, 63: 457–475.

DIMAGGIO, PAUL J., AND WALTER W. POWELL,   "The Iron Cage Revisited: Institutional Isomorphism and Collective Rationality in Organizational Fields," *American Sociological Review*, 1983, 48: 147–160.

DOBB, MAURICE,   *Studies in the Development of Capitalism*, London: Routledge and Kegan Paul, 1963.

DOERINGER, PETER B., AND MICHAEL J. PIORE, *Internal Labor Markets and Manpower Analysis,* Lexington, MA: D. C. Heath, 1971.

DOOLEY, PETER, "The Interlocking Directorate," *American Economic Review,* 1969, 59: 314–323.

DORE, RONALD, *British Factory, Japanese Factory,* Berkeley: University of California Press, 1973.

DORNBUSCH, SANFORD M., "The Military Academy as an Assimilating Institution," *Social Forces,* 1955, 33: 316–321.

DUBICK, MICHAEL A., "The Organizational Structure of Newspapers in Relation to Their Metropolitan Environment," *Administrative Science Quarterly,* 1978, 23: 418–433.

DUBIN, ROBERT, "Industrial Workers' Worlds: A Study of the 'Central Life Interests' of Industrial Workers," *Social Problems,* 1956, 3: 131–142.

DUBIN, ROBERT, JOSEPH E. CHAMPOUX, AND LYMAN W. PORTER, "Central Life Interests and Organizational Commitment of Blue-Collar and Clerical Workers," *Administrative Science Quarterly,* 1975, 20: 411–421.

DUNCAN, ROBERT, "Characteristics of Organizational Environments and Perceived Environmental Uncertainty," *Administrative Science Quarterly,* 1972, 17: 313–327.

EDELSTEIN, J. DAVID, "An Organizational Theory of Union Democracy," *American Sociological Review,* 1967, 32: 19–31.

EDELSTEIN, J. DAVID, *Comparative Union Democracy: Organization and Opposition in British and American Unions,* New York: Wiley, 1976.

EDWARDS, RICHARD, *Contested Terrain,* New York: Basic Books, 1979.

EITZEN, D. STANLEY, AND NORMAN R. YETMAN, "Managerial Change, Longevity, and Organizational Effectiveness," *Administrative Science Quarterly,* 1972, 17: 110–116.

ELDER, GLEN H., JR., *Children of the Great Depression,* Chicago: The University of Chicago Press, 1974.

EMERSON, ROBERT M., "On Last Resorts," *American Journal of Sociology,* 1981, 86: 1–22.

EMERSON, RICHARD M., "Power-Dependence Relations," *American Sociological Review,* 1962, 27: 31–41.

EMERSON, ROBERT M., AND SHELDON L. MESSINGER, "The Micro-Politics of Trouble," *Social Problems,* 1977, 25: 121–135.

EMERY, FRED E., AND E. L. TRIST, "The Causal Texture of Organizational Environments," *Human Relations,* 1965, 18: 21–32.

ERMANN, M. DAVID, AND RICHARD J. LUNDMAN (EDS.), *Corporate and Governmental Deviance,* New York: Oxford University Press, 1978.

ETZIONI, AMITAI, "Basic Human Needs, Alienation, and Inauthenticity," *American Sociological Review,* 1968, 33: 870–885.

ETZIONI, AMITAI, *A Comparative Analysis of Complex Organizations,* New York: Free Press of Glencoe, 1961.

ETZIONI, AMITAI, *A Comparative Analysis of Complex Organizations, Revised and Enlarged Edition,* New York: Free Press, 1975.

ETZIONI, AMITAI, "Two Approaches to Organizational Analysis: A Critique and a Suggestion," *Administrative Science Quarterly,* 1960, 5: 257–278.

EVAN, WILLIAM M., "The Organization-Set: Toward a Theory of Inter-Organizational Relations," in James D. Thompson (ed.), *Approaches to Organizational Design,* Pittsburgh Press, 1966, pp. 175–190.

EVAN, WILLIAM M., *Organization Theory,* New York: Wiley, 1976.

FAGERHAUGH, S., AND ANSELM STRAUSS, *The Politics of Pain Management,* Reading, MA: Addison-Wesley, 1977.

FAIA, MICHAEL A., "Selection by Certification: A Neglected Variable in Stratification Research," *American Journal of Sociology,* 1981, 86: 1093–1111.

FARBERMAN, HARVEY A., "A Criminogenic Market Structure: The Automobile Industry," *Sociological Quarterly,* 1975, 16: 438–457.

*Federal Support to Universities, Colleges, and Selected Nonprofit Institutions, Fiscal Year, 1979, Final Report,* NSF 81-308, February, 1981, Superintendent of Documents, U.S. Government Printing Office, Washington, D.C., 20402.

FENNELL, MARY C., "The Effects of Environmental Characteristics on the Structure of Hospital Clusters," *Administrative Science Quarterly,* 1980, 29: 489–510.

FERRARI, MICHAEL R., *Profiles of American College Presidents,* East Lansing, Mich.: Graduate School of Business Administration, Michigan State University, 1970.

FICHTER, JOSEPH H., *Social Relations in the Urban Parish,* Chicago: The University of Chicago press, 1954.

FINN, PETER, "The Effects of Shift Work on the Lives of Employees," *Monthly Labor Review,* 1981, 104: October, 31–35.

FIREMAN, BRUCE, AND WILLIAM GAMSON, "Utilitarian Logic in the Resource Mobilization Perspective," in Mayer Zald and John D. McCarthy (eds.), *The Dynamics of Social Movements,* Cambridge, MA: Winthrop, 1979, pp. 8–44.

FRANKE, RICHARD HERBERT, AND JAMES D. KAUL, "The Hawthorne Experiments: First Statistic Interpretation," *American Sociological Review,* 1978, 43: 623–643.

FRANKLIN, J. L., "The Normative Organization: An Empirical Test of Etzioni's Compliance Theory." Revision of papers read at 1972 meetings of Midwest Sociological Society and the American Sociological Association, 1972. Cited in Etzioni, 1975, p. 507.

FREEDMAN, MARCIA K., *Labor Markets: Segments and Shelters,* Montclair, NJ: Allanheld, Osmun and Co., 1976.

FREEMAN, JOHN H., AND MICHAEL T. HANNAN, "Growth and Decline Processes in Organizations," *American Sociological Review,* 1975, 40: 219–228.

FREIDSON, ELIOT, "Dominant Professions, Bureaucracy, and Client Services," in Yeheskel Hasenfeld and Richard A. English (eds.), *Human Service Organizations,* Ann Arbor: The University of Michigan Press, 1974, pp. 428–447.

FREIDSON, ELIOT, "Are Professions Necessary?" in Thomas L. Haskell (ed), *The Authority of Experts,* Bloomington, Ind: Indiana University Press, 1984, pp. 3–27.

FREITAG, PETER J., "The Myth of Corporate Capture: Regulatory Commissions in the United States," *Social Problems,* 1983, 30: 480–491.

FRENCH, WENDELL L., *The Personnel Management Process,* Boston: Houghton Mifflin, 1982.

FRENCH, WENDELL, AND CECIL H. BELL, JR., *Organization Development: Behavioral Science Intervention for Organization Improvement,* Englewood Cliffs, NJ: Prentice-Hall, 1978.

GAERTNER, KAREN N., "The Structure of Organizational Careers," *Sociology of Education,* 1980, 53: 7–20.

GALASKIEWICZ, JOSEPH, AND PETER J. MARSDEN, "Interorganizational Resources Networks: Formal Patterns of Overlap," *Social Science Research,* 1978, 7: 89–107.

GALBRAITH, JAY, *Designing Complex Organizations,* Reading, MA: Addison-Wesley, 1973.

GALBRAITH, JAY, *Organization Design,* Reading, MA: Addison-Wesley, 1977.

GAMSON, WILLIAM A., AND NORMAN A. SCOTCH, "Scapegoating in Baseball," *American Journal of Sociology*, 1964, 70: 69–72.

GAMSON, ZELDA, "Utilitarian and Normative Orientation Toward Education," *Sociology of Education*, 1966, 39: 46–73.

GAMSON, ZELDA, "Performance and Personalism in Student-Faculty Relations," *Sociology of Education*, 1967, 40:279–301.

GARABEDIAN, PETER G., "Social Roles in a Correctional Community," *Journal of Criminal Law, Criminology and Police Science*, 1964, 55: 338–347.

GARDNER, BURLEIGH B., *Human Relations in Industry*, Chicago: Richard D. Irwin, 1945.

GARSON, BARBARA, *All the Livelong Day*, Garden City, NY: Doubleday, 1975.

GEORGIOU, PETRO, "The Goal Paradigm and Notes Towards a Counter-Paradigm," *Administrative Science Quarterly*, 1973, 18: 291–310.

GEORGOPOULOS, B. S., AND ARNOLD S. TANNENBAUM, "A Study of Organizational Effectiveness," *American Sociological Review*, 1957, 22: 534–540.

GERSTL, JOEL E., "Determinants of Occupational Communities in High Status Occupations," *Sociological Quarterly*, 1961, 2: 37–48.

GHISELLI, EDWIN E., "The Validity of Occupational Aptitude Tests, New York: Wiley, 1966.

GHORPADE, JAISINGH (ED.), *Assessment of Organizational Effectiveness*, Pacific Palisades, CA: Goodyear, 1971.

GIALLOMBARDO, ROSE, *Society of Women*, New York: Wiley, 1966.

GIFFORD, DICK, "A. T. Kearney/Modern Healthcare Compensation and Benefits Survey," *Modern Healthcare*, 1979, 9: 59.

GLASER, EDWARD M., *Productivity Gains Through Worklife Improvements*, New York: Harcourt Brace Jovanovich, 1976.

GLENN, EVELYN NAKANO, AND ROSLYN L. FELDBERG, "Proletarianizing Clerical Work: Technology and Organizational Control in the Office," in Andrew Zimbalist (ed.), *Case Studies on the Labor Process*, New York: Monthly Review Press, 1979, pp. 51–72.

GLISSON, CHARLES A., AND PATRICIA YANCEY MARTIN, "Productivity and Efficiency in Human Service Organizations as Related to Structure, Size, and Age," *Academy of Management Journal*, 1980, 23: 21–37.

GOFFMAN, ERVING, "On the Characteristics of Total Institutions: The Inmate World," in Donald R. Cressey (ed.), *The Prison: Studies in Institutional Organization and Change*, New York: Holt, Rinehart, and Winston, 1961.

GOFFMAN, ERVING, *Frame Analysis*, New York: Harper and Row, 1974.

GOLDTHORPE, JOHN H., AND OTHERS, *The Affluent Worker: Industrial Attitudes and Behavior*, New York: Cambridge University Press, 1968.

GOODE, WILLIAM J., "Community Within a Community: The Professions," *American Sociological Review*, 1957, 22: 194–200.

GOODMAN, PAUL S., JOHANNES M. PENNINGS, AND ASSOCIATES (EDS.), *New Perspectives in Organizational Effectiveness*, San Francisco: Jossey-Bass, 1979.

GORDON, GERALD, AND SELWYN BECKER, "Careers, Organizational Size, and Succession," *American Journal of Sociology*, 1964, 70: 216–222.

GOSS, MARY E., "Influence and Authority Among Physicians in an Outpatient Clinic," *American Sociological Review*, 1961, 26: 39–50.

GOULDNER, ALVIN W., *Patterns of Industrial Bureaucracy*, Glencoe, Ill: Free Press, 1954.

GOULDNER, ALVIN W., "Metaphysical Pathos and the Theory of Bureaucracy," American Political Science Review, 1955, 49: 496–507.

GOULDNER, ALVIN W., "Cosmopolitans and Locals: Toward an Analysis of Latent Social Roles," *Administrative Science Quarterly*, 1957–58, 2: 281–306 and 444–480.

GRANDJEAN, BURKE D., "History and Career in a Bureaucratic Labor Market," *American Journal of Sociology*, 1981, 86: 1057–1092.

GREENE, C., AND D. W. ORGAN, "An Evaluation of Causal Models Linking the Received Role with Job Satisfaction," *Administrative Science Quarterly*, 1973, 18: 95–103.

GROSS, BERTRAM, *The Managing of Organizations*, New York: Free Press of Glencoe, 1964.

GROSS, EDWARD, "Sources of Lateral Authority in Personnel Departments," *Industrial Relations*, 1964, 3: 121–133.

GROSS, EDWARD, "When Occupations Meet: Professions in Trouble," *Hospital Administration*, 1967, 12: 40–59.

GROSS, EDWARD, "Incentives and the Structure of Organizational Motivation," *Hospital Administration*, 1971, 16: 8–20.

GROSS, EDWARD, "Organizational Crime: A Theoretical Perspective," in Norman Denzin (ed.), *Studies in Symbolic Interaction*, Vol. 1, Greenwich, Conn: JAI Press, 1978, pp. 55–85.

GROSS, EDWARD, "Sport Leagues: A Model for a Theory of Organizational Stratification," *International Review of Sport Sociology*, 1979, 2 (14), 103–112.

GROSS, EDWARD, "Organizational Structure and Organizational Crime," in Gilbert Geis and Ezra Stotland (eds.), *White Collar Crime: Theory and Research*, Beverly Hills, CA: Sage, 1980, Chap. 3.

GROSS, EDWARD AND PAUL V. GRAMBSCH, *Changes in University Organization*, 1964–1971, New York: McGraw-Hill, 1974.

GROSS, EDWARD, AND JAMES C. McCANN, "Careers of Academic Administrators in the U.S.A.: An Approach to Elite Study," *Research in Sociology of Education and Socialization*, Vol. 2, JAI Press, 1981, pp. 127–162.

GRUSKY, OSCAR, "Corporate Size, Bureaucratization, and Managerial Succession," *American Journal of Sociology*, 1961, 67: 261–269.

GRUSKY, OSCAR, "Managerial Succession and Organizational Effectiveness," *American Journal of Sociology*, 1963, 69: 21–31.

GRUSKY, OSCAR, "The Effects of Succession: A Comparative Study of Military and Business Organization," in Morris Janowitz (ed.), *The New Military*, New York: Russell Sage, 1964, pp. 83–109.

GULICK, LUTHER AND L. URWICK (eds.), *Papers on the Science of Adminstration* (New York: Institute of Public Administration, Columbia University, 1937).

GUEST, ROBERT H., "Managerial Succession in Complex Organizations," *American Journal of Sociology*, 1962, 68: 47–54.

GUSFIELD, JOSEPH R., *Symbolic Crusade*, Urbana, Ill.: University of Illinois Press, 1963.

HAAS, JACK, AND WILLIAM SHAFFIR, "The Professionalization of Medical Students: Developing Competence and a Cloak of Competence," *Symbolic Interaction*, 1977, 1: 71–88.

HAAS, JACK AND WILLIAM SHAFFIR, "The 'Fate of Idealism' Revisited," *Urban Life*, 1984, 13: 63–81.

HACHEN, DAVID, "A Framework for the Analysis of Work Organizations in Capitalist Societies," Paper presented at meetings of the Midwest Sociological Society, 1982.

HACKMAN, J. R., "On the Coming Demise of Job Enrichment," in E. Cass (ed.), *Men and Work in Society*, New York: Van Nostrand Reinhold, 1975.

HAGE, JERALD, AND MICHAEL AIKEN, "Relationship of Centralization to Other Structural Properties," *Administrative Science Quarterly*, 1967, 12: 72–91.

HAGE, JERALD, AND MICHAEL AIKEN, *Social Change in Complex Organization*, New York: Random House, 1970.

HALL, RICHARD H., Organizations: *Structure and Process*, Englewood Cliffs, NJ: Prentice-Hall, 1982, 3rd ed.

HALL, RICHARD H., JOHN P. CLARK, PEGGY C. GIORDANO, PAUL V. JOHNSON, AND MARTHA VAN ROEKEL, "Patterns of Interorganizational Relationships," *Administrative Science Quarterly*, 1977, 22: 457–474.

HALL, RICHARD H., J. EUGENE HASS, AND NORMAN JOHNSON, "Organizational Size, Complexity, and Formalization," *American Sociological Review*, 1967, 32: 903–912.

HALL, RICHARD H., J. E. HASS, AND N. J. JOHNSON, "An Examination of the Blau-Scott and Etzioni Typologies," *Administrative Science Quarterly*, 1967, 12: 118–139.

HALL, RICHARD H., AND CHARLES R. TITTLE, "Bureaucracy and Its Correlates," *American Journal of Sociology*, 1966, 72: 267–272.

HANNAN, MICHAEL T., AND JOHN FREEMAN, "The Population Ecology of Organizations," *American Journal of Sociology*, 1977, 82: 929–964.

HANNAN, MICHAEL AND JOHN FREEMAN, "Structural Inertia and Organizational Change," *American Sociological Review*, 1984, 49:149–164.

HARRIS, RICHARD, *The Police Academy: An Inside View*, New York: Wiley, 1973.

HARRISON, PAUL M., "Churches and the Laity Among Protestants," *Annals of the American Academy of Political and Social Science*, 1960, 332: 37–49.

HASENFELD, YEHESKEL, "People Processing Organizations: An Exchange Approach," *American Sociological Review*, 1972, 37: 256–263.

HAY, GEORGE, AND DANIEL KELLEY, "An Empirical Study of Price-Fixing Conspiracies," *Journal of Law and Economics*, 1974, 17: 13–39.

HECHTER, MICHAEL (ED.), *The Microfoundations of Macrosociology*, Philadelphia: Temple University Press, 1983.

HEFFERNAN, ESTHER, *Making It in Person: The Square, the Cool, and the Life*, New York: Wiley, 1972.

HEISKANEN, IKKO, "Theoretical Approaches and Scientific Strategies," in *Administrative and Organizational Research: A Methodological Study*, 1967, 39, No. 2, Helsinki: Commentationes Humanarum Litterarum, Soecietas Scientiarum Fennica.

HELMICH, DONALD L., AND WARREN B. BROWN, "Successor Type and Organizational Change in the Corporate Enterprise," *Administrative Science Quarterly*, 1972, 17: 371–381.

HENRY, JULES, "The Formal Structure of a Psychiatric Hospital," *Psychiatry*, 1954, 17: 139–151.

HENRY, STUART, *The Hidden Economy: The Context and Control of Borderline Crime*, Oxford: Martin Robertson, 1978.

HENRY, STUART, *Informal Institutions*, New York: St. Martin's Press, 1981.

HERMAN, EDWARD S., *Corporate Control, Corporate Power*, Cambridge: Cambridge University Press, 1981.

HERZBERG, FREDERICK, *Work and the Nature of Man*, New York: Crowell, 1966.

HERZBERG, FREDERICK, B. MAUSNER, AND B. SNYDERMAN, *The Motivation to Work*, New York: Wiley, 1959.

HEYDEBRAND, WOLF V., "Organizational Contradictions in Public Bureaucracies: Toward a Marxian Theory of Organizations," *Sociological Quarterly*, 1977, 18: 83–107.

HICKSON, DAVID J., C. R. HININGS, C. A. LEE, R. A. SCHNECK, AND J. M. PENNINGS, "A Strategic Contingencies Theory of Intraorganizational Power, *Administrative Science Quarterly*, 1971, 16: 216–229.

HIRSCH, PAUL, "Processing Fads and Fashions: An Organization-Set Analysis of Cultural Industry Systems," *American Journal of Sociology*, 1972, 77: 639–659.

HIRSCH, PAUL M., "Organizational Effectiveness and the Institutional Environment," *Administrative Science Quarterly*, 1975, 20: 327–344.

HIRSCHMAN, ALBERT O., *Shifting Involvements*, Princeton, NJ: Princeton University Press, 1982.

HOCHSCHILD, ARLIE RUSSELL, *The Managed Heart: Commercialization of Human Feeling*, Berkeley: University of California Press, 1983.

HODGKINS, B. J., AND R. E. HERRIOTT, "Age-Grade Structure, Goals, and Compliance in the School: An Organizational Analysis," *Sociology of Education*, 1970, 43: 90–105.

HOFSTEDE, GEERT, "Hierarchical Power Distance in Forty Countries," in Cornelis J. Lammers and David J. Hickson (eds.), *Organizations Alike and Unlike: International and Interinstitutional Studies in the Sociology of Organizations*, London: Routledge and Kegan Paul, 1979.

HOFSTEDE, GEERT, *Culture's Consequences:* International Differences in Work-Related Values, Beverly Hills, CA: Sage, 1980.

HOLLINGER, RICHARD C., AND JOHN P. CLARK, "Formal and Informal Social Controls of Employee Deviance," *Sociological Quarterly*, 1982, 23: 333–343.

HOMANS, GEORGE C., *The Human Group*, New York: Harcourt Brace, 1950.

HOMANS, GEORGE C., *Social Behavior: Its Elementary Forms, Rev. Ed.*, New York: Harcourt, Brace, Jovanovich, 1974.

*Hospital Statistics*, 1977 Edition.

HSU, CHENG-KUANG, ROBERT M. MARSH, AND HIROSHI MANNARI, "An Examination of the Determinants of Organizational Structure," *American Journal of Sociology*, 1983, 88: 975–996.

HUDSON, W. W. "Commitment and Alienation in a Public Welfare Agency," PhD. dissertation. The University of Chicago, 1973.

IRWIN, JOHN, AND DONALD R. CRESSEY, "Thieves, Convicts, and the Inmate Culture," *Social Problems*, 1962, 10: 142–155.

JAMOUS, H., AND B. PELOILLE, "Changes in the French University Hospital System," in J. A. Jackson (ed.), *Professions and Professionalization*, London: Cambridge University Press, 1970, pp. 111–152.

JENNINGS, ELIZABETH, AND FRANCIS JENNINGS, "Making Human Relations Work," in Edward C. Bursk (ed.), *Human Relations for Management*, New York: Harper, 1956.

JONSSON, EGON, AND DUNCAN NEUHAUSER, "Structural Differences Between Swedish and U.S. Hospitals," in Cornelis J. Lammers and David J. Hickson (eds.), *Organizations Like and Unlike: International and Interinstitutional Studies in the Sociology of Organizations*, London: Routledge and Kegan Paul, 1979.

JOY, DENNIS S., "The Maintenance of Order on an Adolescent Inpatient Unit: An Analysis of Work on the Evening Shift," *Psychiatry*, 1981, 44: 253–262.

JULIAN, JOSEPH, "Compliance Patterns and Communication Blocks in Complex Organizations," *American Sociological Review*, 1966, 31: 382–389.

JULIAN, JOSEPH, "Organizational Involvement and Social Control," *Social Forces*, 1968, 47: 12–16.

JURKOVICH, RAY, "A Core Typology of Organizational Environments," *Administrative Science Quarterly*, 1974, 19: 380–394.

KAHN, ROBERT L., DONALD M. WOLFE, ROBERT P. QUINN, J. KIEDRICK SNOEK, AND ROBERT A. ROSENTHAL, *Organizational Stress: Studies in Role Conflict and Ambiguity*, New York: Wiley, 1964.

KAMENS, DAVID H., "Legitimating Myths and Educational Organizations: The Relationships Between Organizational Ideology and Formal Structure," *American Sociological Review*, 1977, 42: 208–219.

KANTER, ROSEBETH M., *Men and Women of the Corporation*, New York: Basic Books, 1977.

KAPLAN, H. ROY, AND CURT TAUSKY, "Humanism in Organizations: A Critical Appraisal," *Public Administration Review*, 1977, 37: 171–180.

KATZ, DANIEL, AND ROBERT L. KAHN, *The Social Psychology of Organizations*, New York: Wiley, 1978.

KATZ, ELIHU, AND BRENDA DANET (EDS.), *Bureaucracy and the Public*, New York: Basic Books, 1973.

KATZ, FRED E., "Nurses," in Amitai Etzioni (ed.), *The Semi-Professions and Their Organization*, New York: Free Press, 1969, Chap. 2.

KATZ, RALPH, "Managing Careers: The Influence of Job and Group Longevities," in Ralph Katz (ed.), *Career Issues in Human Resource Management*, Englewood Cliffs, NJ: Prentice-Hall, Inc., 1981, pp. 154–181.

KATZELL, RAYMOND A., PENNEY BIENSTOCK, AND PAUL H. FAERSTEIN, *A Guide to Worker Productivity Experiments in the United States, 1971–1975*, New York: New York University Press, 1977.

KEELEY, MICHAEL, "Impartiality and the Participant-Interest Theories of Organizational Effectiveness," *Administrative Science Quarterly*, 1984, 29: 1–25.

KERBO, HAROLD R., AND L. RICHARD DELLA FAVE, "Corporate Linkage and Control of the Corporate Economy: New Evidence and a Reinterpretation," *Sociological Quarterly*, 1983, 24: 201–218.

KERR, CLARK, AND ABRAHAM SIEGEL, "The Interindustry Propensity to Strike—An International Comparison," in Arthur Kornhauser, Robert Dubin, and Arthur M. Ross (eds.), *Industrial Conflict*, New York: McGraw-Hill, 1954.

KIMBERLY, JOHN R., AND MICHAEL J. EVANISKO, "Organizational Innovation: The Influence of Individual, Organizational, and Contextual Factors in Hospital Adoption of Technological and Administrative Innovations," *Academy of Management Journal*, 1981, 24: 689–713.

KING, MICHAEL, MICHAEL A. MURRAY, AND TOM ATKINSON, "Background, Personality, Job Characteristics, and Satisfactions with Work in a National Sample," *Human Relations*, 1982, 35: 119–133.

KLATZKY, SHEILA, "The Relationship of Organizational Size to Complexity and Coordination," *Administrative Science Quarterly*, 1970, 15: 428–438.

KOHN, MELVIN L., "Bureaucratic Man: A Portrait and Interpretation," *American Sociological Review*, 1971, 36: 461–474.

KOHN, MELVIN, AND CARMI SCHOOLER, "Job Conditions and Personality: A Longitudinal Assessment of Their Reciprocal Effects," *American Journal of Sociology*, 1982, 878: 1257–1286.

KOONTZ, HAROLD, AND CYRIL O'DONNELL, *Principles of Management*, New York: McGraw-Hill, 1972.

KORNHAUSER, WILLIAM, *Scientists in Industry*, Berkeley: University of California Press, 1963.

KRIESBERG, LOUIS,   "Careers, Organizational Size, and Succession," *American Journal of Sociology*, 1962, 68: 355–359.

KRONUS, CAROL,   "Occupational Values, Role Orientations, and Work Settings: The Case of Pharmacy," *Sociological Quarterly*, 1975, 16: 173–183.

KUHN, THOMAS M.,   *The Structure of Scientific Revolutions*, Chicago: The University of Chicago Press, 1970.

KURTZ, DAVID L., AND LOUIS E. BOONE,   "A Profile of Business Leadership," *Business Horizons*, 1981, 24: 28–32.

KUSTERER, KEN C.,   *Know-How on the Job: The Important Working Knowledge of "Unskilled" Workers*, Boulder, COLO: Westview Press, 1978.

LADD, EVERETT CARLL, JR., AND SEYMOUR MARTIN LIPSET,   *The Divided Academy*, New York: McGraw-Hill, 1975.

LAMMERS, CORNELIS J., AND DAVID J. HICKSON,   "A Cross-National Cross-Institutional Typology of Organizations," in Cornelis J. Lammers and David J. Hickson, *Organizations Like and Unlike: International and Interinstitutional Studies in the Sociology of Organizations*, London: Routledge and Kegan Paul, 1979.

LAMMERS, CORNELIS J., AND DAVID J. HICKSON (EDS.),   *Organizations Alike and Unalike: International and Interinstitutional Studies in the Sociology of Organizations*, London: Routledge and Kegan Paul, 1979.

LANDSBERGER, HENRY A.,   "The Horizontal Dimension in Bureaucracy," *Administrative Science Quarterly*, 1961, 6: 299–332.

LAUMANN, EDWARD O., AND FRANZ U. PAPPI,   *Networks of Collective Action*, New York: Academic Press, 1976.

LAWLER, EDWARD E., III, AND LYMAN W. PORTER,   "The Effect of Performance on Job Satisfaction," in G. A. Yukl and K. N. Wexley (eds.), *Readings in Organizational and Industrial Psychology*, New York: Oxford University Press, 1971.

LAWRENCE, PAUL R., AND JAY W. LORSCH,   *Organization and Environment*, Cambridge, MA: Harvard University Press, 1967.

LEFTON, MARK, AND WILLIAM R. ROSENGREN,   "Organizations and Clients: Lateral and Longitudinal Dimensions," *American Sociological Review*, 1966, 31: 802–810.

LEIGHTON, ALEXANDER H.,   *The Governing of Men: General Principles and Recommendations Based on an Experience in a Japanese Relocation Camp*, Princeton, NJ: Princeton University Press, 1945.

LESERMAN, JANE,   *Men and Women in Medical School: How They Change and How They Compare*, New York: Praeger, 1981.

LESTER, RICHARD,   "Pay Differentials by Size of Establishment," *Industrial Relations*, 1967, 7: 57–67.

LEVINE, SOL, AND PAUL E. WHITE,   "Exchange as a Conceptual Framework for the Study of Interorganizational Relationships," *Administrative Science Quarterly*, 1961, 5: 583–601.

LEWIN, KURT,   "Group Decision and Social Change," in G. E. Swanson, T. M. Newcomb, and E. L. Hartley (eds.), *Readings in Social Psychology*, New York: Holt, 1952.

LIEBERSON, STANLEY, AND JAMES F. O'CONNOR,   "Leadership and Organizational Performance: A Study of Large Corporations," *American Sociological Review*, 1972, 37: 117–130.

LIKERT, RENSIS,   *New Patterns of Management*, New York: McGraw-Hill, 1961.

LIKERT, RENSIS,   *The Human Organization*, New York: McGraw-Hill, 1967.

LIPSET, SEYMOUR M., MARTIN TROW, AND JAMES S. COLEMAN,   *Union Democracy*, Glencoe, Ill: Free Press, 1956.

LITWAK, EUGENE, AND LYDIA F. HYLTON, "Interorganizational Analysis: A Hypothesis on Co-ordinating Agencies," *Administrative Science Quarterly,* 1966, 11: 31–58.

LOCKE, E. A. "Personnel Attitudes and Motivation," *Annual Review of Psychology,* 1976, 26: 457–480.

LONG, J. SCOTT, "Productivity and Academic Position in the Scientific Career," *American Sociological Review,* 1978, 43: 889–908.

LONG, J. SCOTT, AND ROBERT MCGINNIS, "Organizational Context and Scientific Productivity," *American Sociological Review,* 1981, 46: 422–442.

LOOMIS, CAROL J., "The Madness of Executive Compensation," *Fortune Magazine,* July 12, 1982, pp. 42–52.

LORTIE, DAN C., "Laymen to Lawmen: Law Schools, Careers, and Professional Socialization," *Harvard Educational Review,* 1959, 29: 352–369.

LORTIE, DAN C., "The Balance of Control and Autonomy in Elementary School Teaching," in Amitai Etzioni (ed.), *The Semi-Professions and Their Organization,* New York: Free Press, 1969, Chap. 1.

LOVELL, JOHN P., "The Professional Socialization of the West Point Cadet," in Morris Janowitz (ed.), *The New Military,* New York: Wiley, 1964.

LUNSFORD, TERRY, "Authority and Ideology in the Administered University," in Carlos E. Kruytbosch and Sheldon L. Messinger (eds.), *The State of the University,* Beverly Hills, CA: Sage, 1970.

LUPTON, T., *On the Shop Floor,* New York: Macmillan, 1963.

LYTLE, WILLIAMS, "Obstacles to Job and Organization Design: A Case," in L. E. Davis and A. B. Cherns (eds.), *Quality of Work Life,* New York: Free Press, 1975.

MACAROV, DAVID, Worker Productivity: *Myths and Reality,* Beverly Hills, CA: Sage, 1982.

MACK, RAYMOND, "Ecological Patterns in an Industrial Shop," *Social Forces,* 1954, 32: 351–356.

MANIHA, JOHN, AND CHARLES PERROW, "The Reluctant Organization and the Aggressive Environment," *Administrative Science Quarterly,* 1965, 10: 230–257.

MANNHEIM, KARL, "The Problem of Generations," in P. Kecskemeti (ed.), *Essays on the Sociology of Knowledge,* New York: Oxford University Press, 1952, pp. 276–322.

MARGLIN, STEPHEN A., "What Do Bosses Do? The Origins and Functions of Hierarchy in Capitalist Production," *The Review of Radical Political Economics,* 1974, 6: 33–50.

MARIOLIS, PETER, "Interlocking Directorates and Control of Corporations, The Theory of Bank Control," *Social Science Quarterly,* 1975, 56: 425–439.

MARIOLIS, PETER, AND MARIA H. JONES, "Centrality in Corporate Interlock Networks: Reliability and Stability," *Administrative Science Quarterly,* 1982, 27: 571–584.

MARS, GERALD, *Cheats at Work,* London: George Allen and Unwin, 1982.

MARS, GERALD, AND MICHAEL NICOD, "Hidden Rewards at Work: The Implications from a Study of British Hotels," in Stuart Henry (ed.), *Can I Have It in Cash?* London: Astragal Books, 1981, Chap. 3.

MARSDEN, PETER V., "Restricted Access in Networks and Models of Power," *American Journal of Sociology,* 1983, 88: 686–717.

MARSH, ROBERT, AND HIROSHI MANNARI, *Modernization and the Japanese Factory,* Princeton, NJ: Princeton University Press, 1976.

MARTIN, PATRICIA YANCEY, "Size in Residential Service Organizations," *Sociological Quarterly,* 1979, 20: 565–579.

MARX, GARY T., "Alternative Measures of Police Performance," in Emilio Viano (ed.), *Criminal Justice Research,* Lexington, MA: Lexington Books, 1975, Chap. 17.

MASLOW, ABRAHAM, "A Theory of Human Motivation," *Psychological Review,* 1943, 40: 370–396.

MASLOW, ABRAHAM, *Motivation and Personality,* New York: Harper, 1954.

MAURER, JOHN G., DONALD J. VREDENBURGH, AND RICHARD L. SMITH, "An Examination of the Central Life Interests Scale," *Academy of Management Journal,* 1981, 24: 174–182.

MAYNARD, DOUGLAS W., "Social Order and Plea Bargaining in the Courtroom," *Sociological Quarterly,* 1983, 24: 233–251.

MCCAFFREY, DAVID P., "Corporate Resources and Regulatory Pressures: Toward Explaining a Discrepancy," *Administrative Science Quarterly,* 1982, 27: 398–419.

MCCARTHY, JOHN D., AND MAYER ZALD, "Resource Mobilization and Social Movements: A Partial Theory," *American Journal of Sociology,* 1977, 82: 1212–1241.

MCCLEERY, R. H., *Policy Change in Prison Management,* East Lansing: Michigan State University Press, 1957.

MCGREGOR, DOUGLAS, *The Human Side of Enterprise,* New York: McGraw-Hill, 1960.

MCHENRY, DEAN E., AND ASSOCIATES, *Academic Departments,* San Francisco: Jossey-Bass, 1977.

MECHANIC, DAVID, "Sources of Power of Lower Participants in Complex Organizations," *Administrative Science Quarterly,* 1962, 3: 349–364.

MELBIN, MURRAY, "Night as Frontier," *American Sociological Review,* 1978, 43: 3–22.

MELTZER, LEO, AND JAMES SALTER, "Organization Structure and the Performance and Job Satisfaction of Physiologists," *American Sociological Review,* 1962, 27: 351–362.

MERTON, ROBERT K., "Bureaucratic Structure and Personality," in Robert K. Merton, *Social Theory and Social Structure,* New York: Free Press, 1957.

MERTON, ROBERT K., AILSA P. GRAY, BARBARA HOCKEY, AND HANAN C. SELVIN (EDS.), *Reader in Bureaucracy,* Glencoe, Ill: Free Press, 1952.

MERTON, ROBERT K., G. G. READER, AND PATRICIA L. KENDALL, *The Student Physician,* Cambridge, MA: Harvard University Press, 1957.

MEYER, ALAN D., "Adapting to Environmental Jolts," *Administrative Science Quarterly,* 1982, 27: 515–537.

MEYER, JOHN W., AND BRIAN ROWAN, "Institutionalized Organizations: Formal Structure as Myth and Ceremony," *American Journal of Sociology,* 1977, 83: 340–363.

MEYER, JOHN W., AND W. RICHARD SCOTT, WITH THE ASSISTANCE OF BRIAN ROWAN AND TERRENCE E. DEAL, *Organizational Environments,* Beverly Hills, CA: Sage, 1983.

MEYER, MARSHALL W., "Size and Structure of Organizations: A Causal Analysis," *American Sociological Review,* 1972, 37: 434–440.

MEYER, MARSHALL, AND M. CRAIG BROWN, "The Process of Bureaucratization," *American Journal of Sociology,* 1977, 83: 364–385.

MICHELS, ROBERT, *Political Parties,* New York: Free Press, 1962.

MILETI, D. S., DAVID G. GILLESPIE, AND J. E. HAAS, "Size and Structure in Complex Organizations," *Social Forces,* 1977, 56: 208–217.

MILLER, GALE, "Holding Clients Accountable: The Micropolitics of Trouble in a Work Incentive Problem," *Social Problems,* 1983, 31: 139–151.

MILLER, GEORGE A., "Professionals in Bureaucracy: Alienation among Industrial Scientists and Engineers," *American Sociological Review,* 1967, 32: 755–768.

MILLMAN, MARCIA, *The Unkindest Cut: Life in the Backrooms of Medicine,* New York: Morrow, 1977.

MINTZ, BETH, AND MICHAEL SCHWARTZ, "Interlocking Directories and Interest Group Formation," *American Sociological Review,* 1981, 46: 851–869.

MINTZBERG, HENRY, *The Structuring of Organizations,* Englewood Cliffs, NJ: Prentice-Hall, 1979.

MORRISON, J. L., AND C. P. FREEDMAN, "Community College Faculty Attitudes, Socialization Experiences, and Perceived Teaching Effectiveness," *Community Junior College Research Quarterly,* 1978, 2: 119–138.

MORTIMER, JAYLAN T., AND ROBERTA G. SIMMONS, "Adult Socialization," *Annual Review of Sociology,* 1978, 4: 421–454.

MOTT, PAUL E., *The Characteristics of Effective Organizations,* New York: Harper and Row, 1972.

MOTT, P. E., F. C. MANN, Q. MCLOUGHLIN, AND D. P. WARWICK, *Shiftwork: The Social, Psychological, and Physical Consequences,* Ann Arbor: University of Michigan Press, 1975.

MULFORD, C., G. KLONGLAN, G. BEAL, AND J. BOHLEN, "Selectivity, Socialization, and Role Performance," *Sociology and Social Research,* 1968, 53: 68–77.

MULFORD, C., G. KLONGLAN, R. WARREN, AND P. SCHMITZ, "A Causal Model of Organizational Effectiveness in Organizations," *Social Science Research,* 1972, 1: 61–78.

NEWCOMER, MABEL, *The Big Business Executive,* New York: Columbia University Press, 1955.

NEWMAN, KATHERINE, "Incipient Bureaucracy: The Development of Hierarchies in Egalitarian Organizations," in Gerald M. Britan and Ronald Cohen (eds.), *Hierarchy and Society,* Philadelphia: Institute for the Study of Human Issues, 1980, pp. 143–163.

NOBLE, DAVID F., "Social Choice in Machine Design: The Case of Automatically Controlled Machine Tools," in Andrew Zimbalist (ed.), *Case Studies on the Labor Process,* New York: Monthly Review Press, 1979, pp. 18–50.

OLDHAM, GREG R., AND DANIEL J. BRASS, "Employee Reactions to an Open Office Plan: A Naturally Occurring Quasi-Experiment," *Administrative Science Quarterly,* 1979, 24: 267–284.

OLDHAM, GREG R., AND NANCY L. ROTCHFORD, "Relationships between Office Characteristics and Employee Reactions: A Study of the Physical Environment," *Administrative Science Quarterly,* 1983, 28: 542–556.

OLSON, MANCUR, *The Logic of Collective Action: Public Goods and the Theory of Groups,* Cambridge, MA: Harvard University Press, 1965.

ORZACK, LOUIS H., "Work as a 'Central Life Interest' of Professionals," *Social Problems,* 1959, 7: 125–132.

O'TOOLE, RICHARD, AND ANITA WERNER O'TOOLE, "Negotiating Interorganizational Orders," *Sociological Quarterly,* 1981, 22: 29–41.

OUCHI, WILLIAM G., "The Relationship between Organizational Structure and Organizational Control," *Administrative Science Quarterly,* 1977, 22: 95–113.

OUCHI, WILLIAM G., AND MARY ANN MAGUIRE, "Organizational Control: Two Functions," *Administrative Science Quarterly,* 1975, 20: 559–69.

PARSONS, H. M., "What Happened at Hawthorne?" *Science,* 1974, 183: 922–932.

PARSONS, TALCOTT, *The Social System,* Glencoe, Ill: The Free Press, 1951.

PARSONS, TALCOTT,    "Suggestions for a Sociological Approach to the Theory of Organizations," Parts I and II, *Administrative Science Quarterly*, 1956, 1: 63–85 and 225–239.

PARSONS, TALCOTT, ROBERT F. BALES, AND EDWARD A. SHILS,    *Working Papers in the Theory of Action*, Glencoe, Ill: Free Press, 1953.

PASMORE, WILLIAM, AND FRANK FRIEDLANDER,    "An Action-Research Program for Increasing Employee Involvement in Problem Solving," *Administrative Science Quarterly*, 1982, 27: 343–362.

PENNINGS, JOHANNES M.,    "The Relevance of the Structural-Contingency Model for Organizational Effectiveness," *Administrative Science Quarterly*, 1975, 20: 393–410.

PENNINGS, JOHANNES M.,    *Interlocking Directorates*, San Francisco: Jossey-Bass, 1980.

PERKINS, JAMES A. (ED.),    *The University as an Organization*, New York: McGraw-Hill, 1973.

PERLMAN, BARON, AND E. ALAN HARTMAN,    "Burnout: Summary and Future Research," *Human Relations*, 1982, 35: 283–305.

PERROW, CHARLES,    "The Analysis of Goals in Complex Organizations," *American Sociological Review*, 1961, 26: 856–866.

PERROW, CHARLES,    "Organizational Prestige: Some Functions and Dysfunctions," *American Journal of Sociology*, 1961, 66: 335–347.

PERROW, CHARLES,    *Organizational Analysis: A Sociological View*, Belmont, CA: Brooks, Cole, 1970.

PERROW, CHARLES,    *Complex Organizations*, Glencoe, Ill: Scott, Foresman, 1979, 2nd ed.

PERROW, CHARLES,    "The Organizational Context of Human Factors Engineering," *Administrative Science Quarterly*, 1983, 28: 521–541.

PERROW, CHARLES,    *Normal Accidents: Living with High-Risk Technologies*, New York: Basic Books, 1984.

PFEFFER, JEFFREY,    "Merger as a Response to Organizational Interdependence," *Administrative Science Quarterly*, 1972, 17: 382–394.

PFEFFER, JEFFREY,    *Organizations and Organization Theory*, Boston: Pittman, 1982.

PFEFFER, JEFFREY,    "Organizational Demography," in L. L. Cummings and Barry M. Staw (eds.), *Research in Organizational Behavior*, Vol. 5, Greenwich, CT: JAI Press, 1983.

PFEFFER, JEFFREY, AND WILLIAM L. MOORE,    "Average Tenure of Academic Department Heads: The Effects of Paradigm, Size, and Departmental Demography," *Administrative Science Quarterly*, 1980, 25: 387–406.

PFEFFER, JEFFREY, AND PHILLIP NOWAK,    "Joint Ventures and Interorganizational Interdependence," *Administrative Science Quarterly*, 1976, 21: 398–418.

PFEFFER, JEFFREY, AND GERALD R. SALANCIK,    *The External Control of Organizations: A Resource Dependence Perspective*, New York: Harper and Row, 1978.

PITCHER, BRIAN L.,    "The Hawthorne Experiments: Statistical Evidence for a Learning Hypothesis," *Social Forces*, 1981, 60: 133–149.

PORTER, BRUCE D.,    "Parkinson's Law Revisited: War and the Growth of American Government," *The Public Interest*, 1980, 60: 50–68.

POSNER, RICHARD,    "A Statistical Study of Antitrust Enforcement," *Journal of Law and Economics*, 1970, 13: 365–420.

PRESTHUS, ROBERT, *The Organizational Society,* New York: St. Martin's Press, 1978, rev. ed.

PRICE, JAMES L., *Organizational Effectiveness,* Homewood, ILL: Richard D. Irwin, 1968.

PRICE, JAMES L., *The Study of Turnover,* Ames, IA: Iowa State University Press, 1977.

PSATHAS, GEORGE, "The Fate of Idealism in Nursing Schools," *Journal of Health and Social Behavior,* 1968, 9: 52–65.

PUGH, DEREK S., D. J. HICKSON, C. R. HININGS, AND C. TURNER, "Dimensions of Organizational Structure," *Administrative Science Quarterly,* 1968, 13: 65–105.

QUINN, R. P., AND L. SHEPARD, *The 1972–73 Quality of Employment Survey,* Ann Arbor: Survey Research Center, University of Michigan, 1974.

QUINN, R. P., G. L. STAINES, AND M. R. MCCULLOUGH, *Job Satisfaction: Is There a Trend?* Washington, D.C., U.S. Department of Labor, Manpower Administration, Research Monograph No. 30, 1974.

RADMONDT, JOOP, "Workers' Self-Management and Its Constraints: The Yugoslav Experience," *British Journal of Industrial Relations,* 1979, 17: 83–94.

RANDALL, RONALD, "Influence of Environmental Support and Policy Space on Organizational Behavior," *Administrative Science Quarterly,* 1973, 18: 236–247.

RANDELL, S. "On Some Social Influence of the Military Organization," in Torben Agersnap (ed.), *Contributions to the Theory of Organizations,* Vol. I. Copenhagen, Denmark: Scandinavian University Books, 1968, pp. 58–74.

RESKIN, BARBARA F., "Academic Sponsorship and Scientists' Careers," *Sociology of Education,* 1979, 52: 129–146.

RICHMAN, BARRY M., AND RICHARD N. FARMER, *Leadership, Goals, and Power in Higher Education,* San Francisco: Jossey-Bass, 1974.

RIESMAN, DAVID, "Predicaments in the Career of the College President," in Carlos E. Kruytbosch and Sheldon L. Messinger (eds.), *The State of the University,* Beverly Hills, CA: Sage, 1970.

RITZER, GEORGE, *Working,* Englewood Cliffs, NJ: Prentice-Hall, 1977.

RITZER, GEORGE, AND HARRISON M. TRICE, *An Occupation in Conflict: A Study of the Personnel Manager,* Ithaca, NY: New York State School of Industrial and Labor Relations, Cornell University, 1969.

ROBINSON, J. P., "Occupational Norms and Differences in Work Satisfaction: A Summary of Survey Research Evidence," in J. P. Robinson, et al. (eds.), *Measures of Occupational Attitudes and Occupational Characteristics,* Ann Arbor: University of Michigan, 1969.

ROETHLISBERGER, F. J., AND W. J. DICKSON, *Management and the Worker,* Cambridge, MA: Harvard University Press, 1939.

ROGERS, CARL, *Counseling and Psychotherapy,* Boston: Houghton Mifflin, 1942.

ROKEACH, MILTON, "Change and Stability in American Value Systems, 1968–1971," *Public Opinion Quarterly,* 1974, 38: 222–238.

ROSE, VICKI MCNICKLE, AND SUSAN CAROL RANDALL, "The Impact of Investigator Perceptions of Victim Legitimacy on the Processing of Rape/Sexual Assault Cases," *Symbolic Interaction,* 1982, 5: 23–36.

ROSETT, ARTHUR I., AND DONALD R. CRESSEY, *Justice by Consent: Plea Bargains in the American Courthouse,* Philadelphia: Lippincott, 1976.

ROSSEL, R., "Instrumental and Expressive Leadership in Complex Organizations," *Administrative Science Quarterly,* 1970, 15: 306–316.

ROSSI, PETER H., H. E. FREEMAN, AND S. R. WRIGHT,   *Evaluation: A Systematic Approach*, Beverly Hills, CA: Sage, 1979.

ROTH, JULIUS,   "Some Contingencies of the Moral Evaluation and Control of Clientele: The Case of the Hospital Emergency Service," *American Journal of Sociology*, 1972, 77: 839–856.

ROTHSCHILD-WHITT, JOYCE,   "The Collectivist Organization: An Alternative to Rational-Bureaucratic Models," *American Sociological Review*, 1979, 44: 509–527.

ROY, DONALD,   "Efficiency and 'The Fix': Informal Intergroup Relations in a Piecework Machine Shop," *American Journal of Sociology*, 1954, 60: 255–266.

RYDER, NORMAN B.,   "The Cohort as Concept in the Study of Social Change," *American Sociological Review*, 1965, 30: 843–861.

SALAMAN, GRAEME,   *Community and Occupations: An Exploration of Work/Leisure Relationships*, London: Cambridge University Press, 1974.

SAROFF, JEROME R.,   "Is Mobility Enough for the Temporary Society? Some Observations Based Upon the Experience of the Federal Executive Institute," *Public Administration Review*, 1974, 34: 480–486.

SAYLES, LEONARD R.,   *Behavior of Industrial Work Groups*, New York: Wiley, 1958.

SCHEFF, THOMAS J.,   "Control Over Policy by Attendants in a Mental Hospital," *Journal of Health and Human Behavior*, 1961, 2: 93–105.

SCHERER, F. M.,   *Industrial Market Structure and Economic Performance*, Boston: Houghton Mifflin, 1980.

SCHMIDT, STUART M., AND THOMAS A. KOCHAN,   "Interorganizational Relationships: Patterns and Motivations," *Administrative Science Quarterly*, 1977, 22: 220–234.

SCHRAG, CLARENCE,   "Leadership among Prison Inmates," *American Sociological Review*, 1954, 19: 37–42.

SCHRAG, CLARENCE,   "A Preliminary Criminal Typology," *Pacific Sociological Review*, 1961, 4: 11–16.

SCOTT, MARVIN B., AND STANFORD LYMAN,   "Accounts," *American Sociological Review*, 1968, 33: 46–62.

SCOTT, W. RICHARD,   "Professionals in Bureaucracies: Areas of Conflict," in Howard M. Vollmer and Donald L. Mills, (eds.), *Professionalization*, Englewood Cliffs, NJ: Prentice-Hall, 1966, pp. 265–275.

SCOTT, W. RICHARD,   "Professional Employees in a Bureaucratic Structure: Social Work," in Amitai Etzioni (ed.), *The Semi-Professions and Their Organization*, New York: Free Press, 1969, Chap. 3.

SCOTT, W. RICHARD,   *Organizations: Rational, Natural, and Open Systems*, Englewood Cliffs, NJ: Prentice-Hall, 1981.

SCOTT, ROBERT,   "The Factory as a Social Service Organization," *Social Problems*, 1967, 15: 160–175.

SCUDDER, J. J.,   "The Open Institution," *Annals of the American Academy of Political and Social Science*, 293, 1954, pp. 80–82.

SCULL, ANDREW T.,   *Decarceration*, Englewood Cliffs, NJ: Prentice-Hall, 1977.

SEASHORE, S. E., AND T. D. TABER,   "Job Satisfaction Indicators and Their Correlates," in A. D. Biderman and T. F. Drury (eds.), *Measuring Work Quality for Social Reporting*, New York: Wiley, 1976.

SEASHORE, STANLEY E., AND EPHRAIM YUCHTMAN,   "Factorial Analysis of Organizational Performance," *Administrative Science Quarterly*, 1967, 12: 377–395.

SELZNICK, PHILIP,   "Foundations of the Theory of Organizations," *American Sociological Review*, 1948, 13: 25–35.

SELZNICK, PHILIP, *The Organizational Weapon*, New York: McGraw-Hill, 1952.
SHEPARD, J. M., "On Alex Carey's Radical Criticism of the Hawthorne Studies," *Academy of Management Journal*, 1971, 14: 23–32.
SHORTER, EDWARD, AND CHARLES TILLY, *Strikes in France: 1830–1968*, Cambridge: Cambridge University Press, 1974.
SILLS, DAVID L., *The Volunteers*, New York: Free Press, 1957.
SILVERMAN, DAVID, *The Theory of Organizations*, New York: Basic Books, 1971.
SILVERMAN, DAVID, AND J. JONES, *Organizational Work: The Language of Grading/The Grading of Language*, London: Collier-Macmillan, 1976.
SIMON, HERBERT A., "On the Concept of Organizational Goal," *Administrative Science Quarterly*, 1964, 9: 1–22.
SIMON, HERBERT A., *Administrative Behavior*, New York: Free Press, 1976, 3rd ed.
SIMPSON, IDA HARPER, "Patterns of Socialization into Profession: The Case of Student Nurses," *Sociological Inquiry*, 1967, 37: 47–54.
SIMPSON, RICHARD L., AND IDA HARPER SIMPSON, "Women and Bureaucracy in the Semi-Professions," in Amitai Etzioni (ed.), *The Semi-Professions and Their Organization*, New York: Free Press, 1969, Chap. 5.
SMIGEL, ERWIN O., "Public Attitudes Toward Stealing as Related to the Size of the Victim Organization," *American Sociological Review*, 1956, 21: 320–337.
SMIGEL, ERWIN, *The Wall Street Lawyer: Professional Organization Man?* Bloomington, IN: Indiana University Press, 1964.
SMITH, HARVEY L., "Two Lines of Authority Are One Too Many," *Modern Hospitals*, 1955, 84: 54–64.
SMITH, R., *Why Soldiers Fight: Causes of Fighter Spirit*, Draft of Monograph 1, Social and Policy Research, Santa Barbara, CA, 1973.
SMYTH, D. S., "The Relationship between Size and Performance of Mail Sorting Offices," *Human Relations*, 1982, 35: 567–586.
SNYDER, DAVID, AND WILLIAM R. KELLY, "Industrial Violence in Italy, 1887–1903," *American Journal of Sociology*, 1976, 82: 131–162.
SOFER, C., "Reactions to Administrative Change," *Human Relations*, 1955, 8: 229.
SOSIN, MICHAEL, "Organizational Maintenance, Sensitivity to Clients, and Vulnerability: Some New Suggestions about a Traditional Concept," *Sociological Quarterly*, 1981, 22: 347–358.
SPANGLER, EVE, MARSHA A. GORDON, AND RONALD M. PIPKIN, "Token Women: An Empirical Test of Kanter's Hypotheses," *American Journal of Sociology*, 1978, 84: 160–170.
SPENCE, A. MICHAEL, *Market Signaling: Informational Transfer in Hiring and Related Screening Processes*, Cambridge, MA: Harvard University Press, 1974.
STANTON, A. H., AND M. S. SCHWARTZ, *The Mental Hospital*, New York: Basic Books, 1954.
STARBUCK, WILLIAM H., "Organizations as Action Generators," *American Sociological Review*, 1983, 48: 91–102.
STAW, BARRY M., PAMELA I. MCKECHNIE, AND SHEIL M. PUFFER, "The Justification of Organizational Performance," *Administrative Science Quarterly*, 1983, 28: 582–600.
STAW, BARRY M., AND EUGENE SZWAJKOWSKI, "The Scarcity-Munificence Component of Organizational Environments and the Commission of Illegal Acts," *Administrative Science Quarterly*, 1975, 20: 345–354.
STEELE, J. E., AND L. B. WARD, "MBA's: Mobile, Well Situated, Well Paid," *Harvard Business Review*, January–February, 1974: pp. 9–109.
STEERS, RICHARD M., *Organizational Effectiveness: A Behavioral View*, Pacific Palisades, CA: Goodyear, 1977.

STERN, ROBERT N.,   "The Development of an Interorganizational Control Network: The Case of Intercollegiate Athletics," *Administrative Science Quarterly*, 1979, 24: 242–266.

STEWMAN, SHELBY, AND SURESH L. KONDA,   "Careers and Organizational Labor Markets: Demographic Models of Organizational Behavior," *American Journal of Sociology*, 1982, 88: 637–685.

STINCHCOMBE, ARTHUR L.,   "Social Structure and Organization," in James G. March (ed.), *Handbook of Organizations*, Chicago: Rand McNally, 1965.

STOGDILL, RALPH,   *Handbook of Leadership: A Survey of Theory and Research*, New York: Free Press, 1974.

STOLLBERG, R.,   "Job Satisfaction and Relationship to Work," in Marie R. Haug and Jacques Dofny (eds.), *Work and Technology*, Beverly Hills, CA: Sage, 1977, pp. 107–121.

STOLZENBERG, ROSS M.,   "Bring the Boss Back In: Employer Size, Employees' Schooling, and Socioeconomic Achievement," *American Sociological Review*, 1978, 43: 813–828.

STRAUSS, ANSELM L.,   *Negotiations*, San Francisco: Jossey-Bass, 1978.

STRAUSS, GEORGE,   "Tactics of Lateral Relationships: The Purchasing Agent," *Administrative Science Quarterly*, 1962, 7: 161–186.

STRAUSS, GEORGE, "The Personality-versus-Organization Theory," in Leonard R. Sayles (ed.), *Individualism and Big Business*, New York: McGraw-Hill, 1963, Chap. 8.

STRAUSS, GEORGE,   "Job Satisfaction, Motivation, and Job Redesign," in *Organizational Behavior: Research and Issues*, Madison, WIS: Industrial Relations Research Association, 1974.

STREET, DAVID, ROBERT VINTER, AND CHARLES PERROW,   *Organizations for Treatment*, New York: The Free Press, 1966.

SUDNOW, DAVID,   "Normal Crimes: Sociological Features of the Penal Code in a Public Defender Office," *Social Problems*, 1965, 12: 255–276.

SYKES, GRESHAM G.,   *Society of Captives*, Princeton, NJ: Princeton University Press, 1958.

SYKES, GRESHAM, AND SHELDON L. MESSINGER,   "The Inmate Social System," in Richard A. Cloward et al. (ed.), *Theoretical Studies in Social Organization of the Prison*, New York: Social Science Research Council, 1960, pp. 5–19.

TABER, W.,   "Normative Authority of College Faculty: Bases, Manifestations, and Limitations," PhD. dissertation, Columbia University, 1969. Discussed in Etzioni, 1975, pp. 373–376.

TAUSKY, KURT,   *Work Organizations: Major Theoretical Perspectives*, Itasca, Ill: Peacock, 1978.

TAYLOR, FREDERICK W.,   *Scientific Management*, New York: Harper, 1947.

TERREBERRY, SHIRLEY,   "The Evolution of Organizational Environments," *Administrative Science Quarterly*, 1968, 12: 590–613.

THIELENS, W., JR.,   "Some Comparisons of Entrants to Medical and Law School," *Journal of Legal Education*, 1958, 2: 153–170.

THOMAS, CHARLES W., AND SAMUEL S. FOSTER,   "The Importation Model Perspective on Inmate Social Roles," *Sociological Quarterly*, 1973, 14: 226–234.

THOMPSON, JAMES D.,   *Organizations in Action*, New York: McGraw-Hill, 1967.

THOMPSON, KENNETH A.,   "Religious Organizations," in John B. McKinlay (ed.), *Processing People: Cases in Organizational Behaviour*, London: Holt, Rinehart, and Winston, 1975, pp. 1–40.

TICHY, NOEL M., MICHAEL L. TUSHMAN, AND CHARLES FOMBRUN,   "Social Network Analysis for Organizations," *Academy of Management Review*, 1979, 4: 507–519.

TILLY, CHARLES, *From Mobilization to Revolution,* Reading, MA: Addison-Wesley, 1978.

TOSI, HENRY, RAMON ALDAG, AND RONALD STOREY, "On the Measurement of the Environment: An Assessment of the Lawrence and Lorach Environmental Subscale," *Administrative Science Quarterly,* 1973, 18: 27–36.

TURK, HERMAN, *Organizations in Modern Life,* San Francisco: Jossey-Bass, 1977.

TURNER, RALPH H., "The Navy Disbursing Officer as a Bureaucrat," *American Sociological Review,* 1947, 12: 342–348.

U.S. DEPARTMENT OF COMMERCE, BUREAU OF THE CENSUS, *County Business Patterns,* 1980.

U.S. DEPARTMENT OF COMMERCE, BUREAU OF THE CENSUS, *Enterprise Statistics,* Part 1, 1972.

U.S. DEPARTMENT OF JUSTICE, *Federal Prison System Statistical Report,* Fiscal Year, 1975.

VAN MAANEN, JOHN, "Observations on the Making of Policemen," *Human Organization,* 1973, 32: 418.

VAN MAANEN, J., "Breaking In: Socialization to Work," in Robert Dubin (ed.), *Handbook of Work, Organization, and Society,* Chicago: Rand McNally, 1976, pp. 67–130.

VAUGHAN, DIANE, "Crime Between Organizations: Implications for Victimology," in Gilbert Geis and Ezra Stotland (eds.), *White-Collar Crime: Theory and Research,* Beverly Hills, CA: Sage, 1980, Chap. 4.

VOGEL, EZRA (ED.), *Modern Japanese Organization and Decision-Making,* Berkeley: University of California Press, 1975.

VOLLMER, HOWARD M., *Employer Rights and the Employment Relationship,* Berkeley: University of California Press, 1960.

VROOM, VICTOR, *Work and Motivation,* New York: Wiley, 1964.

WALKER, CHARLES R., AND ROBERT H. GUEST, *The Man on the Assembly Line,* Cambridge, MA: Harvard University Press, 1952.

WALKER, NIGEL, *Morale in the Civil Service,* Edinburgh: The University Press, 1961.

WALL, T., AND G. STEPHENSON, "Herzberg's Two-Factor Theory of Job Attitudes: A Critical Evaluation and Some Fresh Evidence," *British Journal of Industrial Relations,* 1970, 8: 41–65.

WALLACE, MICHAEL, AND ARNE L. KALLEBERG, "Industrial Transformation and the Decline of Craft: The Decomposition of Skill in the Printing Industry, 1931–1978," *American Sociological Review,* 1982, 47: 307–324.

WALSH, EDWARD J., AND REX H. WARLAND, "Social Movement Involvement in the Wake of a Nuclear Accident: Activists and Free Riders in the TMI Area," *American Sociological Review,* 1983, 48: 764–780.

WALTERS, VIVIENNE, "Company Doctors' Perceptions of and Responses to Conflicting Pressures from Labor and Management," *Social Problems,* 1982, 30: 1–12.

WARD, DAVID A., AND GENE K. KASSEBAUM, *Women's Prison,* London: Weidenfeld and Nicolson, 1965.

WARDWELL, WALTER I., "Critique of a Recent Professional 'Put-Down' of the Hawthorne Research," *American Sociological Review,* 1979, 44: 858–861.

WARNER, W. LLOYD, AND J. O. LOW, "The Factory in the Community," in William F. Whyte (ed.), *Industry and Society,* New York: McGraw-Hill, 1946.

WARNER, W. LLOYD, AND J. O. LOW, *The Social System of the Modern Factory,* New Haven, Conn.: Yale University Press, 1947.

WARNER, W. LLOYD AND OTHERS, *The Emergent American Society,* New Haven, Conn.: Yale University Press, 1967, Vol. 1.

WEAVER, CHARLES N., "Relationships Among Pay, Race, Sex, Occupational Prestige, Supervision, Work Autonomy, and Job Satisfaction in a National Sample," *Personnel Psychology*, 1977a, 30: 437–445.

WEAVER, CHARLES N., "Occupational Prestige as a Factor in the Net Relationship Between Occupation and Job Satisfaction," *Personnel Psychology*, 1977b, 30: 607–612.

WEBBER, ROSS A., *Management: Basic Elements of Managing Organizations*, Homewood, Ill: Richard D. Irwin, 1975.

WEBER, MAX, *The Protestant Ethic and the Spirit of Capitalism*, New York: Scribner's, 1958 (first pub. in 1904–1905).

WEBER, MAX, *Economy and Society*, Guenther Roth and Klaus Wittich (eds.), New York: Bedminster Press, 1968.

WEICK, KARL E., "Educational Organizations as Loosely Coupled Systems," *Administrative Science Quarterly*, 1976, 21: 1–19.

WEICK, KARL E., "Enactment Processes in Organizations," in M. Staw and Gerald R. Salancik (eds.), *New Directions in Organizational Behavior*, Chicago: St. Clair, 1977, pp. 263–300.

WEIMANN, GABRIEL, "Dealing with Bureaucracy: The Effectiveness of Different Persuasive Appeals," *Social Psychology Quarterly*, 1982, 45: 136–144.

WEISS, PAUL R., AND ROBERT R. FAULKNER, "Credits and Craft Production: Freelance Social Organization in the Hollywood Film Industry, 1964–1978," *Symbolic Interaction*, 1983, 6: 111–123.

WESTLEY, WILLIAM A., *Violence and the Police*, Cambridge, MA: MIT Press, 1970.

WHEELER, STANTON, "Socialization in Correctional Institutions," in David A. Goslin (ed.), *Handbook of Socialization Theory and Research*, Chicago: Rand McNally, 1969, Chap. 25.

WHITT, J. ALLEN, "Is Oil Different? A Comparison of the Social Backgrounds and Organizational Affiliations of Oil and Non-Oil Directors," *Social Problems*, 1981, 29: 142–150.

WILKINS, ALAN L., AND WILLIAM G. OUCHI, "Efficient Cultures: Exploring the Relationship Between Culture and Organizational Performance," *Administrative Science Quarterly*, 1983, 28: 468–481.

WILLIAMSON, OLIVER E., *Markets and Hierarchies*, New York: Free Press, 1975.

WILLIAMSON, OLIVER E., "The Economics of Organization: The Transactions Cost Approach," *American Journal of Sociology*, 1981, 87: 548–577.

WHYTE, WILLIAM FOOTE, *Money and Motivation*, New York: Harper, 1955.

WILSON, LOGAN, *The Academic Man*, London: Oxford University Press, 1942.

WITTE, JOHN F., *Democracy, Authority, and Alienation in Work*, Chicago: The University of Chicago Press, 1980.

WOOD, STEPHEN (ED.), *The Degradation of Work?* London: Hutchinson, 1982.

WOODWARD, JOAN, *Industrial Organisation: Theory and Practice*, London: Oxford University Press, 1965.

*Work in America*, U.S. Department of Health, Education, and Welfare, Cambridge, MA: MIT Press, 1972.

*World of Work Report*, "Flexiplace," May 1982.

YANKELOVICH, DANIEL, *New Rules*, New York: Bantam Books: 1982.

*Yearbook of American and Canadian Churches*, Nashville, Tenn.: Abington Press, 1977.

YUCHTMAN, EPHRAIM, AND STANLEY E. SEASHORE, "A System Resource Approach to Organizational Effectiveness," *American Sociological Review*, 1967, 32: 891–903.

ZABLOCKI, BENJAMIN, *Alienation and Charisma*, New York: Free Press, 1980.

ZALD, MAYER, "Political Economy: A Framework for Comparative Analysis," in Mayer N. Zald (ed.), *Power in Organizations,* Nashville, Tenn.: Vanderbilt University Press, 1970.

ZALD, MAYER N., AND MICHAEL A. BERGER, "Social Movements in Organizations: Coup d'Etat, Insurgency, and Mass Movements," *American Journal of Sociology,* 1978, 83: 823–861.

ZALD, MAYER N., AND PATRICIA DENTON, "The YMCA: From Evangelism to General Service," *Administrative Science Quarterly,* 1963, 8; 214–234.

ZALEZNIK, ABRAHAM, C. R. CHRISTENSEN, AND F. J. ROETHLISBERGER, *The Motivation, Productivity, and Satisfaction of Workers: A Prediction Study,* Boston: Harvard University Graduate School of Business Administration, 1958.

ZEITZ, GERALD, "Structural and Individual Determinants of Organizational Morale and Satisfaction," *Social Forces,* 1983, 61: 1088–1108.

ZIMMERMAN, DON, "The Practicalities of Rule Use," in Jack Douglas (ed.), *Understanding Everyday Life,* Chicago: Aldine, 1970.

ZURCHER, L. A., "The Naval Recruit Training Center: A Study of Role Assimilation in a Total Institution," *Sociological Inquiry,* 1967, 37: 85–96.

ZWERMAN, WILLIAM L., *New Perspectives in Organizational Theory,* Westport, Conn: Greenwood, 1970.

# INDEX

## NAME INDEX

## SUBJECT INDEX